Dictionary of
Design

BROCKHAMPTON PRESS
LONDON

Editorial note

In this dictionary, architects, sculptors and artists are included primarily for their contribution to design and not for their buildings or fine-art work.

This edition published 1997 by Brockhampton Press, a member of the Hodder Headline PLC Group

ISBN 1 86019 730 2

Printed and bound in India

A

Aalto, Hugo Alvar Henrik (1898–1976) Outstanding Finnish architect, born in Helsinki, who eventually became professor of architecture at the Massachusetts Institute of Technology. He was also a designer of bentwood and laminated plywood furniture, influenced by the style of the BAUHAUS. His *Paimio* (Scroll) chair of 1930 was made from a single sheet of undulating plywood and pioneered techniques for shaping solid wood. He and his wifa, Aino Aalto, established one of the first modern furniture shops, in Helsinki, and he went on to produce a range of furnishings, including glassware, often inspired by natural shapes and the Finnish countryside. At the 1937 Paris Exhibition of Arts and Crafts of Modern Life he exhibited glassware inspired the leather trousers of an Eskimo woman, the first of an important series in clear and coloured glass. In his architecture, organic forms were often an inspiration and he pioneered the use of exposed brickwork.

Aarnio, Eero (1932–) Finnish interior and industrial designer, best known for his chair designs, made from synthetic materials. The best-known include the 1963 womb-like *Globe* chair, made from fibreglass, with built-in stereo speakers and telephone. His work has been widely exhibited, including shows at the Whitechapel Gallery, London (1983) and the Cooper-Hewitt Museum, New York (1983). In 1969, he received the American Interior Design International Award.

Abramovitz, Gerald (1928–) South African-born architect, trained in Pretoria and at the Royal College of Art, London. His designs including seating for KNOLL, a chair receiving the 1963 international furniture award sponsored by the *Daily Mirror,* and his cantilevered desk lamp, produced by Best and Lloyd, which won the 1966 Design Centre Award.

Acanthus A plant motif emphasizing the bold indentations of the scrolled leaves. A common element in Greek and Roman ornament. It features on the classical Corinthian column and was widely used in BAROQUE design.

Acerbis Influential Italian furniture manufacturer founded in 1870 by a cabinet maker of that surname. His grandson **Lodovico Acerbis** (1939–) designed his first furniture for the company when aged seventeen and in 1992 produced the notable *Granducale* collection to honour Kazimir Malevich.

Ackermann, Rudolf (1764–1834) German-born coach designer who settled in London where he opened his first shop, Repository of the Arts, selling books, prints and related articles. He designed Admiral Nelson's funeral carriage in 1806 and founded a magazine, named after his shop and dedicated to the Prince of Wales, which was devoted to the promotion of art and design. Emphasis was given to architecture and furniture design in the classical tradition. The GOTHIC Revival was promoted by the articles and illustrations of A. C. PUGIN. He was a pioneer of lithographic printing and in his later years did much charitable work in his native country.

Acking, Carl-Axel (1910–) Swedish architect who became influential in furniture design, interior design for ships of the North Star Line and furnishings for the Hotel Malmen, Stockholm . His bentwood furniture is widely used, as are designs for wallpaper and textiles.

Adam, Robert (1728–92) Born in Kirkaldy, Fife, Scotland, he was the son of **William Adam** (1689–1754), the leading architect of the age. As a result of the Grand Tour he undertook with the Hon. Charles Hope, in 1754, he was introduced to NEO-CLASSICISM and became a close friend of PIRANESI. Returning home he became architect to Edwin Lascelles, later Lord Harewood, and other aristocrats. He built Syon House for the Duke of Northumberland and was noted for his extensive use of light and elegant ornaments in the classical tradition. The same ornaments were soon employed in the design of chairs, tables, carpets and other furnishings. He was important in the development of the use of colour in interior decoration, supervizing personally every aspect of the design and construction of a building. He employed the most noted painters, decorators, plasterers and cabinet makers of the age, most notably Thomas CHIPPENDALE. By the end of the eighteenth century his work was going out of fashion, regarded as too fussy, but his designs were featured in the Great Exhibition of 1862, thereafter experiencing a flourishing revival.

Adnet, Jacques (1900–84) French architect, born in Chatillon-Coligny. He worked in Paris, creating modern furniture designs and accessories in metal and glass, which he often incorporated into his furniture. In 1922, he became director of the decorating studio of the department store, Galeries Lafayette, where he collaborated with his younger brother, Jean, who was head of the window display department. He designed the public rooms of the liner *Ile-de France* and President Auriol's residence at Chateau Rambouillet, becoming Director of the National High School for Decorative Arts in 1970.

Aesthetic Movement An informal group of British artists who wished to break away from the rigidity of Victorian design, being in favour of freer expression. The group embraced the ideas of the ARTS AND CRAFTS MOVEMENT led by William MORRIS and the PRE-RAPHAELITE painters Dante Gabriel ROSSETTI and Edward BURNE-JONES. The drawings of Aubrey BEARDSLEY and the writing of Oscar Wilde also came within this sphere of influence. Christopher DRESSER's *Art of Decorative Design* embodied many of the principles of the movement.

Aido, Yusuke (1931–) Japanese designer of ceramics. He left Japan in 1961 to work for Bennington Potters, Vermont, USA, where he established popular, industrially-produced, pottery, which is still manufactured. When he returned to Japan in 1965 he reverted to studio pottery, creating large ceramic panels for hotels in Nagoya and Osaka. He became director of the Japan Craft Design Association in 1976.

Aitchison, George (1825–1910) British architect trained at the Royal Academy Schools and University College, London. After continental travel with William BURGES, he consciously included decorative designs in his buildings, most notable among these was the house for Sir Frederick, later Lord, Leighton, in Holland Park, London. The Arab Hall incorporates authentic Moorish tiles.

Alavoine Interieurs French interior decoration company, influential from the 1920s to the 1970s. The company recreated historic styles, ranging from Mock Tudor to Neo-Turkoman. Based in

Paris, they opened offices on New York's Fifth Avenue as early as 1893, with a façade designed by René LALIQUE. Rooms created by the company in New York have been installed in the Brooklyn Museum.

Albers, Josef (1888–1976) German painter and designer, closely connected with the BAUHAUS, who produced MODERNIST tableware and glassware. He emigrated to America in 1933 and taught at the progressive Black Mountain Art College in North Carolina and then at Harvard University, where he refined his minimalist colour theories.

Albert, Prince (1819–61) Born at Rosenau, Saxe-Coburg, he married Queen Victoria in 1840, three years after her succession to the British throne. He promoted all the arts and sciences, himself, designing silverware, jewellery and furniture, such as the billiard table at Osborne House, Isle of Wight. He became President of the Royal Society of Arts and in 1848 set in motion a plan for a series of national design exhibitions. The first was the 1851 London Exhibition, after which he presided over the foundation of the School of Design, which would evolve into the Royal College of Art, and the South Kensington Museum, now the Victoria and Albert Museum. The 1862 Great Exhibition in London was a fitting memorial to his influence on design in every field.

Albertus, Gundorph (1887–1970) Danish silversmith who was the brother-in-law of Georg JENSEN, being responsible for designing the Jensen Silverworks' first stainless steel kitchenware. The *Cactus* platter is still in production. His brother, **Wilhelm** (1878–1963), worked closely with him.

Albinson, Don (1915–) American furniture designer who collaborated principally with Charles EAMES, creating the fibreglass shell, often credited to Eames alone. He became head designer at KNOLL, designing a stacking chair in 1965 which set standards for the industry. He extended his influence into office seating and furniture systems as a consultant to Westinghouse.

Allen, Davis (1916–) American interior designer, born in Iowa who worked in New York. While studying in Stockholm, he visited Finland and met Alva AALTO, who became an influence upon him. He worked for the KNOLL company, as interior designer, and

with Raymond LOEWY's industrial design team. He also designed
furnishings for the General Assembly Building of the United Nations in New York.

Alma-Taderna, Sir Lawrence (1836–1912) Dutch painter.and
furniture designer who was educated in Antwerp, before moving
to London, having gained a reputation as a painter of classical
scenes After he was elected to the Royal Academy, he designed
his first piece of furniture, a Byzantine style piano and seat for his
own use. For his new house at 17 Grove End Road, London, he
designed couches in exaggerated classical styles, exhibiting one
at the 1893 London Arts and Crafts Exhibition. Other private
commissions followed, including a Neo-Classical piano and seat
for Henry G. Marquand of New York.

American Designers' Gallery One of the first attempts to accord
design its rightful status as a creative art. Founded in 1928 in
New York, its first exhibition, featuring fifteen American designers, was mounted in the Chase Manhattan Building.

American Society of Interior Designers American professional
association founded in 1975 by existing design groups. It supports educational initiatives and promotes business ethics and
procedures within the interior decorating world.

Andersen, Ib Joust (1884–1943) Danish painter and sculptor who
became a designer of pewter, setting up his company in 1918. He
also adapted his designs for the JENSEN Silver Company.

Antonini, Carlo (*fl.*1775–90) Publisher of the *Manual of Various
Ornament* over a twelve year period from 1777, with title pages
by Giovanni PIRANESI and plates detailing decoration including
antique rosettes, candelabra and sundials for the guidance of
sculptors, architects, masons, wood-carvers and cabinet makers.
They were largely derived from ancient Roman collections, but
also included decoration from foreign sources as far afield as
England, where his manual was reprinted, but did not achieve
great success, only four of the 213 original plates being included.

Arabesque An elegant flourish used in design, deriving from
Moresque patterns of the 16th century.

Arabia Ceramics The company was founded in 1873 and after
years of innovative design became a seminal influence in the es-

tablishment of Modern Scandinavian design almost a century later under the guidance of Ulla PROCOPÉ, who designed the 1957 *Liekki* suite of flameproof dinnerware, as well as the 1960 *Ruska* stoneware range

Arad, Ron (1951–) Israel-born designer, working principally in London. His best-known designs include the 1985 *Roverchair,* constructed from a salvaged automobile seat, fixed to a tubular steel frame. Other one-off or limited editions followed (limited through restricted original source materials) before he created unusual chairs such as the *Big Easy Red* vinyl chair, manufactured (and very popular) in Italy. It remains a design symbol of the 1980s.

Arbus, André (1903–69) French decorator, initially trained as an architect in Toulouse, his birthplace. Produced elegant furniture for *Epoque,* his shop in Paris, harking back at times to the style of Louis XV. He designed public areas of the liner *Ile-de-France* in 1926, using rare and exotic materials. Other liners in later years included *Provence* and, in 1961, *France* (the first-class section).

Armstrong, John (1893–1973) British painter and designer who studied law at Oxford University before studying art at the St Johns Wood School. He designed the set for Frederick Ashton's ballet *Façade,* and painted murals for Shell-Mex House, London. He designed posters for Shell, as well as for Korda Films such as *The Private Life of Henry VIII, Rembrandt* and *The Shape of Things to Come.* He also designed ceramics under the direction of Clarice CLIFF in the *Bizarre* range. He was an official war artist during the Second World War.

Arp, Jean (1886–1966) French sculptor and painter, born in Strasbourg. Influenced by Paul KLEE, Wassily KANDINSKI and Robert Delauney, he became one of the founders of the *Blaue Reiter* group of painters in Munich and collaborated with the Zurich Dada group from 1916–19, illustrating publications and embarking on a series of sculptures to decorate public buildings such as the Aubette Dance Hall in Strasbourg.

Art Déco An international art and design style, so named in the 1960s after the Paris 1925 *Exposition Internationale des Arts Decoratifs et Industriels Modernes,* which brought together all aspects of design: fashion, interior, printed, architectural and industrial. The distinctive, angular patterns were a direct reaction against the swirling curves of ART NOUVEAU. The main influences on this style were the Fauve painters, who used the bold palette favoured by the designers of the Russian Ballet, introduced to Paris by Serge Diaghilev in 1908, and the Cubists. In fashion, Paul POIRET showed his luscious style, while enamaliers and sculptors used exotic materials such as ebony, ivory and rich coloured lacquers. The movement was influential well into the 1930s, with its distinctive style finding its way into many homes, on linoleum and everyday pottery, as well as furniture. Typical Art Déco buildings include the Chrysler Building in New York, the Bijenkorf department store in the Hague and the Hoover Building, just outside London. Art Déco style enjoyed a great revival in the 1960s, with many pastiche pieces being produced.

Art Nouveau A design movement encompassing all the visual arts. Its title is derived from the name of the gallery opened by Samuel BING in 1895 in Paris. Known in Britain as Modern Style, in Germany as Jugendstil (after the magazine *Jugend*) and Stile Liberti in Italy, derived from the Liberty department store in London, which was one of the prime promoters of the style in fabrics and fashion. The distinctive shapes and patterns of Art Nouveau were curvilinear and sinuous, inspired by natural shapes: plants, the sea and the sky. Lasting little more than ten years, the movement became very important across Europe and to a lesser extent America. In Britain, artists such as Aubrey BEARDSLEY and Walter CRANE worked in Art Nouveau style, with Alphonse MUCHA producing archetypal posters, paintings and stage designs in Austria and France. European architects included Antonio GAUDÍ in Spain, Victor HORTA in Belgium and Otto Wagner in Austria. In Scotland, Charles Rennie MACKINTOSH refined Art Nouveau ideas in his buildings, furniture, jewellery and other artefacts. Emile GALLÉ was the leading glassware designer in this style, with William MORRIS being heavily influenced in Britain.

Arts and Crafts Movement The Arts and Crafts Society was started by the illustrator Walter CRANE and the painters, George Clausen and William Holman-Hunt, in 1886, to promote fine and decorative arts, as a reaction to the badly designed, factory produced goods which were prevalent at the time. Their manifesto was inspired by the writings of A. W. N. PUGIN and John RUSKIN. William MORRIS was the leading member of the Society, serving as President from 1893 to 1896. The aim was to lead designers of all types, furniture, carpets, stained glass, fabric and wall-coverings, to a more craft-based approach. To this end they mounted exhibitions in Britain; the first was held at the New Gallery in London's Regent Street in 1888. They also took British design abroad, notably to the 1902 Turin Exhibition and the 1904 St Louis Exhibition in America.

Ashbee, Charles Robert (1963–1942) British architect who turned to furniture and furnishing design. He was a leading force in the ARTS AND CRAFTS MOVEMENT, influenced by the writings of John RUSKIN. He founded the Guild of Handicraft in 1888 at Toynbee Hall, London, designing metalwork and furniture in the style of William MORRIS. The school moved to Chipping Camden, in the Cotswolds, in 1902. However, the Guild went into voluntary liquidation in 1908, and Ashbee returned to architecture.

Ashley, Laura (1926–88) British fashion and fabric designer, born in Merthyr Tydfil, Wales. Revived the English country cottage design in the early 1950s, adapting 19th-century fabric designs for her dresses, the first of which was marketed in 1968. The company established a manufacturing arm in Machynlleth, Wales and opened a chain of shops which, by 1990, had over 450 branches worldwide. Her design range was extended to include household furnishings, paint and perfume, alongside her perennial hallmark, chintzes.

Astori, Antonia (1940–) Italian designer who worked for DRADE, a company she founded with her brother, Enrico. Their designs were heavily influenced by the DE STIJL group and Mondrian. They pioneered the use of hand-coated board for furniture, which was sold flat-packed.

Audsley, George Ashdown (1838–1925) British architect who incorporated decorative work into his buildings, largely influenced by Christopher DRESSER. He designed and printed several books chromolithographically, including *The Sermon on the Mount* and several studies of Japanese art.

B

B2 French design partnership, so called after Bruno Berrione and Bruno Lefebre who founded it in 1980. They were influenced by Philippe STARCK, the minimalist designer, and Arne JACOBSEN. Their chair fashioned from a large slice of tree trunk, sheet and tubular metal, won the French Industrial Design Award in 1987.

Backstrom, Monica (1939–) Swedish glassware designer. Her distinctive designs for BODA often incorporate metal flakes or objects and can have enamelled surfaces. She has also created large glass decorations for public buildings and Swedish liners.

Backstrom, Olaf (1922–) Swedish engineer who turned to designing kitchen tools, first in wood and then in Melamine. His ergonomic scissors and shears of 1963 and 1967 were first a success in Sweden and then produced in large quantities by Wilkinson Sword.

Bacon, Francis (1909–1992) Irish painter, based in London, notorious for his grotesque paintings. He started out as a designer of modern furniture and carpets, in 1930. He also produced woven rugs of his own designs.

Baillie Scott, Mackay Hugh (1865–1945) British-born architect, who collaborated with Archibald KNOX, designing stained glass and ironwork. As well as his extensive architectural commissions, he designed church mosaics, furniture and wallpaper. His glowing colours and symbolism made him popular in Europe, where he decorated the drawing room and sitting room of the Grand Duke of Hesse's palace at Darmstadt. He was keen on the use of appliquéed embroidery in furnishings. He also designed a forest hideaway, Le Nid, for Queen Marie of Romania, including all the fittings.

Bakelite A synthetic resin named after its inventor Dr Leo Baekeland. It was patented in 1907 and was first produced commercially at Yonkers, near New York. It is produced by combining phenol (a coal-tar by-product) with formaldehyde. It was used in a wide range of hues, by designers of radios, early televisions and costume jewellery.

Bakst, Leon (1886–1924) Russian stage and costume designer, notably for Serge Diaghilev's Ballets Russes. His rich stage designs for ballets such as *Scheherazade and The Firebird* changed the face of interior design in the years before the First World War. Innovations included the use of bright colour schemes and stencilled patterns.

Baldwin, Billy (1903–84) A leading American interior designer in the 1930s, noted for his exquisite use of British and French antiques, shown off against less conventional wall coverings and curtains of cotton . His most publicized designs were for the apartment of Cole Porter, with its unusual brass-tube bookcases.

Ballantine, James (1808–77) Scottish house painter who took up drawing at the Edinburgh Trustees Academy, becoming involved in a revival of the art of stained glass. His company won the competition to make stained glass for the House of Lords, in 1843.

Ballin, Mogens (1871–1914) Danish metalworker, based in Copenhagen. His workshop produced copper and pewter items as well as silver. Georg JENSEN made his first jewellery designs in Ballin's smithy in 1901, before setting up in business himself.

Bang & Olufsen Danish electronics manufacturers were always in the forefront of technological developments from their founding in 1925, but by the early 1960s they made a significant breakthrough in the design and streamlining of their radios, turntables, amplifiers and speakers. The technicians closely liaised with the designers from an early stage, the elegant result being of exquisite simplicity.

Barbe, Pierre (1900–1995) French architect and designer. Specializing in furniture, he produced exhibition-quality pieces in a simple style, using plate glass and formed steel tubing.

Barnack, Oscar (1879–1936) German industrial designer, who created the first Leica 35mm camera which revolutionized photography, replacing the previous, cumbersome models.

Baroque The term baroque is thought to have more than one source, either the Italian word for a tortuous device in logic or the Spanish and Portuguese word for a misshapen pearl. From about 1855 onwards, it became the accepted term to describe 17th-century art and design. The Carracci family of painters from Bologna returned to the grander style of Raphael, based on the ideals of classical antiquity. It was also promoted by Rubens and Bernini. Scrolls, ACANTHUS, masks and putti made frequent appearances in baroque paintings and designs for artefacts. As styles inevitably change, the excesses to which baroque was prone began to fall out of fashion and gradually lead into the ROCOCO style.

Barraband, Jacques (*c.*1767–1809) born in Aubusson, into a family of tapestry makers. He worked variously as a flower painter at the Sèvres porcelain factory (for which he won the Gold Medal at the Paris Salon in 1804) and as a designer at the Gobelin tapestry factory. In 1807, he was appointed Professor of Floral Design at the newly-founded Lyon Ecole des Beaux Arts.

Barrau, Gerard (1945–) French industrial designer, specializing in store layouts, notably those for the clothing company La Chemise Lacoste and the electric goods chain, Darty.

Barron, Phyllis (1890–1964) British textile designer who explored old methods of block printing, using natural dyes. She employed her large collection of old French blocks mingled with blocks cut herself in similar style. Amongst her commissions were the soft furnishings for the Duke of Westminster's yacht *The Flying Cloud* and the Senior Common Room of Girton College, Cambridge.

Bastide, Thomas (1954–) French glass designer, born in Biarritz, who joined BACCARAT in 1981, becoming Head of Design in 1983. His signature piece is the 1986 *Triangle* drinking glass.

Battersby, George Martin (1914–1982) British illustrator and exhibition designer, trained at the Regent Street Polytechnic and the Royal Academy of Dramatic Art, London. He worked briefly at LIBERTY's before designing the 1938 production of *Hamlet* at the Old Vic. An early collector of ART NOUVEAU, about which he became a recognized expert, he also worked as a set designer with Cecil BEATON, painted many murals for private clients, as well as those in the Carlyle Hotel, New York. Designed many exhibitions for the Brighton Festival, England, including 'The Jazz Age' in 1969 and 'Follies and Fantasies' in 1971.

Bauhaus An art school founded in Weimar, Germany, by the leading architect Walter GROPIUS in 1919. It grouped together two schools of fine arts and crafts. Its aim was to revive the lost unity of the arts, in relation to modern architecture on the one hand and the needs of industry on the other. It was a self-contained centre of artistic instruction and culture, with tremendous breadth of scope. The leading teachers, together with Gropius, were artists of the first rank, Lionel Feininger (painting), Paul KLEE (painting and design), Oskar Schlemmer (painting and theatre design), Wassily KANDINSKY (theory and monumental painting) and Ladislaus MOHOLY-NAGY (early photograms and montages) . The school was obliged to move to Dessau in 1929, and was closed down by the Nazis in 1933.

Baumann, Hans Theo (1924–) Swiss ceramic artist who works largely in Germany. Principal clients included ROSENTHAL and Thomas, for whom he designed both ceramic and glassware, most notably his 1958 *Berlin* dinner service. For Arzwald he designed the 1971 *Brasilia* coffee and tea services, amongst many others.

Bawden, Edward (1903–1995) British painter who studied at Cambridge Art School and the Royal College of Art, London, under Paul NASH. He designed many seminal advertising campaigns, notably for the Westminster Bank and Shell-Mex. He also designed wallpapers for Cole, posters for London Transport, decorated pottery for Wedgwood, and made tile decorations for London Underground's Victoria Line.

Bayer, Herbert (1900–1985) Austrian born designer, trained at the BAUHAUS under KANDINSKY and MOHOLY-NAGY . He took charge of the typographic workshop at the Bauhaus in Dessau, designing much printed material, including their *Journal*. In 1925, he designed a new sans-serif typeface, *Universal,* which he revised in 1928, before leaving to set up his own studio in Berlin. In 1838, he left for America and became involved with the Museum of Modern Art Bauhaus Exhibition. He later moved to Aspen, Colorado.

Beardsley, Aubrey Vincent (1872–88) British illustrator and graphic designer. Self-taught, he was encouraged by the painter Edward Burne-Jones. His first major work was *Morte d'Arthur* in 1891-2, which was publicized in the first issue of *The Studio* magazine, for which he designed covers. His highly erotic works were influenced by orientalism, appearing in the notorious *Yellow Book*.

Beaton, Cecil (1904–80) British dilettante designer and photographer. His photographs of royalty, celebrities and fashion graced the pages of smart magazines such as *Vogue* and *Vanity Fair* for nearly four decades. He also designed sets and costumes for the films *Gigi* (1959) and, most famously, *My Fair Lady* (1965), both of which earned him Oscars. His country homes, Ashcombe and, later, Broadchalke in Wiltshire, were decorated in voluptuous styles, by friends such as Rex WHISTLER and Oliver MESSEL.

Beene, Geoffrey (1927–) American fashion designer, born in Louisiana. He worked for Samuel Winston before setting up his own studio in New York, together with his boutiques, Beene Bazaar and Beenebag. He designed furniture such as the *Shoe Heel* stool and the *Leg* table in 1991, together with a range of Drum porcelain in 1993.

Behrens, Peter (1868–1940) German designer, based in Darmstadt, who worked on factory buildings, electrical goods and publicity for AEG.

Bell, Vanessa (1879–1961) British painter and interior designer, sister of the novelist Virginia Woolf. She studied at the Royal Academy Painting School and the Slade School, London. She was a director of Roger Fry's OMEGA WORKSHOPS, painting furniture and screens. With Duncan GRANT she carried out many interior decoration schemes, including work for Kenneth (later, Lord) Clark. She designed book covers for the Hogarth Press and pottery for A. J. Wilkinson, under the direction of Clarice CLIFF.

Benedictus, Edouard (1878–1930) Prolific French designer of textiles and Art Moderne patterns used in decoration. He also designed rugs and carpets.

Berain, Jean (1640–1711) French engraver and designer, he published designs for gun stock and barrel decorations in 1659.

Berg, G. A. (1884–1957) Swedish furniture designer who revived bentwood furniture, which he sold in the store he opened. An influential MODERNIST in Sweden.

Berlage, Hendrik Petrus (1856–1934) Dutch architect and designer, born and worked in Amsterdam, though trained in Zurich.

He introduced the work of Frank Lloyd WRIGHT to Europe and also designed large items of furniture, ironwork and associated lighting.

Bernadotte, Count Sigvard (1907–1995) Son of King Gustavus VI of Sweden, designer in the Georg JENSEN Silversmithy, using a modern, austere style with simple linear decoration, producing his *Bernadotte* flatware in 1939. In 1949, he started his own studio in Copenhagen, which had branches in Stockholm and New York, producing designs for delicate silver and heavy machinery.

Bernard, Oliver Percy (1881–1939) British architect and designer who started out as a stage set designer, working as far afield as the Boston Opera House and the Theatre Royal, Drury Lane, London. He designed the decorations for the 1924 Wembley 'Empire Exhibition' and introduced steel furniture into London hotels, such as the Strand Palace and Cumberland, as well as several Lyons Corner Houses.

Bernardaud, Porcelaines French ceramics company founded in 1863. It is notably recently for designs by Bernard Buffet and Theo van Dongen. Single pieces have also been designed by Roy LICHTENSTEIN and Jean TINGUELY.

Berthelemy, Jean Simon (1743–1811) French painter who won the Prix de Rome in1767, his decorative painting of the Seige of Calais in 1777, being reproduced as a Gobelins tapestry for Louis XVI . Towards the end of his life he designed costumes for the Paris Opera

Beyer, Johann Christian Wilhelm (1725–1806) German-born sculptor, painter and architect. He designed for the Duke of Wurttemburg's porcelain factory at Ludwigsburg, moving on to Vienna where he created garden statues for Schonbrunn Palace. He published a book of these figures (which had mostly been used at Ludwigsburg), a rare account of ROCOCO designs.

Biedermeyer A term first used in 1853 as the surname of an imaginery poet who 'contributed' to a humorous magazine *Fliegende Blatter*. It is made up of 'bieder' the German adjective meaning plain and unpretentious, and 'Meier' one of the most common German surnames. By the 1890s the term came to refer to the design style of the 1820s and 1830s in a derogatory way.

The style was of great simplicity, most obvious in furniture made by craftsmen for the middle classes. It was a simplified form of French Empire style, making it acceptable to its target market in Germany, Austria and the Scandinavian countries.

Bill, Max (1908–1995) Swiss designer, painter and architect who studied at the BAUHAUS before returning to Zurich in 1929 to practise architecture. He worked for the Wohnbedarf department store, designing all their print material, including a logo. Apart from an extensive architectural practice, he continued with product design, producing his classic stacking chair in 1954.

Bindesboll, Thorvald (1846–1908) Danish architect whose buildings include the Thorvaldsen Museum in Copenhagen. He designed earthenware for the Copenhagen Valby factory, as well as posters, bookbindings, furniture and silverwork for Michelsen, the Danish Court jewellers. He was the most prolific of the Danish ART NOUVEAU designers, the Carlsberg lager label being his longest lasting work.

Bing and Grøndahl Porcelaenfabrik Danish ceramics manufacturer founded in 1853. A notable ART NOUVEAU design was the *Heron* dinner service of 1888. They specialized in figurines of women and children and the work of Jean GAUGUIN. In 1987, the company merged with Royal Copenhagen.

Bing, Samuel (1838–1905) German collector, born in Hamburg. He opened his first shop in Paris in 1877. In 1895, he opened another shop, L'Art Nouveau, which gave its name to that artistic movement. He specialized in glass designed by Emile GALLÉ and René LALIQUE. His son, **Marcel Bing** (1875–1920), took over the shop after his death.

Biro, Laszlo (1889–1965) Hungarian painter, sculptor and inventor, who needed a pen that did not dry up for his artwork. With his brother, Gyorgy, he developed a fast-drying ink that fed a rolling ball at the tip of the pen, through capillary attraction. He patented the instrument in 1938 and it was manufactured in Britain for pilots in the Second World War to mark their charts at high altitude. The basic technology was perfected by Marcel Bich, who introduced the novel, clear crystal plastic body, producing the first Bic pen in 1958.

Bjorn, Acton (1910–92) Founder of Denmark's first industrial design practice in 1949 and designer of metalworks, ceramics, industrial machinery and office equipment. His 1966 *Beolit 500*
transistor radio for BANG & OLUFSEN was a landmark design in
electronics.

Black, Misha (1910-77) British industrial and exhibit designer,
who was born in Baku (Azerbaijan). As an architect he designed
Kardomah coffee shops in London and Manchester and founded
the Industrial Design Partnership with Milner GRAY, the first
multi-skilled design group in Britain. They designed radios and
televisions for Ekco, the 'Britain Can Make It' exhibition at the
Victoria and Albert Museum in 1946, trains and stations for London Underground's Victoria Line and the interiors of London's
buses. From 1959 to 1975 he was professor of industrial design at
the Royal College of Art, London.

Blaich, Robert (1931–) American industrial designer who was appointed design director of Philips Electronics in the Netherlands,
supervizing over 200 designers in 22 countries. Described as the
'world's most influential product designer', he once asserted that
'You can be mass and class.'

Boberg, Ferdinand (1860–1946) Swedish architect and designer
of glassware, ceramics and textiles. Famous for his furniture designs for the Swedish Royal Family and was one of the few designers to produce Modern silver in Sweden at the turn of the century. He used pine branches as part of his decorative silver work.

Boda (Kosta Boda) Swedish glass manufacturer founded in 1864
and based in the village of Boda. Window glass was the first
product, then general household glassware. By the turn of the
century they were producing decorative items, including cameo-
glass vessels and a much-copied glass with a bubble entrapped in
the stem which was produced in 1938. They remained at the forefront of glassware design until well into the 1970s, producing distinctive lines, including their classic cafetiere.

Bodley, George Frederick (1827–1907) British architect and designer, a pupil of GOTHIC architect Sir George Gilbert Scott
(1871–78). His first commission, St Michael's Church, Brighton,
includes some of William MORRIS's earliest stained glass and

decorative work. He founded a church furnishing company, designing metalwork, together with textiles and wall coverings. He also redecorated the Fishmongers' Hall in the City of London.

Boehm, Michael (1944–) German ceramic and glassware designer who joined ROSENTHAL in 1966, where his hallmark designs are inspired by 17th-century Venetian vessels, particularly those involving twisting thread stems.

Bogler, Theodor (1897–1968) German ceramic designer who studied at the BAUHAUS, where he went on to supervise the Ceramic Production Workshop at Dornburg, near Weimar, an annex of the Bauhaus. He also produced commercial designs for several ceramic factories, including the State Majolica factory at Karlsruhe. He became a Benedictine monk in 1932, becoming abbot of the Maria Laach monastery in 1939.

Boiceau, Ernest (1881–1950) Swiss designer who worked in Paris, best known for tapestries and embroidery which he sold in his own shop. He also carried out public commissions and decorating many private apartments, as well as the Hotel de Wendel, Paris. He also designed fabric for the couture house of Worth.

Boissevain, Antoinette (1898–1973) Dutch painter and lighting designer who settled in London in 1918, taking over the management of Merchant Adventurers, importers of European china and glass, in 1924. They imported GISPEN's lighting range in 1930 for the yacht club at Burnham-on-Crouch, which led to extensive commissions to design the lighting fixtures for Shell-Mex, Harrods, the Savoy Hotel and Bush House, all in London.

Bojeson, Kay (1886–1958) Danish silversmith and ceramicist, trained with Georg JENSEN and the Royal Craft School of Precious Metals in Wurttenburg. He pioneered Danish Modern style with simple undecorated forms. He was a consultant to BING AND GRØNDAHL and designed stainless-steel tableware for Universal Steel. He also pioneered simple, modern toy design and was appointed silversmith to the king of Denmark.

Bonfils, Robert (1886–1971) French painter and designer, creating bookbindings and ceramics for Sèvres. He designed the tea room of the Au Printemps department store in Paris, painting the walls with images of the seasons.

Bonnard, Pierre (1867–1947) French painter with a great interest in the decorative arts. In the commercial field be designed a poster for France-Champagne in 1889 and, in 1894, for *La Revue Blanche,* for which he also did illustrations. In 1895, he designed a stained glass window for TIFFANY, which was exhibited by BING. A screen featuring nursemaids and cats was designed in 1894 and lithographed in 1897. In 1904 he designed a bronze table centre-piece.

Bonvallet, Lucien (1861–1919) French designer and master of copperware, he designed mountings for important pieces of glassware by Emile GALLÉ and others.

Boote, T. and R. British ceramics manufacturer, in Burslem, Staffordshire, founded in 1842. It produced tiles and, in collaboration with Boulton and Worthington, patented a new method of tile production, in 1863, which made decorative tiles more widely available. In the 1890s, they produced tiles incorporating the drawings of Walter CRANE, as well as transfer-printed tiles with ART NOUVEAU patterns. Their plain tiles were used to line the Blackwall Tunnel under the River Thames. They also produced Parian ware, exhibiting a copy of the Portland Vase in the Great Exhibition of 1851.

Booth, Charles (1844–93) British stained-glass designer who worked in New York in the 1870s, where he designed windows for the Jefferson Market Courthouse and the Calvary Church. He used Modern GOTHIC style, based on the designs of Christopher DRESSER and the Anglo-Japanese fashions of the 1870s.

Borrelli, Corrado (1947–) Italian industrial and graphic designer working in Milan. He worked as a consultant for many clients, including the *Carlotta* bamboo chair, for Bonacina, and the *Model 1475* television, for AEG.

Borsani, Osvaldo (1911–1995) Italian furniture designer, born in Switzerland, who designed from technological principles rather than aesthetics. He founded his company, Tecno, in 1954, producing an articulated chaise longue and a matching sofa. His rubber-armed chair was described as a 'machine for sitting' and supposedly could assume 486 positions.

Borsato, Giuseppe (1770–1849) Venetian painter who worked in

Rome with Canova, before returning to Venice to work as a decorative painter. He achieved fame by designing for Napoleon I and his circle. In 1815 he designed a table that was presented to Austria as a token of Venice's loyalty, illustrated in his volume, *Opera ornamentale* (Venice, 1822). It includes his designs for church furniture and decoration, silver and life.

Bossanyi, Elvin (1891–1975) Hungarian stained-glass designer who settled in Britain. His work includes glass for the Senate House of London University (1934), Uxbridge Undergound Station (1935) and for the Tate Gallery over a period of four years from 1938. Other commissions include glass for Canterbury Cathedral, the Victoria and Albert Museum, the church at Port Sunlight and York Minster.

Boucher, Guy (1935–1992) French designer and engineer who designed dinnerware for Duralux, drinking glasses for DAUM and the first one-piece pocket lamp, produced by Mazda.

Boulestin, X Marcel (*fl.* 1906–1930) French interior designer, first worked in Paris with Colette and her husband, Willy. Max Beerbohm encouraged him to move to England in 1906, where he set up the *Decoration Moderne* shop in Elizabeth Street, stocking Parisian furniture and furnishings as well as a range of designs by Paul POIRET. Clients included Lady Curzon and the Baroness d'Erlanger. He started the fashion for 'java paper' (silk glued to paper) lampshades. When the shop closed in 1921 he became a restaurateur.

Bradley, Will (1868–1962) American graphic designer who worked in Chicago as a wood-engraver. Influenced by Aubrey BEARDSLEY, his work was of impeccable technical quality. He was also an influential typographer.

Brandt, Edgar (1880–1960) French designer, specializing in metalwork and lighting. The leading exponent of decorative ironwork of his day, his principle commissions included pieces in ART NOUVEAU style for the Paris 1925 Exhibition and the Tomb of the Unknown Soldier at the Arc de Triomphe, Paris.

Brandt, Marianne (1893–1983) German designer and metalworker, who studied at the BAUHAUS from 1923–25. Inspired by MOHOLY-NAGY's Constuctivist geometric forms, she became an industrial designer, mainly of lamps. She became head of the Bauhaus metal workshops in 1928 and worked with its founder, the architect Walter GROPIUS, in Berlin. Some of her designs are still produced, including a 1930s tea set.

Brangwyn, Frank (1867–1956) Belgian-born British artist, who trained as a draughtsman and designed tapestries for William MORRIS. He designed and painted murals for Samuel BING's shop in Paris in 1895, and designed his first bedroom furniture in 1900, which was produced by Norman and Stacey in London. Many and various commissions followed the showing of his murals for the San Francisco International Exposition in 1914, including tableware for Doulton and the Empire Murals for the House of Lords in 1930, which were rejected and were eventually installed in Swansea Town Hall in 1934. Other murals were installed at the Rockefeller Center, New York, the Skinners Hall and the Rowley Gallery, both in London.

Braquernond, Joseph Auguste (1833–1914) French artist and designer who discovered Japanese coloured, woodblock prints in a shop in Paris in 1856. Out of this chance happening grew the French and British enthusiasm for Japanese design, heavily promoted by LIBERTY'S.

Brateau, Jules-Paul (1844–1923) French metalworker and jewellery designer who became head designer at Boucheron, the jewellers. He also made attractive and inexpensive objects in pewter, thus helping to revive interest in this metal.

Braun German domestic appliance maker, founded by Max Braun in Frankfurt in 1921. Their products were always design-led, sometimes appearance being better than performance; their elegant 1961 toaster, with simple unadorned lines, was not tall enough to toast the top of a slice of bread.

Breuer, Marcel Lajos (1902–81) Hungarian-born designer who studied architecture in Vienna before attending the BAUHAUS, where he specialized in the design of furniture. His design from this period is distinctive by the purity of its form. In 1925 he produced the *Wassily* chair, inspired by the technology used in the frame structure of an Adler bicycle; it was the first steel tubular chair. From 1925 Breuer was head of furniture design at the

Bauhaus before leaving to establish his own practice in Berlin in 1928. Until 1931 he continued to design interiors and furniture, including the *Cesca* chair (1928) which proved very successful. In 1935 Breuer worked in England practising as an architect before settling in America where he worked in partnership with Walter Gropius until 1941. He was also professor of architecture at Harvard fom 1937–47. Breuer's importance as a designer has been exemplified by the continued production of his designs.

Breuhaus de Groot, Fritz-August (1883–1960) German architect and designer who worked in Dusseldorf for fellow student Peter Behrens. For Württembergische Metallwarenfabrik, he designed silverware and metalwork, and tubular-steel chairs, parallelling the work of Breuer. He worked on the interior design of the first Zeppelin and on the layout and decorations of the ill-fated Hindenburg dirigible in 1936, making extensive use of aluminium.

Brongniart, Alexandre-Theodore (1739–1813) French architect who designed many buildings in Paris after 1765, his last being the Bourse, which was begun in 1807. He designed for the Sèvres porcelain factory from 1801 until his death. His works included the *Olympic* service, begun in 1804 and Napoleon's private service, began in 1807.

Brown, Eleanor McMillen (1890–1991) American interior designer who studied in New York and at the influential Parsons School of Design in Paris. Her clients included prominent families of American social life; the Winthrops, the Aldriches and the Rockefellers. She also used her bold statements in the design of the house of Mr and Mrs Henry Parish II in the late 1920s. Mrs Parish (aka Sister Parish) became an interior designer herself. Employing mostly students of the Parsons School (of which she was a governor) her design practice became the training ground for further generations of American interior designers.

Brown, F. Gregory (1887–1948) British commercial artist and designer who initially trained as an art metal worker but was soon working as an illustrator for several magazines. His fabrics were roller-printed in highly fashionable black onto white linen and one won a gold medal at the 1925 Paris Exposition of Decorative Arts. His graphic design clients included the major railway companies (prior to nationalization), Mac Fisheries, Derry and Toms and Cadbury.

Brown, Ford Madox (1821–93) Born in France, Brown initially studied painting in northern Europe before travelling to Paris, Rome and eventually to England. In 1848 he met Dante Gabriel ROSSETTI in London and became involved with the PRE-RAPHAELITE movement, although he was never a member of the brotherhood. In 1856 he met William MORRIS and became a founder member of Morris and Co. in 1861. Until the mid-1870s, Brown designed furniture, wallpaper, embroidery, glass and tiles; some pieces of his furniture were shown at the 1890 Arts and Crafts exhibition. He was also commissioned to contribute decorations for Manchester Town Hall.

Buatta, Mario (1936–) American interior designer, working in New York. He designed the interiors of Blair House in Washington, the American government's guest-house for visiting dignitories. The English-inspired designs, employing flower-covered fabrics, led to him being dubbed 'the prince of chintz'. He has designed every conceivable item needed in the home, from coal scuttles to carpets.

Bugatti, Carlo (1855–1940) Italian designer and furniture maker who was born and worked in Milan. Best known as the designer of highly unusual furniture in Futuristic style, combined with Moorish and Japanese styles of the day. His pieces were often asymmetrical and covered with parchment, leather, metal inlays and innumerable other knick-knacks. In 1900, he designed furniture for the Khedive's palace in Istanbul and in 1901 for Lord Battersea in Britain. His most fantastic achievement was the extraordinary Snail Room for the 1912 Turin Exhibition which he designed in its entirety, employing a myriad of materials from inlaid and gilded woods, silver and pewter, insects and flowers. He sold his business in 1904, moving to Paris to work as a designer of silverware. His son, **Ettore** (1881–1947) achieved lasting fame as a car designer.

Bulgari, Sotirio (1857–1932) Greek jeweller who started out selling modest jewels from a stall in Rome, in 1881. After some years he was able to open a shop, near the site of the present-day flagship store, which heads a world-wide chain. Employing notable designers, they have developed a boldly-stated style.

Burckhardt, Ernst F. (1900–1958) Swiss architect and designer who worked in Zurich and London, where he designed sets for two productions at London University. In Zurich he designed for the Krater Cabaret, which he headed, and designed the interiors of the Wohnbedarf department store. His buildings include the Zurick Volkstheater (1950) and the Dublin University Theatre (1956).

Burges, William (1827–81) British architect who won the international competition to build Lille Cathedral, although the design was never executed. A friend of the PRE-RAPHAELITES, he was involved in the GOTHIC revival movement. Outside architecture his work embraced medieval jewellery design, antique metalwork, stained glass, ceramics and painted furniture. Principal buildings include Cardiff Castle, Cork Cathedral and his own house in Holland Park, London.

Burne-Jones, Edward (1838–1898) British artist and designer. He met William MORRIS at Oxford University, where he also discovered the writings of John RUSKIN. Though best-known as a painter, a pupil of Dante Gabriel ROSSETTI, he also designed stained-glass windows and figurative tapestries for the William Morris company. He was commissioned by John Ruskin to design the Whitelands College medal and he designed a range of jewellery featuring leaf and bird designs.

Busquet, Edouard Wilfred (*fl.* 1920s) French lighting designer who patented the first anglepoise lamp in 1925, one of the most popular lamps of the period, much admired by architects such as BREUER.

Butterfield, William (1814–1900) British GOTHIC Revival architect who made effective use of patterned brickwork, the best example being Keble College, Oxford.

C

Caelani, Michelangelo [Duke of Sermoneta] (1803–83) Italian patron, painter and jewellery designer who supported the Fortunato

Pio Castellini family and company. He designed many of their Neo-GOTHIC and Italian medieval style jewels.

Calder, Alexander (1898–1976) American sculptor, painter and designer, famed for his decorative mobiles which were a feature of the 1950s. They were inspired by images created by painters such as Paul KLEE and Joan Mirò. In 1969, he designed porcelain for Sèvres and airplane fuselages for Braniff Airlines. He also designed for the stage, working in primary colours, which were also a feature of his paintings.

Cailleres, Jean Pierre (1941–) French architect and designer who set up his own studio, Papyrus, in 1979, to specialize in office, shop and hotel interiors, and related furniture. He designed dinner services in unusual triangular and asymmetric shapes and some of the first dishes specifically designed for microwave ovens.

Callot, Jacques (1592–1635) French engraver, originally apprenticed as a goldsmith. He settled in Florence in 1612 and produced prints incorporating many cartouches, often of a macabre nature, which were the inspiration for designs by many goldsmiths and at the porcelain factories of Meissen, Vienna and Chelsea.

Cameron, Charles (*c.*1743–1812) London-born son of a Scottish carpenter and builder, he trained as an architect, specializing in the Palladian style. He edited Lord Burlington's edition of Palladio's drawings and, in Rome, published his own *The Baths of the Romans,* which he dedicated to Lord Bute. In 1778, he went to work for Catherine the Great in Russia, designing a pavilion at the Winter Palace at Tsarskoe Selo. In 1781, he designed the palace at Pavlovsk for the Grand Duke Paul, who, on becoming Tsar, dismissed him. He returned to favour when Paul's son, Alexander, came to the throne. He died while working in St Petersburg.

Carder, Frederick C. (1863–1963) British glassware designer who, dissatisfied with production standards in Britain, joined Thomas Hawkes in America to found the STEUBEN Glassworks, named after Steuben County, New York. They introduced new techniques, including irridescent glass known as Aurene, as well as cameo glass based on 18th-century Chinese styles. He is regarded as the father of modern glass-making in America.

Cardew, Michael (1901–83) British ceramicist, a pupil of Bernard

LEACH who revived the art of British slip-ware. He also set up potteries in Commonwealth countries, including Nigeria and Ghana.

Carême, Marie Antoine (1714–1833) French designer, son of a street cleaner. He was abandoned at the age of ten, but rose to become the greatest cook of the age. He studied architecture from volumes at the Bibliotheque Royale, to facilitate the design of elaborate table decorations built out of icing sugar. He published plans for real buildings in Paris and St Petersburg.

Carnegie, Hattie (1886–1956) Born Henrietta Kanengeiser in Austria, Carnegie worked as a clothing and jewellery designer New York. She opened her first shop, Carnegie-Ladies' Hatters, in 1909, which she expanded into a chain by 1929. She survived the stock market crash by launching her ready-to-wear line of originals and copies of French fashions.

Carr, Alwyn C. E. (1872–1940) British silversmith, who worked in London at the company formed in partnership with Omar Ramsden, named St Dunstan's, after the patron saint of silversmiths. Their style was that of the ARTS AND CRAFTS MOVEMENT.

Carrier-Belleuse, Albert-Ernest (1824–87) French ceramicist and modeller who studied and worked in Paris before joining MINTON in Britain where he designed majolica and Parian wares. He also designed for Wedgwood and continued to send designs for metalwork to Paris.

Carter, John (1748–1817) British architect and antiquarian, trained as a marble carver and mason. In 1786, the Society of Antiquaries commissioned him to prepare drawings and etchings of current trends in monumental design. He was elected a Fellow in 1795, supported by Sir John Soane and Horace Walpole.

Carter, Ronald (1926–) British furniture designer who started out as a designer with the Corning Glassworks, New York, before setting up businesses in London and Birmingham. He has designed mass production furniture for Sir Terence CONRAN's Habitat chain and has worked on corporate commissions for the BBC, the Victoria and Albert Museum and Terminal Four of Heathrow Airport.

Cartier French court jewellers, originally based in Paris. The company was originated by **Pierre Cartier**, built up by his son **Louis-**

François (1819–1904) to become the most successful jeweller of the Second Empire, through the patronage of Princess Mathilde Bonaparte, a cousin of Napoleon I. The Franco-Prussian War of 1870 led Louis-François to open a shop in London. The New York Cartier house was bought in 1917, reputedly for a double string of pearls. Cartier's style became more distinct in the 1920s and 1930s. In 1917, they created the *Tank* watch to honour the American Tank Corps and they became known for their ART DÉCO mantel clock with its invisible movement. The 1923 interlaced three-band ring, made of three shades of gold, was wrongly accredited to Jean COCTEAU, who did receive one of the first produced. **Louis Cartier** (son of Louis-François) was the creative force of the company and responsible for the Art Déco and Art Moderne designs. Their leading freelance designer during this period was Jeanne Toussaint, who eventually took over the Paris shop in 1942. Many of the most striking pieces of the 1930s and 1940s were commissioned by the Duke of Windsor for his Duchess. The separate, Paris, London and New York shops were brought together as Cartier International when they were acquired by Robert Hocq, the French industrialist, in 1972 and 1976.

Carwardine, George (1887–1948) British automobile engineer and lighting designer. He produced the first commercially successful anglepoise lamp in 1934 based on the constant-tension principles of the human arm, its springs being the equivalent of muscles.

Cellini, Benvenuto (1500–71) Italian goldsmith, born in Florence where he worked before leaving for Bologna and Rome. His designs in MANNERIST style, for vases and centrepieces, and enjoyed great success in Italy and France. He also wrote a colourful autobiography.

Cerri, Pierluigi (1939–) Italian architect, industrial, graphic and exhibition designer. Designed the 1976 Venice Biennale and the Alexander CALDER exhibition in 1983. Designed for Electa, the publishing company, and designed and edited the magazine *Casabella*. Industrial clients include Fiat, IBM and Missoni.

Chalon, Louis (1866–1916) French painter and designer who worked in Paris. He started out as a painter and illustrator, but soon became active as a gemsetter, couturier, ceramicist and sculptor. He also produced models for a range of bronzes. His most popular items had a *femme-fleur* theme, his lighting fixtures featured bronze nymphs or naiads holding torches and women holding flowers, the petals surrounding electric bulbs.

Champion, Georges (1889–1940) French decorator and furniture designer who worked in Paris. He produced many pieces, largely for the firm of G. et G. Guerin, in severe geometric shapes, using contrasting colours, influenced by the DE STIJL group. In 1930, he opened Studio 75 and managed the magazine *L'Art Vivant,* which published the work of young artists and designers.

Chan, Kwok Hoi (1939–87) Chinese architect and interior designer, trained in Hong Kong. He designed furniture for Air India and the IBM offices in Hong Kong. In London, he collaborated on the design of some interiors for the liner, *Queen Elizabeth II.* Signature pieces include the cantilevered, tubular steel, *Pussy-Cat Chair* in 1969.

Chanaux, Adolphe (1887–1965) French designer and interior decorator, creator of exquisitely matched veneers in vellum, ivory, marquetry and leather. He designed chairs for the competition organized by the Paris Museum of the Decorative Arts in 1924. In 1932, he opened a shop on the Rue du Faubourg Saint-Honoré, with Jean-Michel FRANK, to sell his designs and those of friends such as the GIACOMETTI brothers. In 1941, Chanaux became artistic advisor to the House of Guerlain in Paris.

Charalambides Divanis, Sonia (1948–) Greek furniture designer who studied architecture and computer science in Paris, combining these two disciplines to research design methods and the use of computers in architecture. She returned to Athens to set up an architectural practice and design furniture, including *First,* a one-piece tubular armchair and *Animate*, a birch and steel chair, in 1987.

Charpentier, Alexandre (1856–1909) French sculptor, medallist, designer and decorator, much associated with BING and his shop, L'Art Nouveau. He designed furniture, interiors, metalwork, ceramics and lighting and was considered one of the best representatives of the Parisian ART NOUVEAU style.

Chase, William Merritt (1849–1916) American artist and teacher who influenced a whole generation of artists and designers, encouraging a lively approach and experimentation in colouration at the New York School of Fine and Applied Art, which he founded. One of his teachers of interior design was Frank PARSONS.

Chauchet-Guillere, Charlotte (1878–1964) French artist, decorator and furniture designer. From 1913 to 1939 she was artistic director of the Primavera workshop of the Au Printemps department store, Paris. She designed a bedroom for the Paris *Exposition Internationale des Arts Decoratifs et Industriels Modernes* in 1925.

Cheret, Joseph (1834–94) French sculptor and ceramicist designed many models and decorations for Sèvres where, in 1887, he succeeded his father-in-law, CARRIER-BELLEUSE, as artistic director of the modelling studio. He also designed in pewter, produced designs for BACCARAT and designed bronzes and electric sconces for the Soleau foundry.

Chermayeff, Serge Ivan (1900–1995) Russian architect and designer who settled in London in 1910, moving to America in 1939. His buildings in Britain include the Cambridge Theatre, London, in 1929–30, and the Earl de la Warr Pavilion, Bexhill-on-Sea, in 1933–35. He designed many fixtures and fittings, including carpets woven by Wilton Royal Carpets and radio cabinets for Ecko. He also pioneered the design of tubular steel furniture and designed ART DÉCO furniture for Waring and Gillow. In America, he was a professor at various colleges including Harvard and Yale.

Chessa, Paolo Antonio (1922–) Italian architect who turned to furniture design in the late 1940s, best known for his *Butterfly* chair, formed from lacquered plywood. He moved on to designing household furniture in plastic, his ideas being taken up by other designers.

Cheti, Fede (1905–78) Italian textile designer, based in Milan and backed by Gio PONTI, noted for her large motifs, printed and painted chintzes and rich velvets and silks, the popularity of which spread outside Italy. She also produced fabrics designed by artists such as Raoul DUFY and Georges de Chirico.

Cheval, Ferdinand (1836–1924) French postman who taught himself architecture, which he put into practice by building an extensive folly, his *Palais ideal,* at Hauterives. It drew upon European, African and Oriental architecture and consists of labyrinths, galleries and connecting steps. It was to become his tomb and was designated an historic monument in 1969.

Chevalier, Georges (1894–1987) French designer who worked with Leon Bakst, adding stage design to his knowledge of architecture and fine art. His interpretation of Cubism and orientalism was expressed in his work for Baccarat, with whom he was connected for most of his working life. Some of his pieces, such as the 1937 *Panther* and the 1949 *Stag's Head,* are still in production.

Chippendale, Thomas (1718–79) British furniture designer and cabinetmaker. He worked in London under the patronage of Lord Burlington, financed by his Scottish partner, James Rannie. His book, *The Gentleman and Cabinet-maker's Director, is* one of the most important pattern books of the century. His first major commission, by the architect Robert Adam, was for the furnishing of Dumfries House.

Cibic, Aldo (1955–) Italian architect working in Milan, he specialized in store design for Fiorucci and Esprit, watches for Tissot, and the furniture and ceramics for the Memphis group.

Clendenning, Max (1924–) British architect noted for his distinctive interiors using minimal furniture, often made of plywood, and the use of white. He has also designed a range of furniture for Liberty's.

Clerget, Charles Ernest (b. 1812) French designer of porcelain for the Sèvres factory and tapestry for the Gobelins factory. He produced books of ornaments, published designs for wallpapers and goldsmith's work.

Cliff, Clarice (1899–1972) British ceramicist and painter who produced distinctive, brilliantly-coloured, geometric patterns, very much her own vision of Art Déco. From 1929 to 1935 she worked at the Newport pottery, in Stoke-on-Trent, where she produced her highly-successful *Bizarre* pattern, creating such an enormous demand that extra painters had to be hired. Other successful patterns, including *Fantasque* and *Biarritz,* followed. In 1934, she became artistic director of ceramicists, overseeing designs by artists such as Paul NASH, Laura Knight, Duncan GRANT and Vanessa BELL. Until 1963, she continued to paint at the Royal Staffordshire Pottery.

Cobden-Sanderson, Thomas James (1840–1922) British bookbinder and printer, co-founder of the Dove Press. He is credited with coining the title of the ARTS AND CRAFTS MOVEMENT. His earlier bindings were decorated with gold ART NOUVEAU motifs.

Cocteau, Jean-Maurice-Clement-Eugene (1889–1963) French intellectual *agent provocateur,* who both created works himself and encouraged others. His graphic works were prolific; he called them 'graphic poems'. Many items were inspired by his drawings; furniture and jewellery, ceramics and fabric. He drew the original logo for the Edinburgh International Festival, Scotland.

Codman Jr., Ogden (1863–1951) American interior designer and architect who swept aside the heavy, cluttered interior decor of the Edwardian era, replacing it with white paint and light flowered fabrics, set in airy rooms. He wrote the influential book *The Decoration of Houses* (1897), with the novelist Edith Wharton. As an architect, his masterwork is considered to be *Leopolda,* a large chateau he built for himself at Villefranche-sur-Mer on the Cote d'Azur, France, in 1930. He later rented it to the Duke and Duchess of Windsor.

Colani, Luigi (1928–) German designer of speedboats, fashion, furniture and ceramics. The teapot of his *Drop* dinner service for ROSENTHAL had the handle near the centre of gravity to ease pouring, it was of thin-walled porcelain to retain heat and the cups had 'feet' to stop liquid collecting in the saucer. He designed the 1981 tea service produced by Melitta and, in 1986, pens for Pelikan.

Cole, Eric Kirkham (1901–65) British electronics industrialist who founded Ecko Radio, the earliest in wooden casings copying conventional furniture. He was the first British manufacturer to set up a plastics moulding plant, although the early bakelite sets did not sell well. Cole commissioned new designs from CHERMAYEFF with imaginative results, breaking away from the conventional 'furniture' look.

Cole, Sir Henry (1808–82) British soldier and administrator who published and promoted many aspects of design, including illustrated children's books and, in 1843, the first Christmas card, designed by J. C. Horsley. He was admired by PRINCE ALBERT and was on the committee to organize the 1851 Great Exhibition, and was general adviser to the 1862 Exhibition. He created his own museum in South Kensington, London, in 1852, which has developed into the Victoria and Albert Museum.

Colefax, Sybil (c.1875–1950) British designer who established salons at Onslow Square and Argyll House, London, which rivalled those of Ladies Oxford, Asquith and Cunard. In 1933, she began to work as an interior designer, setting up as Colefax and Fowler, with John Fowler, in 1934. She designed exquisitely detailed decors, often in unconventional colours, for her large circle of wealthy and well-connected friends.

Colonna, Edward (1862–1948) Born Edouard Klonne in Germany, Colonna moved to America in 1882, where he worked for Associated Artists, headed by Louis Comfort TIFFANY. Originally trained as an architect, his design work included railroad cars and railway stations. In 1898, he moved to Paris where he worked for BING's L'Art Nouveau shop, designing jewellery, fabrics and dinner services, as well as Bing's pavilion at the 1900 Paris Universal Exhibition. When Bing's shop closed, he returned to America as an interior designer, but his later ART DÉCO designs lacked originality.

Conran, Sir Terence Orby (1931–) British designer and entrepreneur, initially trained as a textile designer. After working for the Rayon Centre and for the architect, Dennis Lennon, he founded his own design group. He opened the first of the Habitat stores in 1964 to sell modestly-priced, well-designed furniture and furnishings. They influenced a whole generation of young people, furnishing their first homes. His Foundation funded the Boilerhouse project at the Victoria and Albert Museum, to promote good design. From this evolved the Design Museum at Butler's Wharf, London.

Cooper, Susan Vera (1902–1996) British ceramicist who started her career as a dress designer. From 1922 to 1929, she worked as a decorator, becoming the chief designer of the A. E. Gray company and the first woman to have her name, Susie Cooper, stamped on wares. In 1929, she set up her own pottery, moving in 1931 to Burslem, where she stayed for fifty years. At first she painted designs by hand, later using a lithographic transfer process. The John Lewis stores were her first major customer, soon followed by all the major British department stores. She designed elegant tableware for Imperial Airways and for the Royal Pavilion at the 1951 Festival of Britain. Her 1933 *Curlew* and 1935 *Kestrel* designs remain classics.

Coper, Hans (1921–1981) German-born ceramicist who settled in Britain in 1939 and was inspired to take up pottery by the works of Lucy RIE in 1946, with whom he eventually collaborated. His works were influenced by the Orient, as well as the modern, including the sculptors Alberto GIACOMETTI and Constantin Brancusi (1876–1957). In 1962, his candlesticks were installed in Coventry Cathedral.

Coray, Hans (1906–1991) Swiss designer who promoted the use of aluminium in furniture design. His 1939 *Landi* chair was designed for use at the Swiss National Exhibition and, until 1980, was made exclusively by a Swiss cookware manufacturer. It weighed 2.9 kilos (6.4 lbs) and was water-resistant.

Cottier, Daniel (1838–91) British stained-glass designer and decorator who worked initially in his home city of Glasgow, producing windows for Aberdeen cathedral and painted decorations for Downahill Church and the United Presbyterian Church, Queen's Parish, in Glasgow. In 1873, he opened a shop in New York, selling Venetian glass, Oriental rugs and a range of furniture. In 1878, he was commissioned to design a window for the Green Memorial Alcove in the New York Society Library. Others followed including the Calvary Church, Gramercy Park and the Grace Church, Brooklyn.

Cranach, Wilhelm Lucas von (1861–1918) German painter, jeweller and decorator. He designed ART NOUVEAU jewellery in the French and Belgian style, distinguished by a voluptuousness that was missing from the work of some of his contemporaries.

Crane, Walter (1845–1915) British illustrator and designer, initially apprenticed to a wood-engraver. He first came to prominence with his highly original children's books, which showed Japanese influences. A founding member of the Art Workers' Guild, he became an important propagandist for the ARTS AND CRAFTS MOVEMENT. He was one of the most versatile of the late-Victorian decorative artists, producing stained glass, ceramics, tiles, textiles, mosaics and plaster work. In 1895, his work was on show at BING's shop, L'Art Nouveau and as an honourary member of the Vienna Sezession, he designed the 1898 cover of its magazine *Jugend.*

Crotti, Jean (1878–1958) Swiss painter and stained glass craftsman who worked in Paris. Married to the sister of the artist Marcel Duchamp (1887–1968), he espoused Cubism and was active in the Dada movement. He created the *gemail* technique of assembling stained glass without the use of leading.

Cuvilliés, Jean François Vinzent Joseph (1695–1768) French-born architect who was court dwarf to Elector Max Emanuel of Bavaria in 1706. He was sent to Paris to develop his natural talents in 1683. After he returned to Munich, he designed several ROCOCO buildings, including the theatre of the Munich Residenz, now named after him. He was a prolific designer of furniture, snuff-boxes, picture frames, ormulu and plaster work.

D

Dair, Thomas (1954–) American industrial designer who studied at Syracuse University, New York State. He has worked as a designer of computer and medical products ranging from sewing machines to sunglasses, and for clients including Corning Glass, 3M, Singer and KNOLL. He has taught product design at the Parsons School of Design, New York.

Dali, Salvador (1904–88) Spanish painter, engraver, writer and book designer. Famed for his surrealist paintings, he was originally a book and magazine illustrator. Designs inspired by his paintings included the 1934 sofa for Edward James in the shape of Mae West's lips, the 1936 Lobster telephone and Hands chair.

He designed the dream sequence in Alfred Hitchcock's 1945 film, *Spellbound*. He also designed surrealist jewellery and glassware for such manufacturers as Steuben and Simpson's of New York and for Daum in France.

Dalpayrat, Pierre-Arden (1844–1910) French porcelain painter and ceramicist born in Limoges, France. He settled near Paris in 1889 and specialized in stoneware, developing his own colour, Dalpayrat rouge, a copper-red glaze which he used to create marble effects. The forms of his pots were influenced by Japanese design, often of gourds, figures, animals and fruits.

Dalton, William Bower (1868–1965) British watercolourist and potter, principal of Camberwell School of Art, 1899–1919, then curator of the South London Art Gallery. He also published three influential books on pottery design.

Darwin, Robin (1910–1974) British design educator, the great-grandson of Charles Darwin and great-great grandson of Josiah Wedgwood. He studied at Cambridge and the Slade School of Art, London. During the Second World War he served in the camouflage directorate, after which he taught at the Royal College of Art in London, eventually becoming Rector in 1948. His work emphasized the importance of industrial design, using the most up-to-date technology.

Daum, Auguste (1853–1909), **Antonin** (1864–1930) and **Paul** (d.1943) French glassware designers and manufacturers, based in Nancy. Father and sons produced everyday glassware, but gradually assembled a team of designers and artisans, becoming famous for fine, cut, etched and gilt glassware. Influenced by Émile Gallé, they opened a decorative studio which specialized in long-necked vases and lamps, often involving cameo-work. The company suffered badly during the economic depression of the 1920s, but they were rescued by an order for 70,000 sets of crystal for the liner Normandie. After the Second World War they returned to decorative porcelain, employing Salvador Dali amongst others. The company continues and has produced designs by Hilton McConnico and Philippe Starck.

Davis, Owen William (1838–1913) British architect noted for his fabric and wallpaper designs, with carefully concealed repeats.

He also designed furniture and metalwork for major manufacturers.

Dawson, Nelson Ethelrad (1889–1942) British architect, more interested in painting and silversmithing. With his wife, Edith, he set up a workshop in London, where she did most of the enamelling. In 1901, they founded the Artificers' Guild. Their designs, which often featured in The Studio and the Art Journal, often incorporated delicate enamels into their architecture-inspired silverware.

Day, Lewis Foreman (1845–1910) British designer of stained glass in the ARTS AND CRAFTS tradition. His first pattern book, *Instances of Accessory Art* (1880), shows the heavy influence of Japanese art.

Day, Lucienne (1917–) British textile designer who studied at the Royal College of Art, London. After some years of teaching, she began designing fabrics, wallpapers and carpets for many clients, including EDINBURGH WEAVERS, Wilton Royal Carpets, John Lewis and HEAL's. Her *Calyx* pattern for the Festival of Britain, London, 1951, is an archetypal image for the 1950s. Married to Robin DAY, with whom she collaborated on stained-glass, textile and wallpaper designs.

Day, Robin (1915–) British furniture designer. Following his exhibit at the international competition at the New York Museum of Modern Art in 1948, he became a consultant to HILLE, designing contract furniture. His propylene chairs sold over 12,000 copies. In 1951, he designed the seating for the Royal Festival Hall and, in 1968, for the Barbican Centre, both in London. He designed interiors for many aircraft, including the Super VC10. In 1962, he became a consultant to the John Lewis department store chain.

de Boer, Antoinette (1939–) German textile designer who studied under Margret HILDEBRAND in Hamburg, and succeded her as artistic director of the Stuttgarter Gardinenfabric. Architectural motifs feature in her designs, as in her 1969 Zazi range.

de Castelbajac, Jean-Charles (1949–) French fashion designer, born in Casablanca. He studied in Limoges, where he founded his first ready-to-wear company, Ko. From 1968, he worked as a freelance designer for companies including Max Mara, Levi-

Strauss, Jesus Jeans, Ellesse and Etam. His designs have used unconventional materials, including canvas, parachute cloth, plastics and car upholstery. After setting up a chain of boutiques in
the 1970s, he designed costumes for several films, including
Annie Hall and Who Killed My Husband?, as well as the TV series, Charlie's Angels. He has also designed costumes for Rod
Stewart, Elton John and Talking Heads. In 1979, he produced his
furniture range, featuring reversible, multicoloured, leather upholstery.

de Feure, George (1868–1928) Dutch decorative artist who
worked in Paris. He designed furniture, posters, glassware and
ceramics in the ART NOUVEAU style, first for Maison Fleury before
joining BING's shop, L'Art Nouveau, in Paris, becoming head of
design in 1924. He designed all the furniture in the fashion house
of Madeleine Vionnet.

de Lanux, Eyre 'Lise' (1894–1995) American designer who
worked in Paris in the 1920s, designing furniture in the Cubist
style, together with geometric-patterned rugs. She was a close
confidante of some of the greatest figures of the period, including
André Gide, Ernest Hemingway, Matisse, Pablo PICASSO and
Bernard Berenson. She left her husband, the diplomat Pierre de
Lanux, to live with Evelyn Wyld, with whom she worked. She
opened the fashionable shop, Decor, in Cannes and, when it
closed, moved to Rome where she designed for society friends. In
the 1960s, she contributed stories to the New Yorker magazine.

De Maestra, Georges (*fl.*1940s–50s) Swiss inventor of the tape
fastener known as Velcro, comprising of tiny hooked elements,
which cling to a fuzzy counterpart. Inspired by plant burrs, it was
designed in 1948 and patented in 1953.

De Morgan, William (1839–1917) British painter, ceramicist and
tilemaker, who was born and worked in London. He began working for William MORRIS in the early 1860s, painting tiles, but also
worked on stained glass. He later specialized in highly decorative
tile designs, some 300 being recorded in his pattern book of
1872–81. In his tiles, as with his pottery, he was heavily influenced by Islamic designs. He also produced decorations for
twelve liners of the P&O line.

Del Marie, Felix (1889–1952) French painter and designer who espoused Italian Futurism and became a follower of Piet Mondrian and the DE STIJL Group. He designed chairs in two or three colours and in tubular steel. He also experimented with the use of wrought iron and frosted glass in lighting design.

Denis, Maurice (1870–1943) French decorator who, together with Paul Serusier and Paul GAUGUIN and others, founded the NABIS group in the late 1880s. He illustrated books by Paul Verlaine and André Gide and designed stained glass and wallpaper. He painted friezes for the Church of St Paul in Geneva and his former home, the priory of St-Germain-en-Laye, near Paris, is now the Musée Symbolistes et Nabis.

DePree, Dirk Jan (1891–1990) American furniture manufacturer who worked in Michigan at his company, named after his father-in-law, Herman Miller, who had no other connection with the firm. He engaged Gilbert ROHDE as design director in 1931, eventually producing some of his MODERNIST designs. Following the death of Rohde, he employed a stream of eminent consultants including Charles EAMES, Isamu NOGUCHI, and the textile designer Robert PROPST. His association with Propst produced the Action Office, an open-plan office system which transformed the office environment.

Despres, Jean (1889–1980) French airplane pilot and aeronautical draughtsman who turned to silver- and gold-smithing. He specialized in severe, geometrical shapes, intended to look as though they had been made by machine.

De Stijl Dutch art and design movement founded in 1917 and the name of a magazine that expounded the views of the group, which included the painter Piet Mondrian. The group was strongly influenced by Cubism and the architectural designs were characterized by angular, smooth, cubic formations. The founder of the group and editor of the magazine, which ran from 1917 to the late 1920s, was the Dutch architect Theo VAN DOESBURG.

De Wolfe, Elsie (1865–1950) American interior designer who worked in New York, Paris and Los Angeles. Originally an actress, at a time when it was not a very respectable occupation, she moved into the house of her long-time companion and theatrical agent, Elisabeth Marbury in 1892, transforming its dark interiors (it had reputedly been the house of Washington Irving) with light shades and French furnishings, often painted white. In 1904, she retired from the stage, to become effectively, America's first professional interior designer. She opened, and decorated, a woman's club, The Colony. She introduced indoor-outdoor effects, involving trellis work and *trompe l'oeil* decoration. Henry Frick commissioned her to design the private rooms of his house on Fifth Avenue, New York. In 1926, she married the British diplomat, Sir Charles Mendl, becoming Lady Mendl. At their house in Beverly Hills she recreated the white effect.

Dinh Van, Jean (1927–) French jewellery designer who started as an apprentice at CARTIER, Paris. He set up his own workshop in 1965 and opened a boutique in 1976. Early pieces included a ring made of extruded gold, mounted with an iron pearl. He is noted for his simple, innovative shapes.

Dixon and Sons, James British silversmiths in Sheffield, founded in 1806. They produced many pieces designed by Christopher DRESSER from 1879 onwards and, later, pieces in both ART NOUVEAU and ART DÉCO styles.

Dobson, Frank (1888–1963) British painter and sculptor, active in many of the artists' groups of the early 1920s. He designed the ceramic reliefs on the, now fashionable, Hays Wharf building in London. Throughout the 1920s and 30s he designed several fabric ranges in batik, silk-screen and lino-cut. In 1935 he designed the *Calix Majestatis* silver-gilt cup, commissioned by the National Jewellers' Association for presentation to King George V.

Dohner, Donald R. (1907–44) American industrial designer who worked in Pittsburgh, Pennsylvania. An influential teacher at the Carnegie Institute of Technology, he was also a consultant to the Westinghouse Corporation, designing over 120 productions, ranging from vacuum cleaners to diesel-electric locomotives.

Dominique French interior design company, founded in 1922 by Andre Domin and Marcel Genevriere in the Rue du Faubourg Saint-Honoré, Paris. Their furniture was created out of exotic woods, often with pearl or brass inlay and applied carved relief mouldings. They also incorporated shagreen, an untanned, rough-surfaced lather. They furnished four grand apartments on the liner *Normandie*. After the Second World War, they designed furniture for the Elysée Palace in Paris.

Donald Brothers Scottish fabric manufacturers, based in Dundee, who employed notable designers of the 1930s, including Marion DORN and P. A. Staynes. Their range was described as 'Old Glamis Fabrics' and included high-quality art canvas, decorative linens and natural cotton and jute. *Festoon* was their most popular pattern.

Dorn, Marion Victoria (1899–1964) American-born fabric and carpet designer, who was married to E. McKnight KAUFFER. She worked in Paris from 1921 to 1925, producing batik designs with Matisse-inspired motifs. She designed fabric and Carpets for the Savoy, Claridges and Berkeley hotels in London and for liners including Orion and Queen Mary. With her husband she designed for the Wilton Royal Carpet factory and, by the mid-1930s, was the best-known carpet designer in Britain. Her white carpet was a feature of Syrie MAUGHAM's living room and, on her return to America, she was commissioned to design carpets for the diplomatic lounge of the White House.

Dorner, Marie-Christine (1960–) French designer, born in Strasbourg and trained in Paris. She went to Tokyo in 1986, where she designed a 13-piece suite of furniture, inspired by origami shapes, as well as interiors of boutiques and restaurants. She returned to Paris in 1987 to design furniture for a wide range of clients, including the Au Printemps department store. In 1989 she designed the furniture for the restaurant of the Comedie Française.

Dossi, Dosso (d.1542) Italian painter who worked in Mantua, Ferrarra, Florence and Venice, where he became friendly with the painter Titian. He designed tapestries, majolica, horse armour, coins and court entertainments, often in collaboration with his brother, Battista, who had worked in Raphael's workshop.

Doucet, Jacques (1853–1929) French couturier and patron of the arts. He encouraged Paul POIRET and Madeleine Vionnet. He built up a large collection of 18th-century art, which he sold in 1912, using the proceeds to amass an important library of art and design, which he gifted to the University of Paris in 1918. As an art patron, he once owned Pablo PICASSO's Les Demoiselles d'Avignon, commissioning furniture from Paul IRIBE, lacquers by Eileen GRAY and bookbindings and furniture from Paul-Émile Legrain. His 1926 villa at Neuilly had LALIQUE glass doors, a black glass staircase and a Lipchitz chimneypiece.

Draper, Dorothy (1889–1969) American interior designer, who became well-known after the renovation of her own house on the Upper East Side of New York. She established the Architectural Clearing House in 1925, to match architects with appropriate commissions. In 1929 she designed the public rooms of the Carlyle Hotel, New York, in a style christened 'Roman Deco', boldness being its hallmark. Her designs for the Hampshire House Hotel included cabbage rose chintzes, which became Schumacher's most popular design. Other hotels ranged from the Mark Hopkins in San Francisco, to Petropolis, near Rio de Janeiro. In 1954, she designed the restaurant of the Metropolitan Museum of Art, New York. In the 1940s and 1950s, much of the furniture and textile design in America was by, or inspired by her. She pioneered the picture window, white organdy curtains, outsize fabric motifs and bold, marble, floor tiles.

Dreier, Hans (1885–1966) German film designer, who was trained as an architect. He went to America in 1923 and was head of the design department at Paramount from 1928 to 1951. BAUHAUS furniture from his home featured in *Trouble in Paradise* in 1932 and he supervised the creation of an ART DÉCO Venice for *Top Hat* in 1935.

Dresser, Christopher (1834–1904) British botanist and designer, born in Glasgow and trained in London. While holding the position of professor of botany at several universities, he also had a large design practice, supplying designs for wallpapers, carpets, fabrics, linoleum and furniture. He designed tiles for MINTON and also worked in metal, in cast iron for Coalbrookdale Ironworks and in silver and silver place to Thomas Johnson, London.

Dreyfuss, Henry (1903–1972) American stage designer, who founded an important industrial design studio. He designed Bell telephones, Hoover products and passenger cars for the New

York Central Railroad. His books include *Designing for People* (1955) and *The Measure of Man* (1959). In 1965 he became the first president of the Industrial Designers Society of America. In 1972 he and his business-manager wife committed suicide.

Driade Italian furniture manufacturer set up in 1968 by Enrico ASTORI, his sister Antonia ASTORI and his wife Adelaide. Their many important designers, including Philippe STARCK, used plastic and fibreglass to create innovative furnishings in Pop and Conceptual Art styles. Classic pieces include THE 1977 *Alessio* chair and *Febo* table, together with Starck's series of Ubik furniture, inspired by the science-fiction novels of Philip K. Dick.

Dubois, Ferard (b.1859) Belgian sculptor and metalworker who studied natural sciences before turning to design. He was a medallist and modeller of silver and bronze, producing a wide range of objects, including fans, candelabra, medallions and plaques. His most famous piece is the lively five-branched candelabra in the Horta Museum, Brussels.

Dubreuil, Andre (1951–) French interior and furniture designer who started out in the antiques trade and as a *trompe l'oeil* artist. In 1985 he collaborated on the decoration of the Rococo Chocolats boutique and started designing wrought-iron furniture. His 1987 *Spine* chair was produced in Japan and, in 1990, he designed his first range of Roman-inspired glassware for DAUM.

Duc, Christian (1949–) Vietnamese designer working in Paris. Originally a book illustrator, he designed cinema and café interiors in Berlin, before setting up a gallery in Paris, in 1977. Clients for his lighting, furniture and carpet designs include the Toronto Museum of Modern Art, the Africa Queen restaurant in Paris and Elise Editions Rugs.

Du Cerceau, Jacques Androuet (*c.*1515–*c.*85) Little is known of the beginnings of this important pattern designer, whose ideas were disseminated across Europe by architects and crafsmen. His main body of work appeared *c.*1560 in a frenetic MANNERIST style. One design was used for a table listed in the1601 inventory of Hardwick Hall, Britain.

Dufet, Michel (1888–1985) French interior designer who studied painting and architecture at the Ecole des Beaux-Arts in Paris. In

1913 he established the MAM (Mobilier Artistique Moderne) Studio to produce modern furniture, wallpaper, fabrics and lighting. In 1918 he collaborated with Paul Claudel, André Gide, Marcel Proust and Gabriel Fauré on a revue, Feuillets d'Arts. For two years from 1922 he was head of the Red Star studio in Rio de Janeiro, designing cinemas, bars and stores. Back in Paris, between 1924 and 1929 he designed individual pieces such as the silver-birch desk for the head of Agence Havas and an ebony and zinc veneered desk for Compagne Asturienne des Mines. In 1924 he designed the first Cubist wallpapers and, in 1926, interiors for the liner *Foch*. In 1935 he designed 40 cabins of the liner *Normandie* and a private yacht. His furniture was also influenced by Cubism, often made of exotic woods. In 1933 he became editor-in-chief of Decor d'Aujourd'hui and in 1974 he designed the layout of the museum devoted to the architecture of Antoine Bourdelle, his father-in-law.

Dufrène, Maurice (1876–1955) French designer of furniture, fabrics, wallpapers, ceramic and silverware. In 1940 he founded the Société des Artistes Décorateurs, as a reaction to the excesses of Art Nouveau. He designed plain, solid shapes, with refined lines. From 1921 to 1952 he was design director for the La Maîtrise studio of Galeries Lafayette, Paris. He also undertook major private commissions, such as the townhouse of Pierre David-Weill and, in restrained Art Déco style, the apartment of Pierre Benoit. In the late 1920s he contributed furnishing designs for several French embassies and for the Elysée Palace in Paris.

Dufy, Raoul (1877–1953) French painter, associated with the Fauve school of artists, but active as a designer of letterheads, including that of Paul Poiret, who also commissioned fabric designs from him. From 1912 to 1930 he designed dress fabrics, upholstery textiles and printed patterns from Bianchini-Ferier in Lyons. His all-over patterns have been compared to those of William Morris. He designed curtains for the Boulestin's restaurant in London and 14 large textile hangings for Paul Poiret's barge at the 1925 Paris 'Exposition Internationale des Arts Decoratifs et Industriels Modernes'.

Dulac, Edmund (1881–1953) French illustrator who became a naturalized British citizen in 1912. He produced wax caricatures of celebrities of the time, such as Thomas Beecham. In 1930 he designed the Cathay Lounge on the liner *Empress of Britain*, Dutch banknotes for De La Rue, chocolate wrappers for Cadbury's and, among his many philatelic commissions, stamps for the coronations of George VI and Elizabeth II, and for the 1951 Festival Britain.

Dumas, René (1937–) Greek architect and interior designer who became designer of leather goods for Hèrmes in 1962. In 1983 she started designing the *Pippa* range of furniture for them and also designed the interiors of their shops in Paris, New York, Madrid and Milan.

Dumée, Guillaume (*fl.*1601–1626) French decorative painter who was curator of the royal paintings at Saint-Germain. He worked for the king at the Tuileries and decorated the Grand Cabinet in the Louvre for the queen. In 1610 he became the royal tapestry designer and collaborated with Laurent Guyot on a suite of 26 tapestries on the theme of Il Pastor Fido.

Dumoulin, Georges (1882–1959) French ceramic and glass deigner who worked at Manufacture de Sèvres for nine years. His first glssware was shown before 1925 and pieces were exhibited at the 1937 Paris Exposition, alongside works in enamel on metal.

Dupas, Jean (1882–1964) French artist whose decorations of the Church of Saint-Esprit, in Paris, brought him fame after the 1925 Paris Exposition. He designed the silver room at the royal palace, Bucharest, reception rooms of the Bourse, Bordeaux and designed painted-glass panels for the liner *Normandie*, in 1935.

du Pasquier, Nathalie (1957–) French textile designer who works in Milan. She started her professional career at Memphis fabrics, introducing early silkscreen designs, with vivid overall colours. In 1982 she joined Fiorucci and in 1985 branched out into industrial design, producing cutlery, flatware and pocket knives. She continues to design fashion fabrics for Pink Dragon, Esprit and Missoni.

Dyce, William (1806–64) British painter and educationalist, born in Aberdeen. He studied at Marischal College in his home city, specializing in the sciences. Determined to paint, he studied at the

Royal Academy School, in 1824, and travelled to Rome. In 1826 he decorated a room in his father's house in Aberdeen in the ARA-BESQUE manner. He studied teaching methods at design schools across Europe and presented papers to the London School of Design, outlining how design and industry should work together. In 1838 he was appointed head of the school, resigning for a brief period, before returning as head of the school of ornament. His ideas were widely admired and copied and he was heavily involved in the fresco revival of the 1940s, working on the New Palace of Westminster and Osborne House, where his work was admired by Prince Albert. He also worked on William BUTTERFIELD's All Saint's Church, Margaret Street, London and designed stained glass for Ely Cathedral and Alnwick church.

E

Eames, Charles (1907–78) American architect and one of the most influential furniture designers of the century. A steel mill worker, then technical draughtsman, then architect, he worked in the office of his friend, Eero SAARINEN, collaborating on the design of their first moulded plywood and aluminium chair in 1940. It presaged the design of plastic furniture after the Second World War. That same year he designed the seating for the Kleinhans Music Hall in Buffalo and in 1941 moved to California, where he worked in the art department of Metro-Goldwyn-Mayer, continuing his experiments with moulded plywood. An offshoot of this work was the design of a leg splint for the US Navy. In 1944 he set up a manufacturing plant to produce his wood and bent metal chairs, in styles that greatly influenced Italian designers in the late 1940s. In 1948 he designed his classic fibreglass shell chair, with thin multiple metal rod legs, nicknamed the 'Eiffel tower' base. His tinted fibreglass furniture was very popular in the 1950s, as was his black leather and rosewood veneer ottoman of 1956 and his aluminium table and seating group, of 1958. A prolific film-maker, often using background music composed by Elmer Bernstein, he also designed many notable exhibitions. In

1949 he designed and built his steel-framed, partly prefabricated house in Pacific Palisades, California, influenced by Japanese designs. He was an important spokesman for standards in design, as well as being an influential teacher at the University of California, Los Angeles and Berkeley, the University of Georgia and Yale University.

Eames, Ray (1912–88) The wife of Charles EAMES, after a period spent designing plywood sculpture and editing the journal ARTS AND ARCHITECTURE, she collaborated closely with her husband. From the late 1940s the designs produced by their company should be attributed mutually.

Eastlake, Charles Locke (1836–1906) British architect and administrator who became Secretary to the Institute of British Architects in 1871 and Keeper of the National Gallery in 1878. His *Hints on Household Taste in Furniture, Upholstery and Other Details* was published in 1868, heavily influenced by the style of fellow architects such as Norman SHAW and John SEDDON, it proved a popular and significant guide. It also had great influence in America, with six editions appearing in Boston between 1872 and 1879.

Eberson, John (*fl.*1920s) American designer of fantastic cinema interiors, including the Majestic Theater, Houston, Texas, in 1923. He recreated his vision of the garden of a late-Renaissance palazzo in Italy. His workshop, Michelangelo Studios, designed many others in a variety of styles; Moorish, Dutch, Chinese and Spanish.

Eckmann, Otto (1865–1902) German designer and painter who promoted decorative art inspired by Japanese printmaking. He was professor at the Kunstgewerbeschule in Berlin, specializing in the applied arts. He designed furniture, rugs and textiles, ceramic tiles for VILLEROY ET BOCH and interiors for the Grand Duke of Hesse-Darmstadt. He was one of the main proponents of JUGENDSTIL, the German movement associated with ART NOUVEAU.

Edinburgh Tapestry Company Textile firm established by the 4th Marquess of Bute in 1912, at Dovecot Studios. The first craftsmen came from William MORRIS's studio at Merton Abbey. In recent years, tapestries have been commissioned from designers including Frank Stella, who provided eleven designs for panels for Pepsi-Cola.

Edinburgh Weavers Fabric and carpet manufacturers, based in Carlisle but established in Edinburgh in 1929. With a reputation for the innovative use of Modern avant-garde designs, the company has employed the talents of many designers and artists; the German painter Hans Tisdall created abstract designs, Ashley HAVINDEN, natural forms, including birds in flight, and Marian DORN her distinctive swirling patterns. The artists, Ben NICHOLSON and Barbara HEPWORTH designed the company's 1937 range. The company was taken over by Courtaulds in 1962.

Edis, Robert William (1839–1927) British architect who promoted the red-brick Queen Anne style for buildings and the same middle-brown style for furnishings. His *Decoration and Furniture of Town Houses* of 1881 included interiors and MINTON tiles designed by Edis himself, together with wallpapers by Walter CRANE and furniture by William MORRIS and Gillows.

Edwards, Edward B. (1873–1948) American graphic designer and illustrator who became director of the American Institute of Graphic Art. He designed handbooks for many institutions, including the Metropolitan Museum, New York.

Ehrlich, Franz (1907–1983) German designer, trained at the BAUHAUS. He worked for Walter GROPIUS in Berlin, producing decoration and advertising. In 1936 he was interned at Buchenwald concentration camp by the Nazis, but survived and after the Second World War he worked as an exhibition designer in Leipzig.

Eichler, Fritz (1911–91) German teacher and designer, who worked on stage-set designs, before being hired by Arthur BRAUN in 1954. He was responsible for commissioning designs for radios from the Hochschule fur Gestaltung, Ulm, and establishing the company's distinctive stark forms for shavers, sound equipment and household goods.

Einarsdottir, Sigrun (1951–) Icelandic glassware designer, who set up the first hot-glass workshop in Iceland. She designed both unique pieces and production glassware decorated with fluid human forms.

Einarsson, Gudmundur (1895–1963) Icelandic ceramicist, who studied in Munich. He set up the first ceramic workshop in Iceland in 1927, specializing in double-walled pieces, pierced strapwork and animal figures.

Eisen, Charles (1720–78) French artist, born in Val<u>ci</u>enes, who became a prolific book illustrator, much admired by Voltaire. He became drawing-master to Mme de Pompadour and Dessinateur du Roi. He published designs vases, fountains, cartouches and ornaments in the ROCOCO style. In later years he adopted the NEO-CLASSICAL style, with many of his designs reproduced on Sèvres porcelain. In 1777 he fled to Brussels to escape creditors and died there.

Eitelberger-Edelberg, Rudolf von (1817–85) Austrian teacher who, influenced by the London 1862 Exhibition, published articles which led to the foundation of the Austrian Museum for Art and Industry, the first museum in Europe to be modelled on the South Kensington Museum (now the Victoria and Albert Museum).

Ekco Radio *see* **Cole, Eric Kirkham**.

Electrolux Swedish domestic appliance manufacturer, founded as AB Lux, in 1901. Over the years the company's commitment to good design was expressed through commissions for various items designed by Raymond LOEWY, Carl OTTO, and Sixten Sason of Sweden.

Ellis, Eileen (1933–) British textile designer, who started work for Ascher, designing printed fabrics for, amongs others, Marks and Spencer. In 1960 she formed the Orbit Design Group and designed fabrics for BEA's Trident airliner, for EDINBURGH WEAVERS and for the John Lewis store chain. Other commissions included curtains for the Birmingham Playhouse, In 1970, she formed Weaveplan, working for Irish Ropes (carpet manufacturers) and Hirst's Furnishings.

Ellis, Harvey (1852–1904) American architect who was active as a painter in Rochester, New York, designing posters for the *Rochester Herald* and *Harper's Magazine*. In 1902 he moved to Syracuse, New York, to work for Gustav Stickley's The Craftsman, for which he designed interiors, furniture and textiles, including a child's bedroom with a *Puss-in-Boots* frieze.

Elmslie, George Grant (1871–1952) Scottish architect who moved to America in 1885, joining the Silsbee practice in 1887, at the same time as Frank Lloyd WRIGHT. In 1889 he joined Adler and Sullivan, where he was responsible for designing ornamental details. Here and with other practices, he also designed furniture, stained glass, embroidery, carpets and metalwork.

Erdmannsdorff, Friedrich Wilhelm (1736–1800) German painter and architect, who was sponsored by Duke Friedrich-Franz of Anhalt-Dessau. He travelled to Venice and to England, where he came under the influence of ADAM. On his return to Germany he rebuilt Schloss Dessau in 1767 and, in 1769, his masterpiece, Schloss Worlitz. He designed chairs in the CHIPPENDALE style and adapted the Adam style for German taste. He designed tables in early NEO-CLASSICAL style and, in 1771, he proposed the foundation of a school of design for craftsmen.

Errazuriz, Eugenie (1861–1954) Chilean society hostess, who settled in Paris and became very influential in interior design. Her principle was 'throw out and keep throwing out' and was put into practice in her sparse and simple room arrangements, the peasant style for patricians. She introduced the use of plain, but strong, colours, including her favourite 'Inca Pink', which the couturier Elsa Schiaparelli adopted as 'shocking pink'. In 1900, she moved to Cheyne Walk, London, where she propounded her design views to society friends including the eccentric photographer, Baron de Meyer. On her return to Paris she founded a salon and influenced the styles of painters, including Pablo PICASSO and Braque and writers such as COCTEAU and Radiguet. LE CORBUSIER designed a house for her in Chile, a design never realized, but showing his early interest in primitive technical elements.

Erte (1892–1990) Russian designer, born Romain de Tirtoff, who studied in St Petersburg and Paris. He worked for Paul POIRET as a designer and in 1914 went to Monte Carlo to work as an illustrator and costume designer. His clients included Mata Hari and, in later years, Zizi Jeanmaire. In New York, he designed for the Ziegfeld Follies and George White's Scandals and for the department stores, Bendel's and Altman's. In 1925 he went to Hollywood to design for MGM, largely in an overdecorated and opulent style. After the stock market crash of 1929, he returned to Paris to design costumes for the Bal Tabarin, Folies Bergères and Chatelet Theatre. His erotic alphabet designs remain popular today.

Esslinger, Hartmut (1945–) German designer of radios for Wega, which was taken over by Sony, enabling him to expand into the Japanese market. He opened a studio in California in 1982, where his clients now include Apple Computer, Olympus, AT&T and AEG. In Europe he has designed porcelain for VILLEROY ET BOCH and ROSENTHAL, and lighting for Erco.

Etchells, Frederick (1886–1973) British painter and architect who joined OMEGA WORKSHOPS as a designer in 1913, but left when Wyndham LEWIS resigned.

Eureka Company The American manufacturer, founded in Detroit, in 1909, now located in Bloomington, Illinois. The company sold its vacuum cleaners through door-to-door salesman, accounting for one-third of those in America. By the 1980s they had 40 models, including the colourful, plastic *Mighty Mite* model of 1982.

Evanson, James (1946–) American lighting designer who specialized in large lighting constructions that emulated city skylines. Best-known are his 1985 *Lightstruck* table lamp, the *Hi-beam* floor lamp, and *Light Collection* produced by Art et Industrie.

F

Fabergé, Peter Carl (1846–1920) Russian goldsmith and jeweller, born in St Petersburg, the son of Gustav Fabergé, who opened the family shop in 1842. In 1870, Peter Carl took over the business. Not a silversmith himself, he supplied designs and then oversaw the work, at one time having 500 assistants working for him as modellers, gem-cutters, enamellers and metalsmiths. In 1881, the company were awarded the Imperial Warrant from Tsar Alexander, which was continued by his son, Nicholas II. The most famous jewels produced were the series of miniature Easter eggs, made for the Tsar to present to his wife and mother. A total of 56 were produced, from 1884 onwards, each jewel-encrusted egg containing a miniature palace, ship or similar object. In 1883, Fabergé's younger brother, Agathon, joined the company and widened the range of goods to include cigarette cases, photograph frames, desk accessories and bibelots in precious metals. In 1887, a shop was opened in Moscow, in 1905 in Odessa and Kiev and, in 1906, in London. Work was farmed out to smaller concerns, with Fabergé providing rent-free workshops and the designs, to cope with the great demand for the company's wares. After the 1917 Revolution, the company was closed down because of its Imperial connections and the stock was confiscated. Fabergé fled to Lausanne and, in 1921, his sons set up the business in Paris, under the name of Fabergé et Cie.

Fabiansen, Ib (1927–) Danish architect who designed Illum's Bolighus store. He became consultant designer to BANG & OLUFSEN, responsible for the simple lines of the 1962 *Horizon* TV set. He also designed interiors, garden furniture and lighting.

Fabricius, Preben (1931–) Danish designer who, in 1952, designed seating for the United Nations Building in New York. An influential teacher in Copenhagen, he also set up his own studio. His signature work is the 1962 *Scimitar* chair, with its tractor-like seat.

Fantastici, Agostino (*fl.*1820s) Italian architect who designed elegant furniture in NEO-CLASSICAL style. A volume of his drawings is housed in the Siena public library.

Faulkner, Kate (d.1898) British decorator who painted tiles for her brother's company, Morris, Marshall, Faulkner & Co. She painted tiles and made gesso decorations for Webb's Broadway grand piano, which was shown at the first Arts & Crafts Exhibition in 1898. She also designed wallpapers for MORRIS & Co. Her sister Lucy, as Mrs Orrinsmith, wrote *The Drawing Room, its Decoration and Furniture* in 1878.

Favre-Pinsard, Gisèle (*fl.*1930s–40s) French ceramicist who, with other members of her family, founded Les Quatre Potiers, to produce tableware and bathroom and kitchen fixtures. She designed the interiors of the house of the couturier Andre Courreges.

Fazioli, Domenico (1937–) Italian architect who designed the *Ex-*

ecutive range of office furniture, the *Galileo* range of tables and desks for the MIM group of companies.

Fear, Jeffrey (1945–) Canadian designer of contract furniture, including his 1971 upholstered tubular-steel chair and ottoman, for Kinetics Furniture, Toronto.

Fels, Jerry (1917–1996) American costume jeweller who produced pieces inspired by pop architecture and native, primitive art. He started at Gertz's department store in New York, before going to California were he founded the company, Renoir of Hollywood, which became Renoir of California. His partner, Curt Freiler, cut, soldered, pierced and polished all principal pieces by hand. Mass-produced pieces, though still in fairly limited quantities, were made by Mexican metalworkers and then finished by hand. Until the Korean War many of the pieces were of copper, but shortages made them look to different materials and copper bonded to aluminium. Their popular line in 1952 was *Matisse*, incorporating coloured enamel inserts.

Fennemore, Thomas Acland (1922–55) British pottery, wallpaper and textile designer who worked for the Peter Jones store, London and Lawley (China and Glass) in Stoke-on-Trent, before setting up his own business, Fennemore Hayden. As director of pottery at Brain and Co., Fenton, he commissioned designs from Vanessa BELL and Duncan GRANT. From 1947 to 1953 he was consultant designer to SANDERSON, Antler Luggage, Wilkinson pottery and Lawley pottery. He also designed for the Wilton Royal Carpet Factory, HEAL's and Horrockses.

Feuchère, Leon (1804–57) French architect and deocrator whose first work was for the theatre. His *L'Art Industriel*, of 1842, contains 72 plates, illustrating an imaginary palace, with elaborate furniture, silver, porcelain, lighting and other decorations in the Louis XIV and Louis XV, Byzantine, GOTHIC and Chinese styles, as well as one of the earliest examples of Moorish revival. Hailed as the greatest decorator of his day, he was appointed Conseil Superieur for the French National Manufactures.

Fischer, Uwe (1958–) German designer who set up the Gimbande studio in Frankfurt, creating articulated furniture and, in 1988, the *Tabula Rosa* combination table and bench.

Fisher, Alexander (1864–1936) British silversmith who studied in London and Paris, where he experimented layering translucent enamels. In 1896 he set up a workshop in London and taught at the Central School of Arts and Crafts. In 1904, he founded his own school and taught enamelling. Amongst his most notable works are a girdle with a buckle 4 inches (10cm) high and plaques showing Wagnerian scenes.

Flaxman, John (1755–1826) British sculptor and designer, trained at the Royal Academy Schools. He designed ceramics for Wedgwood and Bentley, with low relief busts and delicate reliefs in the Neo-Classical style. He designed a Gothic chess set for Wedgwood and began to design in silver. Furthering his career as a sculptor, he travelled to Rome and, while there, he designed 213 drawings for the *Odyssey* and the *Iliad*, which were hailed as the 'finest modern imitations of the elegance and beauty of ancient Greek attire and furniture'. He was elected R.A. in 1800 and, in 1810, was appointed Professor of Scuplture at the Royal Academy. Sculpted designs include Josiah Wedgwood's tomb in Stoke-on-Trent. His masterpiece of silver design was the Shield of Achilles, on which he worked from 1810 to 1818. He designed many medals, drawing on classical antiquity for his inspiration.

Flecheux, Luc (1966–) French designer of furniture and tableware, whose 1986 suite of earthenware dinnerplates for Siècle was inspired by designs for an amphitheatre. He has also designed for the theatre.

Fleming, Erik (1894–1954) A Swedish baron who founded the Atelier Borgila, which became one of Sweden's leading Modern silver workshops. His designs from the 1920s were in classical styles, those from the 1930s reflecting his version of Art Déco. In 1932, the Swedish government commissioned him to produce an 800-piece silver set as a wedding present for Prince Gustav Adolf and Princess Sybilla.

Fleuron, The (1923–30) A magazine concerned with all aspects of typography. For the first two years it was edited by Oliver Simon of the Curwen Press, where it was printed. From 1926 to 1930 it was edited by Stanley Morison and published by the Cambridge University Press.

Follot, Paul (1877–1941) French decorative artist whose early work has much in common with the PRE-RAPHAELITES. In 1901, he joined Meier-Graefe's shop La Maison Moderne, Paris, where he met DUFRÈNE and designed bronzes, jewellery and fabrics. He worked in early ART DÉCO style and in 1911 was commissioned by Wedgwood to design a range of ceramics, production being delayed by the First World War. In 1921, he designed cabins for the liner *Paris* and the *appartement de luxe* for the *Normandie* in 1935. In 1923, he became artistic director of Au Bon Marché. In the 1920s he designed silverware for both Christofle and Lapparra. In 1928, he was made co-director, with Serge CHERMAYEFF, of the Modern Art Department of Waring and Gillow, a British company with a branch in Paris, which it opened with a display of 60 furnished Modern interiors.

Fontana, Carlo (1638–1714) Italian draughstman who worked under BERNINI on the colonnades of St Peter's in 1659. He became architect of St Peter's, in Rome, in 1697 and designed ecclesiastical fittings, candlesticks, altars and tombs, as well as secular furniture including chairs, cabinets, frames and pedestals. He also designed ironwork and the papal galley.

Fontenay, Eugene (1823–87) French goldsmith who set up his first workshop in 1847, becoming best-known for his delicate decorations inspired by ancient Etruscan styles. In 1858, he designed a diadem in diamonds, emeralds and pearls for the Empress Eugenie.

Forbicini, Fulvio (1952–) Italian industrial designer who started out with Roche Bobois, before opening his own studio. In 1988 he designed the *Ribalta* sofa, a day-bed with its corners turned up to form six different positions.

Fornasetti, Piero (1913–88) Italian artist taken up by Gio PONTI and for whom he executed several commissions, including frescoes in the Palazzo Bo in Padua. In 1950 he designed interiors for the Casino at San Remo and, in 1952, for the liner *Andrea Doria*. In the 1970s he set up shops in Milan and London to promote his varied designs for books, posters, desk equipment and other artefacts. In New York, he transformed the ballroom of the Time-Life building with Surrealist *trompe-l'oeil* designs applied to walls and all furnishings. His1984 decorated bicycle became a signature piece.

Forseth, Einar (b.1892) Swedish-born son of a Norwegian lithographer, who started out as a church decorator, specializing later in stained glass and mosaics, including those for the Golden Room of Stockholm City Hall. His stained glass can be seen in the English Church in Stockholm and Coventry Cathedral, where he also designed the mosaic floor of the Chapel of Unity. He has also designed Swedish postage stamps and tapestries for the Stockholm Concert Hall.

Forsyth, Gordon Mitchell (1879–1953) Scottish ceramicist, educated at Grays School of Art, Aberdeen. From 1902 to 1905 he was artistic director of MINTON, then artistic director of Pilkington's Royal Lancastrian Pottery, where he specialized in lustreware. He became principal of the Stoke-on-Trent Schools of Art and his *Twentieth Century Ceramics* was published in 1936.

Fortuny y Madrazo, Mariano (1871–1949) Spanish designer most famous for his silk fabric designs which were printed with metallic inks and folded into narrow pleats. He created a secret method for printing and embossing fabric in the style of ancient brocades. His couture designs employing his fabrics, including Empire-style dresses, coats and capes, changed little from the early 1900s until his death. His best-known design was the *Delphos* dress of 1909, the hem weighted by beads to achieve a floating motion. Famously, the fabric kept its shape when folded into a knot and kept in a small box. His home, the Palazzo Orfei in Venice, is now the Fortuny Museum. At the turn of the century he designed opera sets, including those for *Tristan and Isolde* at La Scala, Milan.

Foster, Norman (1935–) British architect, who pioneered HIGH-TECH design. For his buildings he designed the *Nomas* furniture system in 1987, which was produced by Tecno, and lighting, produced by Erco. In 1988, he designed carpets for the German Dialog collection.

Fowler, John (1933–) British interior designer who started out as a printer, then a decorator for the Peter Jones home furnishings store. In 1934 he set up his own studio, going into partnership with Sybil COLEFAX in 1938. His designs were mostly adapted from 18th- and 19th-century pattern books and material fragments. During the Second World War he designed the house of the actor Michael Redgrave, using parachute silk for curtains. The partnership became a major decorator of rooms for high society, from an audience room in Buckingham Palace, to rooms for Lord Rothermere, Mrs James de Rothschild and Mrs Evangeline Bruce, the latter in Albany, London. His most popular chintz design was *Old Rose* and he used dyed tape borders as an edge to patterns such as *Berkeley Sprig*, now the logo of Colefax and Fowler. Another Fowler innovation was the use of silk bows and ribbons as picture-hangers.

Frampton, George (1860–1928) British sculptor and teacher, closely associated with the ARTS AND CRAFTS MOVEMENT. In 1894 was appointed joint head of the Central School of Arts and Crafts in London. His most famous sculpture is *Peter Pan* in Kensington Gardens, London.

Frank, Jean-Michel (1895–1941) French interior decorator who was a great-uncle of Anne Frank. Active in Paris and New York, his work was influenced by the design ideas of Eugenie ERRAZURIZ. He met Adolphe CHANAUX, who had worked on the 1925 Paris Exposition, and formed a partnership to promote their own work, alongside that of Salvador DALI, Christian Berard, the GIACOMETTI brothers and others. He was the first to introduce the use of white-leaded wood in the 1920s, seen to best effect in his magisterial modern interiors for the house of the Vicomte and Vicomtesse de Noailles, in Paris. The walls were covered in beige vellum, to set off the ebony furniture and a huge bronze door was edged with ivory. Seating was upholstered in bleached leather and tables, screens and desk tops were covered in lacquer and shagreen and untanned horse-leather. By the mid-1930s his work was becoming even more theatrical, best shown in the Guerlain salon with *trompe l'oeil* effects. In 1940 he decided to settle in New York but after just one week he threw himself from a window of the St Regis Hotel. Few of his projects are intact today.

Frankl, Paul Theodore (1887–1958) Austrian designer who settled in America in 1914, where his signature designs in the 1920s include the 'skyscraper' bookcases, a large combined desk and bookcase and a chrome, aluminium and leather chair. His writings were influential, including *Form and Re-Form*, published in 1930. In the late 1940s he experimented with the use of cork veneer in his furniture for the Johnson Company. He was the main force behind the formation of the American Designers' Gallery in 1928 and the American Union of Decorative Artists and Designers in 1930.

Fraser, Claud Lovat (1890–1921) British textile and theatre designer and illustrator, influenced by traditional designs. His designs for Nigel Playfair's production of *The Beggar's Opera*, revived in 1920, were a sensation. His fabric designs were produced by William Foxton and he designed many advertisements, including those for HEAL'S, Eno's Fruit Salts and the London Underground.

Frattini, Gianfranco (1926–) Italian architect who also designed many items of furniture, including some in lacquered wood, wicker and plastic for many clients such as Acerbis-Morphos, BERNINI and Fratelli Faber. His *Model 595 Sesann* armchair, in leather and foam on a bent wire frame, was produced by Cassini. Lighting designs for Artemide include the snake-like *Boalamp*. Designs using industrial plastics include hard hats for Montecatini.

Frau, Renzo (b.1880) Italian designer from Sardinia who worked as a joiner in the Italian royal household. In 1912 he founded the furniture company Poltrona Frau, designing the famous *Poltrona* armchair in its first year. In 1926, was appointed supplier to the royal family, continuing interior design for titled clients.

Fremiet, Emmanuel (1824–1910) French sculptor who brought his sculpting talents to lighting design. He also produced animal images including maribou storks, butterflies, pelicans and dragons for friezes and columns of buildings.

Frey, Patrick (1947–) French fabric designer who expanded the family company set up by his father in 1935. From the 1980s the firm's output exceeded 5000 colour ways and 30 designs each year. From 1987 they branched out into upholstered furniture, decorative accessories and household fragrances.

Froment-Meurice, François-Désiré (1802–55) French goldsmith who learned his trade in his step-father's workshop. His first works, in Neo-GOTHIC style were an immediate success and he was dubbed the '19th Century Cellini'. He was influential in Britain after he and his company won prizes at the 1851 Great Exhibition, in London, and the Paris Exhibition of 1855.

Fronzini, A. G. (1923–96) Italian architect and editor of *Casabella*. In 1963 he designed an attache case for Valextra, in 1964 the *Serie 64* furniture for Galli and in 1966, the reading room of the Instituto di Storia dell'Arte. He was consultant designer for Galli's furniture and fittings.

Fry, Roger (1866–1934) British writer and artist who became curator of paintings at the Metropolitan Museum of Art, New York, from 1906 to 1910. In 1913, he opened the OMEGA WORKSHOPS, with the aim of applying Post-Impressionism to the decorative arts. Designers who worked there included Vanessa BELL and Duncan GRANT, together with Wyndham LEWIS. Their printed and woven fabrics, carpets and embroideries were a major influence in British textile design.

Fujie, Kazuko (1947–) Japanese designer who founded the Field Shop Office in 1977, designing furniture for Maezawa Garden House in 1982, Keio University Library in 1982 and for Toyoma Airport, in 1984.

Fuller, Richard Buckminster (1895–1983) American architect, principally known for his geodesic domes, one of which housed the American exhibit at Expo '67 in Montreal.

Fumiani, Giovanni Antonio (1643–1710) Venetian-born painter, famed for his decoration of the church of St Pantaleone and his mosaics in St Mark's. In 1702 he painted a series of designs for torcheres and vases, for Ferdinando de' Medici.

Funakoshi, Saburo (1931–) Japanese glassware designer who joined the staff of the design department, at the Shisuoka Institute after studying at Tokyo University of Arts. From 1957, he worked at Hoya Crystal, becoming head of the design department at Musashi Glass. Here he produced designs for machine- and hand-made items. At Hoya he used sand blasting for designs on soy and other bottles.

Functionalism an architectural theory developed from the idiom that form should reflect function, and generally associated with the architectural and design style of the early-20th century. The notion was first posited in the mid-18th century with the idea that an emphasis should be placed on construction forming the basis of architecture. Functionalism went through various stages of interpretation and in the 19th century it led to a rejection of aggressively ornamented structures in favour of more pure, simple, organic forms. With the development of early-20th century Neo-Classicism by designers such as Behrens, and the emergence of machine-made objects, Functionalism evolved into a style in the 1920s, but it more effectively formed the basis for Modernism.

Furness, Frank (1839–1912) American architect who practised in Philadelphia, designing buildings in an aggressive Gothic style. He worked briefly for Louis Sullivan and was praised by Christopher Dresser for his fine use of ornament.

G

Gabriel, René (1890–1950) French decorator who worked in Paris, designing wallpaper, fabric, rugs, and porcelain (mainly for Sèvres). He produced limited-edition furniture with simple lines, developing into modular elements, known as Editions RG, and subsequently, bent-metal tubular seating. In 1920 he opened an exclusive wallpaper store, Au Sansonnet, and the Ateliers d'Art at Neuilly in 1934. In 1947, he became president of the Société des Artistes Decorateurs.

Gagnère, Olivier (1952–) French student of economics who became a designer with the Memphis Group in Milan, before setting up his own consultancy. A notable piece is his 1984 *Verseuse* teapot using industrial materials.

Gaillard, Eugène (1862–1933) French jewellery designer, associated with Bing's Paris shop L'Art Nouveau. He used soft flowing lines inspired by nature. His elder brother, **Lucien Gaillard**, was an active silversmith, producing pieces influenced by Japanese style.

Gallé, Émile (1864–1904) Influential French glassware designer who learnt his craft in his father's workshop at Saint-Clément and his shop in Nancy. After further studies in the collections at Cluny and the Louvre, he became director of the family firm, exhibiting some 300 pieces of glassware at the 1884 Paris Exposition, some of which were influenced by Islamic and medieval styles. He made a collection of exotic woods to create the bases for his pieces of layered glass, enamelled glass and gold and platinum encrusted glass. In 1884 he began to use these woods for his designs of decorated furniture, some of which reflected 18th-century cabinet work, with Renaissance mouldings. In the same year he began producing his typical smoked glass, making both limited and mass-produced editions, some of which were made by other factories. After this time many of the pieces produced by him were designed by other people. In 1901 he founded the Alliance Provinciale des Industries d'Art, becoming the first president.

Games, Abram (1914–) British graphic artist and industrial designer, best known for his posters in the 1940s and 1950s for the War Office, London Transport, Shell, British Petroleum and Guinness. During the Second World War he designed propaganda material for the Ministry of Information and, in 1951, his graphics were used at the Festival of Britain in London. A key design was the 1947 Cona coffee percolator, which was re-designed in 1959 and is still in production. In the early 1960s he designed the projected new casing for the Gestetner duplicating machine, but production was abandoned due to Gestetner's death.

Garbe, Richard (d.1957) British sculptor who designed for Doulton of Burslem, producing large figures and matt-glazed sculptures including *Spring, Lady of the Rose, Lady of the Snows* and *The Spirit of the Wind* in editions of 50 to 100. He also designed wall masks, while working as a teacher at the Central School of Arts and Crafts from 1929 to 1946, and professor of sculpture at the Royal College of Art, London from 1933 to 1939.

Gardella, Ignazio (1905–95) Italian architect of notable classical façades, including that of the Olivetti headquarters. In the early 1940s he started designing furniture, his first piece being the

1940 Vigano folding butterfly chair. In the 1950s he designed the *Digamma* armchair for Favina and street lighting for the Piazza San Babilia in Milan.

Gardner, James (1907–95) British jewellery designer for CARTIER from 1924 to 1931. He was head of the 75-strong design team for the 1946 'Britain Can Make It' exhibition and designed the Battersea Pleasure Gardens for the 1951 Festival of Britain.

Garrard British goldsmiths and jewellers, founded in London by George Wickes in 1721, and taking on a partner, Edward Wakelin, in 1747. In 1753 they received a royal warrant from Frederick, Prince of Wales. In 1792 Robert Garrard became a partner and when he died his sons took over the company. In 1843 they became the crown jewellers and carried out many commissions for Queen Victoria and Prince Albert. The company's Florence Nightingale jewellery and the collar and badge of the Order of the Star of India were designed by the prince. The company was run by descendants of Robert Garrard until 1952, when it was merged with the Goldsmiths' and Silversmiths' Company, remaining the crown jewellers.

Gaskin, Arthur Joseph (1862–1928) British painter, silversmith and jeweller who studied at Birmingham School of Art where, with fellow students and tutors, he formed the Birmingham Group of Painters and Craftsmen. He met fellow silversmith Georgina Smith at the school and married her in 1894. In 1899 they set up a workshop to produce jewellery to their own designs. Arthur Gaskin's style used curled gold- and silver-wire tendrils, decorated with foliage in coloured semi-precious stones. They were influenced by the PRE-RAPHAELITES, several of whom were their friends. They were also influenced by medievalism of and Eastern motifs. They also designed the *Cymric* range of jewellery for LIBERTY.

Gaudí, Antoni (1852–1926) Spanish architect whose most famous building is the unfinished Sagrada Familia Church in Barcelona. In his highly idiosyncratyic and personal version of ART NOUVEAU, he designed metalwork including cast-iron lamps, partitions and furniture for the Casa Calvet, and benches for the crypt of the Colonia Güell church, near Barcelona. His custom-built chairs for the Casa Calvet were reissued in a limited edition in the 1980s.

Gauguin, Jean (1881–1961) French ceramicist, son of the painter, PAUL GAUGUIN. His most important work was done for BING AND GRØNDAHL, Denmark.

Gauguin, Paul (1848–1903) French painter noted for his portraits of women in the South Pacific, he was also a prolific designer of ceramics, furniture and metalwork. His middle-period work did not sell, so he gave most of it to his family in Copenhagen, retreating to pursue sculpture. Apart from a few stoneware pieces completed around 1894, he abandoned ceramics completely.

Gecchelin, Bruno (1939–) Italian architect who designed refrigerators and stoves for Indesit, glassware for Venini, the Fiat Panda car and typewriters and calculators for Olivetti.

Geddes, Norman Bel (1893–1958) American industrial and theatrical designer who started out in advertising. Before turning to industrial design he was responsible for over 200 theatrical productions, including the setting for Max Reinhardt's *The Miracle*. He also designed for the Metropolitan Opera, New York, before going to Hollywood to work for D. W. Griffith and Cecil B. De Mille. In the 1930s he designed interiors for J. Walter Thompson, radios for Philco, radio cabinets for RCA and metal bedroom furniture for Simmons. He prophesied the coming of the road freeway systems and the use of air-conditioning. He taught Eero SAARINEN and employed Eliot NOYES who designed the first IBM electric typewriter.

Gehry, Frank O. (1930–) Canadian architect who created innovative furniture with sculptural forms, made from inexpensive industrial materials. In the early 1970s he produced corrugated cardboard furniture which was reissued in the 1980s. In 1983 he branched out into lighting design with his first 'fish-light' for Formica in coloured plastic.

Geneviere, Marcel *see* **Dominique**.

Gensoli, Maurice (b.1892) Algerian ceramicist who was a freelance designer, working largely for Sèvres where, after the success of the 1925 Paris Exposition, he became head of the decorating department.

Gentile, Thomas (1936–) American jewellery designer whose pieces have been exhibited in many of the world's leading museums, including the Victoria and Albert, London, the Gulbenkian, Lisbon and the Vancouver Museum.

Gentleman, David (1930–) British painter who studied at the Royal College of Art, London, and has produced designs for wallpaper, postage stamps and books. His best-known work is the series of murals for London Underground in the 1980s.

Germanez, Christian (1940–) French designer of office furniture and the *Half and Half* seat produced by Airborne in 1966. He has designed many public interiors, ceramics for Sèvres, exhibitions at the Paris Grand Palais and stage sets for the choreographer, Maurice Bejart.

Gesamtkunstwerk A concept founded in Germany in the early 19th century, defining a bringing together all the arts, epitomized by the operas of Richard Wagner and, in the field of design, by Frank Lloyd WRIGHT and Josef HOFFMANN in the 20th century. In architecture, it would mean the interior of a building reflecting the exterior, as should the furnishings and decorations.

Giacometti, Alberto (1910–66) and **Diego** (1902–85) Swiss artists and designers who worked in Paris. They designed many lighting fixtures, bronze vases, candlesticks, medallions and other metalwares. When this business declined, Diego went on to design perfume bottles and fashion accessories. Returning to metalwork in the 1950s, he designed bronze furniture and, after Alberto's death, cast replicas of some of his early pieces. Some of these can be seen at the Musée Picasso, Hôtel Salé, Paris.

Gibbons, Cedric (1893–1960) Irish-born, American film set designer. He introduced early three-dimensional sets to replace painted backdrops, as well as detailed set-dressing; he was described as 'the man who put the glove on the mantelpiece'. The 1925 Paris Exposition influenced him, and his films promoted ART DÉCO. His best-known contribution to the film industry was his design of the Oscar statuette for the Academy of Motion Picture Arts and Sciences in the late 1920s. He had screen credits for 1,500 films and won eleven Academy Awards.

Gignoux, Michèle (1944–) French 'Pop romantic' artist who designed the 1967 Cube photo frame for Plexiglas and Bac Design and the 1989 *Vertige* chair in fluorescent Formica.

Gilbert, Alfred (1854–1934) British sculptor whose most famous work is Eros, in Piccadilly Circus, London. He created notable jewellery pieces in the ART NOUVEAU style, including the 1888 badge and chain of office for the Mayor of Preston and the presidential badge of the Royal Institute of Painters in Watercolour.

Gill, Arthur Eric Rowton (1882–1940) British sculptor and engraver whose conversion to Roman Catholicism in 1913 was central to his creative output. Over a five-year period he carved The Stations of the Cross for Westminster Cathedral, London and then founded a semi-religious crafts community a Ditchling, Sussex. He designed and illustrated many books with his woodcuts, for the Golden Cockerel Press, and several typefaces, including his 1927 *Perpetua* and 1928 *Gill Sans*, for Monotype. Other major sculpted works include the façade of BBC Broadcasting House, London and the League of Nations Building, Geneva. He designed the typography and decorations for the 1937 coronation stamps, with the image of King George VI by Edmund DULAC.

Gimson, Ernest (1864–1919) British architect who turned to chair-making, forming a partnership with the Barnsley brothers at Daneway House, Gloucestershire. His designs ranged from simple folk styles to elaborate veneered and inlaid cabinets. He refused to join the Design and Industries Association as he did not approve of machine production.

Girard, Alexander Hayden (1907–93) American architect who worked in Florence, Rome, London, Paris and New York, before setting up his own office in Florence in 1930. In 1937 he moved to Detroit where he designed the interiors of the 1943 Ford and 1946 Lincoln cars. He was a colour consultant to General Motors from 1948 to 1956. At this time he started designing textiles for Herman Miller in Michigan, using exuberant, colourful patterns, influenced by his large collection of North-American folk art. In 1956 he designed the corporate identity for Braniff Airlines and, in 1957, the interiors for the house of the film director Billy Wilder. In 1966 he designed the furniture and decor of L'Etoile restaurant in New York.

Gispen, Willem H. (1890–1981) Dutch metalworker who was influenced by the ARTS AND CRAFTS MOVEMENT when he visited Britain in 1911. In 1915 he opened a factory to make wooden furniture and by 1916 was working in steel, producing domestic and street furniture, including stair rails in Amsterdam and for the Scala Theatre, Rotterdam. He then started producing hand-bent, tubular steel pieces, becoming mechanized in 1924. The same process was used for his 1926 *Giso* range of lighting. He had a showroom in Amsterdam and opened shops in The Hague, Paris, London and Nottingham. In the late 1920s he designed all the lighting and furnishing in tubular steel for the Van Nelle Coffee and Tea Factory in Rotterdam, several of the pieces being produced for the wider public. These included a chair with leather upholstery and a tubular steel framed desk with a black top. He used similar designs for the liner *Dagenham*, owned by the Ford Motor Company. After internment during the Second World War, his company restricted itself to the design of office furniture. In 1951 he briefly retired to paint, making a comeback with a company producing furniture in Scandinavian and Italian designs two years later. He stopped designing in 1960 to make etchings and take on a few private commissions, such as bungalows on the Costa Brava and a house in Amsterdam.

Giugiaro, Giorgio (1938–) Italian car designer who started his career in 1959 with Fiat, moving to work with Nuccio Bertone in 1965. For the next three years he was head designer at Ghia, before forming a partnership, ItalDesign, with Aldo Mantovani in 1968. Thereafter, work is accredited to the partnership and their 200 employees. They were responsible for over 40 cars, including the 1971 Alfa Romeo Alfasud, the 1974 Volkswagen Golf, the 1981 Fiat Panda and the 1983 Fiat Uno. They also designed the 1978 F3 and F4 Nikon cameras, Necchi sewing machines and the Seiko Chronograph watch. In the mid-1980s he designed a range of men's clothing and accessories for Voiello.

Glaser, Milton (1929–) America president of Push Pin Studios in New York from 1954 to 1974, when he set up his own studio. He designed magazines, including *New York*, *Paris Match* and *The Washington Post*. His enlarged graphics decorate the Grand Union grocery chain and the World Trade Center in New York. From the early 1960s he designed over 300 posters, including *Bob Dylan* for Columbia Records.

Glasgow School A group of architect-designers, including Charles Rennie MACKINTOSH, Frances and Margaret MACDONALD, George MACNAIR and George Walton, that developed a conservative version of ART NOUVEAU, incorporating Celtic motifs.

Godwin, Edward William (1833–86) British architect who designed town halls and other buildings in GOTHIC Revival style. In 1866 he started to design wallpapers and furniture in various styles, his best-known being stark Anglo-Japanese 'Art Furniture' made by William Wall at first and, later, Gillow, Collingson and Lock, and Smee. From 1874 to 1878 he collaborated with his friend, the painter James Whistler, on projects which included the Bedford Park Estate, Britain's first garden suburb. He decorated Oscar Wilde's house in Tite Street, London, and towards the end of his life he designed many theatrical productions. He lived for several years with the actress Ellen Terry and they had a son, Edward Gordon Craig.

Goldfinger, Erno (1902–87) Hungarian architect and designer who worked in Paris and London. In 1929 produced the first version of the *Safari* chair, and in 1931 the *Entas* stacking metal chair. In 1934 he settled in London where he concentrated on buildings, including his own controversial house in Hampstead, London.

Goldman, Jonathan (1959–) American artist and performer who devised the 300ft (91m) ribbon for the 1990 opening of the Trump Taj Mahal Casino, Atlantic City, New Jersey. In the 1980s he developed the *Sawtooth* lamp, which incorporated a fan to inflate the shade and cool the bulb. Unorthodox chairs included the *Hairy* chair, which had inflatable yellow spikes, and the *Venus Fly Trap* chair, which had forest green upholstery surrounded by bright blue cones.

Goldsmiths' and Silversmiths' Company British silversmiths, founded in London in 1898. It Produced silverware by a variety of eminent smiths who, in the 1930s, included Bernard Cuzner, Leslie Durbin and A. E. Harvey.

Gooden, Robert Yorke (1909–96) British architect who also designed wallpapers, domestic machine-pressed glassware and, in 1953, hangings in Westminster Abbey for the coronation of Elizabeth II. He designed gold and silver ceremonial items and glassware for King's College, Cambridge and, in 1961, metal-foil murals for the liner *Canberra*. With R. D. Russell he designed the Western Sculpture and Oriental Galleries and the print room of the British Museum. From 1948 to 1971 he was professor at the Royal College of Art, London.

Goossens, Robert (1927–) French jewellery designer who worked for Coco Chanel's supplier in the 1930s, becoming her close collaborator in the 1950s. In the 1960s he produced his hallmark pear/triple-ring-motif barrettes and earrings for Chanel. In 1958 he started to work with Cristobal Balenciaga, refining his style, before going on to work with Yves Saint-Laurent.

Gothic The predominant architectural style of western Europe from the mid-12th century to the beginning of the 16th century, when it was superceded by the Renaissance style of Italy. The Gothic style pervaded all aspects of design and ornamentation and was characterized by the pointed arch, the ribbed vault and the arch buttress. The term 'Gothic' evolved in the 17th century, when the medieval style had become so despised that it was dismissed as barbarous and ugly—the creation of the Goths who had destroyed the Roman Empire. However, Gothic style never completely vanished and in the early-18th century it underwent a revival, particularly in England. In the 19th century, A. W. N. Pugin and Ruskin both advocated Gothic design and craftsmanship. Pugin, Butterfield and others developed a style now referred to as Reformed Gothic, while the influence of Ruskin and William Morris ensured that English Gothic design heavily informed the Arts and Crafts Movement.

Gough, Piers (1946–) British architect who designed the 1987 bent-and-folded-metal chaise longue for Aram Designs.

Gavin, Bernard (1940–) French interior designer who created several furniture ranges, including the 1967 *Asmara* and the 1975 *Satan*, for Ligne Rose. Other designs include beds for Dunlopillo, interiors for the town hall of Orleans and a hotel in Nice.

Grange, Jacques (1944–) French entrepreneur who worked for Yves Saint-Laurent in the 1970s and 1980s, designing his private house, his offices and his boutique, for which he designed a range of one-off furniture. He opened a range of Grange shops worldwide, to sell the furniture he manufactured. He was the interior designer of the Barbizon Hotel, New York.

Grant, Duncan (1885–1978) Scottish painter who studied at the Westminster and Slade schools in London. After meeting Roger FRY in 1912, he designed for OMEGA WORKSHOP, producing textiles, pottery and painted furniture with Vanessa BELL, Wyndham LEWIS, Gaudier-Brzeska and Nina Hamnett. During the 1920s and 1930s he formed a close collaboration with Bell, moving into her house Charleston, in Sussex, which he decorated, using many different techniques and styles. In 1932 he designed the ballet *The Enchanted Grove* for the Sadlers Wells Ballet, as well as printed fabrics, the most popular being the *Daphne and Apollo* motif. In 1934 he produced *Old English Rose* porcelain for Brain's of Fenton and, in 1935, three panels for the liner *Queen Mary*, which were rejected as being 'too modern'.

Grasset, Eugène (1845–1917) Swiss architect who also designed jewellery and textiles. He designed many books and typefaces and was one of the founders of the Société des Artistes Decorateurs. Amongst his many interiors was the complete design of Louis Gillot's photographic studio, in Paris, mixing Renaissance and ART NOUVEAU styles. Stained glass designs include the Joan of Arc windows in the cathedral, Orléans. His books on decorative design were very influential, particularly *Plants and their Ornamental Applications*, published in 1897.

Graves, Michael (1934–) American architect who, by the mid-1970s, was better known for his furniture, interior and industrial design. He produced popular furniture for Memphis and the Post-Modern stainless-steel teapot for Alessi, which sold over 500,000 pieces. He produced office furniture for the Disney Corporation and the *Mickey Mouse* teapot. In 1988 he started designing carpets for Vorwork and ceramics for Swid Powell.

Gray, Eileen Moray (1878–1976) Irish architect who studied at the Slade School, London, settling in Paris in 1909, where she studied lacquer-work. Her first complete object was the 1919-1922 *Le Destin* folding screen for the couturier, Jacques DOUCET. After the First World War, she entered her exotic period, designing luxury pieces which included her *Gondola* day-bed. She opened a shop under the name 'Jean Désert' in 1922, selling unique pieces of furniture, lighting and carpets. In 1923 she was commissioned to produce furnishings for the Vicomte and Vicomtesse de Noailles at Hyeres. Her society clients included Elsa Schiaparelli, Henri Laurens and the Countess of Oxford. In 1924 she designed furniture for the liner *Transatlantique* and, in 1925, her first metal furniture. Her house at Roquebrun-Cap-Martin became a showcase for her ideas. Interiors were sparse, but comfortable, every space being multifunctional, filled with collapsible furniture made out of steel, glass and painted wood. From 1930 she concentrated on architecture, designing only items of furniture for villas she re-modelled. After the Second World War her influence waned, but was revived towards the end of her life.

Gray, Milner Connorton (b.1899) British industrial designer who worked in the Army Camouflage Unit in the First World War, setting up his first studio in 1922. In 1930 he was a founder member of the Society of Industrial Arts. He worked for other studios throughout the 1930s and taught at various colleges, becoming head of the Sir John Cass School, London in 1937. In 1943, he started the Design Research Unit with Misha BLACK, designing propaganda exhibitions for the Ministry of Information, including the classic 'Dig for Victory'. His graphic design commissions included corporate identities for British Rail, Courage Breweries and Austin Reed shops. The partnership designed prototype domestic wares for the 'Ideal' fitted-kitchen at the 1946 'Britain Can Make It' exhibition. They also designed all the signage for the 1951 'Festival of Britain' exhibition. In 1977, he designed the emblem for the Silver Jubilee of Queen Elizabeth II.

Green, A. Romney (1872–1945) British craftsperson and sailor, a proponent of the ARTS AND CRAFTS MOVEMENT in furniture. Eric GILL's woodcuts appeared in his book *Woodwork in Principle and Practice* of 1918.

Grenander, Alfred (1894–1956) German industrial designer, an early member of the Deutscher Werkbund, producing highly functional furniture for Berliner Mobelfabrik, and stations and passenger cars for the Berlin elevated tramway (now replaced).

Gresley, Herbert Nigel (b.1897) British engineer who was carriage and wagon superintendent of the Great Northern Railway from 1905, becoming locomotive superintendent in 1911. He was best-known for his designs of some of Britain's fastest and most powerful steam locomotives, particularly the streamlined *Mallard* class. He designed a special carriage for the fast service between London and Edinburgh, to commemorate the 1936 coronation of King George VI. The *Coronation* was in two shades of blue, using Rexine (a book-binding material) on surfaces and uncut moquette for upholstery and carpets. Chrome-plated metal added to the stream-lining.

Gropius, Walter (1883–1969) German architect who became director of the BAUHAUS at Weimar and Dessau in 1919. Previously, he had designed NEO-CLASSICAL furniture for Hertzfeld and steel furniture for the battleship *Von Hindenberg*. He worked in Britain with Maxwell Fry from 1934 to 1937, when he moved to America. Pieces produced in Britain include the 1936 plywood chair and table and a perforated aluminium waste-bin. In America, he concentrated on architecture and teaching. In 1968 he collaborated on tea and coffee sets for ROSENTHAL. In 1979, Tecta reissued his 1910 *Fagus* chair.

Groult, André (1884–1967) French furniture and textile designer who, in the 1910s and 1920s, worked in the traditional 18th- and early-19th-century style. In 1912 he designed elegant wallpapers and toile (ornate fabric patterns) and published his own drawings, as well as those by Marie Laurenáin and Paul IRIBE. His signature piece was an anthropomorphic chest of drawers shown at the 1925 Paris Exposition. That same year he produced silver designs for Christofle.

Gruber, Jacques (1870–1936) French stained-glass artists who worked for DAUM, in ART NOUVEAU style. He learned the art of engraving while rendering designs for Wagner's operas. In 1900 he set up his own studio to manufacture furniture with acid-etched cameo glass to incorporated into it. He designed the glass for the tea-room and cupola of Les Galeries Lafayette, Paris. After 1914 he restricted himself to the design of stained glass, including the choir of the cathedral of Verdun and various French embassies.

Guimard, Hector (1867–1942) French architect whose signature building is the Castel Bëranger apartment block, with its virtuoso external and internal decorative detailing. His cast-iron details for the Paris Metro are a permanent reminder of his inventiveness.

H

Hadid, Zaha (1950–) Iraqi architect, working in London. She is well-known for her winning design for the 1983 'The Peak' competition in Hong Kong, to build a private club and residential complex. Her furniture design includes the 1987 *Wavy Back Sofa* produced by Edra.

Hadley, Albert (1920–) American interior designer who studied at the Parsons School, New York. He started as a decorator for A. Herbert Rogers and then the McMillen Studio, where he was responsible for the restoration of the Rosedown Plantation, Louisiana. In 1963, he formed a partnership with Mrs Henry 'Sister' PARISH, becoming renowned for their classical approach. They have created interiors for many privileged and wealthy clients.

Haerdtl, Oswald (1899–1959) Austrian architect who became better know as a designer of elegant drinking suites, candlesticks and crystal lighting, including the 1925 *Tableset 240* and the 1950 *Commodore Tableset* for J. and L. Lobmeyr.

Hafner, Dorothy (1950–) American ceramicist and metalworker who produced her first designs by hand, in a Pop-art, comic-book style. In 1982 her domestic wares were mass-produced by ROSENTHAL. She was the first woman designer at Rosenthal and went on to work for TIFFANY.

Hagler and Co. Stanley American jewellery company founded in Hollywood in 1953 by Stanley Hagler and Edward Nakles. Their flamboyant designs reflected the outlook of the 1960s, as did a range of necklaces and medallions for men. After Nackles left, Hagler specialized in multiple-jewellery; necklaces could become bracelets, earrings could become brooches, or be enlarged with additional pieces.

Haines, William (1900–1973) American actor who took up professional interior design when he left MGM in 1930. He set up a business on Sunset Strip dedicated to going back to classical basics, using English antiques. In the 1930s he designed houses for the Jack Warners and George Cukor, in Regency style. He pioneered the use of copper for lighting shades and fireplaces, suede wall-coverings and leather-laced curtains. Amongst his last designs were Walter Annenberg's desert house, 'Sunnylands' in 1966 and, in 1969, 'Winfield House', the home of the American ambassador in Regent's Park, London.

Haite, Georges Charles (1855–1924) The son of a Paisley textile designer, he was influential in textile design at the end of the Victorian era. He published pattern books, including *Plant Studies for Artists, Designers and Students* in 1886.

Hald, Edward (1883–1980) Swedish glassware designer who studied with Matisse. After a freelance career for Rorstrand and Karlskrona porcelain factories, he became head designer at Orrefors Glasbruk in 1924, remaining as managing director until 1944. He developed the *graal* technique of blowing coloured decoration into the walls of vessels. He continued to design for Orrefors until the late 1970s.

Halfpenny, Joseph (1748–1811) British draughtsman and engraver who was the son of the gardener to the Archbishop of York. Apprenticed as a house-painter, he later became a topographical artist and drew the ornaments in York Minster, while scaffolding was erected for its restoration.

Hamada, Shoji (1894–1978) Japanese chemist and potter who carried out important experiments with Korean and Chinese glazes. In 1919 he met Bernard LEACH in Japan and returned to England with him. He worked in St Ives, England, for two years, returning to Japan to found a studio in Mashiko, a traditional village of artisans, north of Tokyo. In the 1910s and 1920s he developed Mingei, 'popular art', creating simple forms, including unu-

sual sake bottles, teapots, vases and plates. His work is characterized by free-flowing shapes and decorations.

Handler, Laura (1947–) American designer who started out with
commissions for Krizia and Pomellato in Milan. She set up her
own studio in New York in 1983 and has produced clocks, leather
goods and housewares, as well as atomizers for Prescription cosmetics and the *Safari* cosmetic range for Ralph Lauren. Other clients include Colgate-Palmolive, Estée Lauder, Revlon, Fabergé
and Calvin Klein.

Harcourt, Geoffrey (1935–) British furniture designer who
worked in Chicago and Copenhagen (for JENSEN) before opening
his own studio in London. First commissions were for Artifort in
the Netherlands and over 20 models of his designs were produced
in Japan. His seating is popular with airport architects.

Haring, Keith (1958–90) American artist of graffiti-like paintings,
who turned to furniture design, producing his 1988 *On Tara* and
On Giro tables and his 1989 nine-piece bronze suite, which included a three-panel screen. He designed ceramics for VILLEROY
ET BOCH, his last commission. He set up an Aids research trust
which uses his images on a range of toys, T-shirts and other items.

Harrison, Marc (1936–) American industrial designer who fo-
cuses on ergonomic concepts. He designed the 1972 American
Red Cross blood-collecting equipment and was also principal designer for Cuisinart household products and food-processing
equipment.

Hartman, Cedric (1929–) American lighting designer whose
award-winning 1966 *Pharmacy* lamp has been widely copied.

Hartwein, Peter (1942–) German industrial designer who trained
as a joiner, before working in several architectural practices and,
in 1970, joining BRAUN, designing their electronic products.

Hasenauer, Karl von (1833–94) Austrian architect who promoted
the importance of decorative aesthetics in the design of his buildings. He was one of the architects of the Vienna Ringstrasse. He
became professor at the Akademie der Bildenden Kunste, Vienna.

Hassall, Thomas (1878–1940) British ceramics designer joined
Spode in 1892, becoming artistic director in 1910. His brother
Joe Hassall was chief engraver.

Haustein, Paul (1880–1944) German enamellist and ceramicist who worked in the Darmstadt artistic colony founded by the Grand Duke Louis IV of Hesse-Darmstadt. His silver designs were produced by the court silversmith and his tureen, shown at the 1910 Brussels Exposition, was one of the first examples of ART DÉCO style.

Havinden, Ashley Eldrid (1903–1973) British painter and graphic designer who first worked in advertising where his clients included the Milk Marketing Board, the General Post Office and Simpson's department store. From 1933 he designed textiles and rugs for the interior decorator J. Duncan Miller, and his designs were manufactured by Campbell Fabrics, London, and the Wilton Royal Carpet Factory. His ribbon-pattern, birds and scroll-design fabrics were produced by EDINBURGH WEAVERS.

Hay, David Ramsay (1796–1866) Scottish interior decorator and scientist, who set up business in Edinburgh in 1828. He wrote several books on the theory of colouring and proportion.

Heal, Ambrose (1872–1959) British designer who served as an apprentice cabinet-maker before joining the family firm in 1893. From 1896 he began to show his work, in a fine ARTS AND CRAFTS idiom. From the 1930s he adopted a more Modern style. He promoted good design for a mass market. Following a visit to Sweden in 1923, for the Gothenburg Exhibition, he introduced Swedish glassware and furniture design to Britain. In the 1950s he encouraged many young British artists and designers to produce distinctive textile ranges. In 1983 Heal's was acquired by the Storehouse Group, then led by Terence CONRAN.

Heath, Adrian (1923–) British industrial designer who worked largely in Denmark, where he taught at the Arhus art school. Specializing in exhibition and furniture design, his signature pieces include the 1968 *Chair 194* in laminated wood and canvas. His wife, Ditte Heath, has collaborated on many designs.

Heaton, Maurice (b.1900) Swiss glassware designer who worked in New York. From the late 1920s he experimented with translucent white glazes, produced bubble-glass sheets and introduced enamel spirals. His most outstanding work was the large glass mural *The Flight of Amelia Earhart Across the Atlantic* for the

1932 interior of the RKO cinema, Rockefeller Center, New York. He was continuing to produce interesting, reasonably-priced glassware well into his eighties.

Hebey, Isabelle (1935–) French industrial designer who designed all Yves Saint-Laurent's boutiques from 1966 to 1990. In 1972 she designed the interior of the Concorde airliner with Aerospatiale and, from 1979 to 1982, interiors of the Honda Accord car. From 1988 to 1990 she produced furniture for the new French Ministry of Finance, as well as the personal desk of Danielle Mitterand, wife of the president. She designed the interior and furnishings of the South Arch of the Arche de la Defense, Paris.

Held, Marc (1932–) French industrial designer who founded Archiform, a study centre for design research, in 1960. In 1965 he founded the magazine *L'Echoppe*, which is also the name of his boutique. Throughout the 1960s he produced designs for three chairs for KNOLL, including the widely-publicized *Culbuto* model of 1967. In the early 1970s he designed much plastic-moulded furniture for his boutique and items, including a tea-cart, writing desk and bed, for distribution by Prisunic. In 1973 he designed a dinner service for LIMOGES and, in 1974, the Lip watch collection. In 1987 he designed the interior of the liner *Wind Star* and headed a team from Archiform which designed the Grand Drawing Room of the Elysée Palace for President Mitterand.

Helios British textile manufacturer, based in Bolton, founded in 1937. It employed important designers, including Marianne STRAUB, who influenced British textile design of the 1930s and 1940s.

Henningsen, Poul (1894–1967) Danish architect whose 1924 *PH* ceiling and table lamp, for Poulson of Copenhagen, is still in production. He edited the magazine *Kritisk Revy* which spread the gospel of functional design. He designed part of the Tivoli Gardens, Copenhagen.

Henrion, Frederick Henri Kay (1914–1996) French exhibition designer who was born in Nuremburg and worked in London. From 1943 to 1945 he designed all the exhibitions of the Ministry of Agriculture and in 1946 became consultant to the American

Office of War Information. His poster designs included those for the General Post Office, BOAC and London Transport. He was responsible for the corporate identity of KLM airline and was president of the Society of Industrial Artists from 1961 to 1963.

Hepworth, Barbara (1903–1975) British sculptor, married first to John Skeaping and then, Ben NICHOLSON, both painters. In 1937 Hepworth and Nicholson were commissioned to design fabrics for EDINBURGH WEAVERS, Hepworth produced *Pillar*, with its highly textured and cropped motifs. She design the 1951 production of Strauss's *Electra* at the Old Vic Theatre and, in 1954, Tippett's *The Midsummer Marriage*, at the Royal Opera House, both in London.

Herbst, René (1891–1982) German architect who worked in London, Frankfurt and Paris. He was a leader of the FUNCTIONALIST movement, shunning ornamentation. His designs incorporated polished and plated metal and for seating he employed rubber tubes wrapped in cloth thread, currently used for bungee jumping. He was window-display adviser to Siégel, Paris, and designed lighting fixtures. In 1930 he designed Prince Aga Khan's apartment in Paris and, in 1932, MODERNIST furniture in chromium-plated steel for the Maharajah of Indore, in India. He was active in many design organizations, including the Union des Artistes Modernes, becoming president and designing all their exhibitions until 1961.

Heritage, Robert (1927–) British designer who studied at Birmingham College of Art and the Royal College of Art, in London. From 1951 to 1953 he was staff designer at Evans Furniture, before setting up his own studio. He was influenced by simple designs and produced pieces for Rotaflex Lighting and RACE Furniture. In 1968 he designed the innovative *QE2* cast-aluminium chair, manufactured by Race, with legs attached with special adhesive.

Herman, Sam (1936–) American glass designer who studied at Wisconsin University, Edinburgh College of Art and the Royal College of Art, London. He became an influential teacher at the latter from 1969 to 1974. In 1969 he and Graham Hughes founded The Glasshouse Gallery and Workshop, London. He

moved to Australia in 1974 where he founded the New Wave
Movement and established the Jam Factory glass workshop, in
Adelaide. He returned to Europe in 1980 and has since worked in
Belgium at Val-Saint-Lambert.

Hermès French leather-goods manufacturer and retailer. Thierry
Hermès founded the firm as a harness-maker, in 1837. From the
1880s they manufactured saddles, branching out into handbags,
travelling bags, couture, jewellery and watches in the 1920s.
Their silk scarves are epitomized by the classical saddlery motifs.
Key pieces include the 1929 white leather hand-sewn desk and in
the 1930s monumental leather double doors by GIACOMETTI. In
1958 they created the *Kelly* bag, named after the actress Grace
Kelly.

Hermes, Gertrude (1902–1994) British illustrator who also designed decorative furnishings. In 1932 she produced the mosaic
floor and carved centre stone and door-furniture for the Shakespeare Memorial Theatre, Stratford-upon-Avon.

Hicks, David Nightingale (1929–) British interior and furniture
designer who became famous through his designs for his mother's house in Eaton Place, London. In 1960 he established the
first of his own studios which would develop into a world-wide
chain. By 1977 he had branched out into the design of costume
jewellery, glasses, shoes and menswear. His hallmark is the luxurious English country-house style, with simplified lines and the
mixing of styles and materials. He has designed for royalty, to
which he is related by marriage, and other wealthy clients. Public
interiors include the first night-club on the 1969 liner *Queen
Elizabeth II*.

Hicks, Sheila (1934–) American textile designer, based in France,
who has taught and worked in many Third World countries, setting up factories to provide employment. In India she produced
one of her most commercially successful fabrics, the 1968
Badagara heavy double-sided cloth with woven reliefs, which is
a popular wall-hanging. Important works include hangings for
the conference room of the Ford Foundation building, New York,
and the conference centre of the United Arab League, Makkah.

High-Tech Architectural and design style developed in the 1970s and 1980s by Richard Rogers, Norman FOSTER and others. Conventional furnishings were replaced by industrial artefacts, bookcases by metal shelving, the skeletons of chairs and sofas were left unadorned and floors were left uncovered or were covered with synthetic carpeting.

Hildebrand, Margret (1917–) German fabric designer who worked for Stuttgarter Gardinenfabrik from 1936, applying the principles of FUNCTIONALISM to mass production. She was managing director of the company from 1956 to 1966 and in the years following the Second World War was Germany's most famous fabric designer.

Hill, Oliver (1887–1968) Briton who took up architecture on the advice of Edwin LUTYENS, becoming a builder's apprentice in 1909. He set up his own practice in 1918 and gained many commissions to design houses and interiors. Significant work includes North House, Westminster, and art historian, Kenneth Clark's house in Hampstead. In the 1930s he designed furniture for HEAL'S.

Hille British furniture manufacturer founded in 1906 by the Russian émigré Salamon Hille, who was a restorer of 18th-century furniture in Whitechapel, London. After the Second World War his grandson, Leslie Julius, introduced Modern furniture by designers including Robin DAY and Roger Dean. Day's polypropylene chair of the 1960s was Hille's best-selling product. In 1983 Hille merged with Ergonom.

Hills, David (1923–) American glassware designer with STEUBEN from 1948 to 1952. He designed more than 20 vessels, candlesticks, vases and urns. His 1949 bud vase is one of Steuben's most popular pieces and is still in production.

Hilton, Matthew (1957–) British designer who worked for CAPA consultancy on HIGH-TECH products, before starting his own studio in 1984. In 1986 produced a range of furniture for Sheridan Coakley, his best-known pieces including the 1987 *Antelope* aluminium and wood side table with animal-like legs, and his 1988 *Flipper* aluminium and glass coffee table with fin-legs.

Hockney, David (1937–) British artist who pioneered British Pop Art after leaving the Royal College of Art in 1962. He has illustrated numerous books and in the mid-1970s started designing for the stage, with Mozart's *The Magic Flute* and Stravinsky's *The Rake's Progress*. In 1988 he designed carpets for Vorwerk's *Dialog* range.

Hoffman, Josef (1870–1956) Moravian-born architect who studied in Vienna and Munich. Along with Gustav KLIMT and others he was a member of the WIENER WERKSTÄTTE. Initially influenced by ART NOUVEAU, his work took on a style that owed much to the influence of Charles Rennie MACKINTOSH. From 1899 until 1941 he held the post of professor of architecture at the School of Applied Arts in Vienna, continuing to design buildings, exhibition rooms and pavilions, furniture, jewellery, metalwork, leatherwork and textiles. His *Kubus* armchair of 1910 was reproduced in 1978.

Hoffmann, Wolfgang (1900–69) Austrian designer who worked extensively in America as an architect of theatres, apartments and stores, mostly in New York. By 1932 he had become interested in the design of lighting, pewter and furniture influenced by Marcel BREUER. In 1936, he patented tubular-metal chairs, including an outdoor chair, an armchair, a club chair and a chaise longue. His wife, **Pola Hoffmann**, collaborated on some accessories and also designed fabrics.

Hogan, James (1883–1948) British glass craftsman who was a member of the Art-Workers' Guild. He became art director at Whitefriars glass, producing domestic and art wares. His most famous commission was his two 100ft (30m) windows of Gilbert SCOTT's Liverpool Cathedral.

Hohulin, Samuel (1936–) American industrial designer with The Eureka Company, Bloomington, Illinois, who designed the 1982 *Mighty Mite* vacuum cleaner, recognized by its bright, plastic case and compact size.

Holbek, Jorgen (1930–) Danish designer of the 1969 *Prism* flatware produced by Georg JENSEN Silversmiths, also known for designing tobacco pipes.

Holiday, Henry George Alexander (1839–1927) British artist who studied alongside Simeon Solomon and William DE MORGAN at the Royal Academy Schools, London, in the mid-1850s. Associated with the PRE-RAPHAELITES, he worked as a stained glass artist for Edward BURNE-JONES at the manufacturers of Whitefriars glass. He employed a freer style than the typical MORRIS product. He also designed embroideries, mosaics and murals.

Hope, Thomas (*c.*1770–1831) British art connoisseur who travelled widely collecting ancient sculpture and works by NEO-CLASSICAL sculptors which he displayed for the edification of artists at his house in Duchess Street, London. His *Household Furniture and Interior Decoration* of 1792 promoted the Neo-Classical style.

Horák, Bohuslav (1954–) Czech sculptor who joined the Atika design group, established in 1987, in Prague. In 1988 he produced his *A Rotten Luck Easy Chair*, made from welded iron and leather, and his *Flammenschrank* stained-wood and metal cupboard. He often incorporates traditional materials and uses non-industrial production methods.

Horne, Herbert Percy (1864–1916) British surveyor who turned to architectural and furnishing decoration. He also designed the popular, swirling fabric design *The Angel with the Trumpet* and strong, leafy-patterned wallpapers for Century Guild. In 1897 he decorated Arnold Dolmetsch's first harpsichord, which was shown at the Arts and Crafts Exhibition that year. In 1900 he moved to Florence and designed a typeface of that name.

Horta, Victor (1861–1947) Belgian architect who specialized in the design of buildings as an entire concept, including all the furnishings and fittings. He pre-dated HIGH-TECH designers by exposing the framework of a building, the balustrades, window frames and girders and joists. He was an outstanding ART NOUVEAU designer and his best work was his own house, which is now the Horta Museum in Brussels.

Horwitt, Nathan (1889–1990) Romanian designer who worked in New York after studying at the University and Art Students' League, also in New York. In 1930 he designed his *Beta* chair and the 'frameless' picture frame. His numberless, black-faced, clock has been widely copied. Its manufacturer, Movado, adapted it to launch a range of related accessories for their boutiques.

Hugo, François (b.1899) French jeweller, friend of many artists including Jean COCTEAU, Max Ernst, André Derain and Jean Arp. He produced Pablo PICASSO's first designs in silver in 1956 and Salvador DALI's 1957 *Mollusc* flatware in silver-gilt and glass.

Hunt, Martin (1942–) British ceramicist who founded the Queensberry Hunt design group with David QUEENSBERRY in 1966. He has worked for BING AND GRØNDAHL, Wedgwood, ROSENTHAL, Doulton and Pilkington Glass. He worked with Colin Rawson on the 1977 *Concept* vitrified-clay dinnerware for Hornsea Potteries and designed the *Tournee* porcelain dinner service for Thomas.

Hunzinger, George (1835–98) American furniture designer who pioneered the use of imitation bamboo made from wood turned on a lathe.

Husson, Thierry (1951–) French architect who designed the 1986 *Babylone* chair produced by Editions AH!, a suite of which was installed in the offices of the French minister of culture, Jack Lang, and in the national assembly.

Hutton, John (1947–) American furniture designer who became design director at Donghia Furniture and Textiles in 1978. He revived 1950 patterns for furnishings, fabrics and wallpaper. Best-known pieces include the 1988 *San Marco* sofa and *Luciano* club chair.

I

Image, Selwyn (1849–1930) British priest who gave up holy orders to become an artist and designer. He worked with Arthur MACKMURDO on the formation of the Century Guild and designed the first edition of the Guild's magazine *The Hobby Horse*. He made designs for embroidery and stained glass, influenced by the work of William MORRIS. He became master of the Art-Workers' Guild in 1910.

Imgrand, Max (1908–69) French glass designer who was responsible for the illuminated glass fountain at the Rond Point, Avenue des Champs-Elysées, Paris. He designed the wavy, thin-walled *Mouchoir* vase (1957) for Fontana Arte and the 1953 stained-glass windows of the church of Saint-Pierre de Montmartre, Paris.

Ingres, Jean Auguste Dominique (1780–1867) French painter who studied in Paris under Jacques David, the pioneer of Neo-Classicism in painting. In 1842 he designed stained glass for the Chapel of Saint-Ferdinand at Neuilly and in 1844 a series of windows for the Chapelle Royale at Dreux, where Delacroix assisted. From 1848 to 1850 five tapestries were woven at Gobelins based on the Dreux designs. He showed 25 stained-glass designs at the 1855 Paris Exhibition. In 1861 he designed a NEO-CLASSICAL cameo depicting the Apotheosis of Napoleon I.

Iosa Ghini, Massimo (1959–) Italian designer and illustrator and member of the Zak-Ark group. He started out as an illustrator of comic-books in Italy and rock magazines in America, and went on to design projects for Centro Moda Firenze and Swatch. He has designed discothéques, video projects and furniture, including Memphis's 1986 *12 New* Collection, the *Roy* wood and metal table and *Bertrand* sideboard. For Fiam he designed the *Genio* and *Incontro* tables.

Iribe, Paul (1883–1935) French designer and illustrator who provided caricatures for journals such as *Le Rirei* and *Le Cris* de Paris. He did fashion illustrations for Paul POIRET and set up a decorating studio to produce wallpapers, fabrics and *objets d'art*. His finely carved furniture was made of exotic woods and veneered with amaranth, ebony, rosewood and shagreen, an untanned leather, often horse. He had theatrical flair as shown in the designs for Jacques DOUCET's house which was completely redecorated when he disposed of his collection of 18th-century furniture. In 1914 he went to Hollywood and worked as designer on Cecil B. De Mille's 1921 *The Affairs of Anatol* and the 1934 *Cleopatra*. In 1930 he returned to France and illustrated books and magazines, the emblem of the couture house Lanvin and costume jewellery for Coco Chanel.

Isäus, Magnus (1841–90) Swedish architect who led the Renaissance revival in architecture during the 1880s. In the early 1870s he designed for the Gustavsberg porcelain factory in Stockholm, working in his version of Louis XVI style.

Ishimoto, Fujiwo (1941–) Japanese fabric designer who works in Finland. In 1970 he joined Decembre, moving to Marimekko in 1974. He is known for his black-and-white palette and themes drawn from nature, not unlike Maija ISOLA. In the early 1980s he added to colour and the Japanese idiom to his range, designing the 1984 *Taival* fabric and 1987 *Uoma* tablecloth.

Isokon *see* **Pritchard, Jack**.

Isola, Maija (1927–) Finnish fabric designer who started at Printex, where her bright and bold printed textiles were widely admired in the 1950s and 1960s. She was innovative in the use of bed sheeting on which to silk-screen big geometric designs. From 1951 she also produced similar designs for Marimekko. Later influences were Byzantine decorations and Finnish folk motifs, from the province of Karelia.

Isozaki, Arata (1931–) One of Japan's best known architects of the last quarter of the century. He has worked as a visiting professor at major universities worldwide, including California, Hawaii and New York. In 1988 he designed the *Dialog* range of rugs for Vorwerk and, in 1981 *Fuji* cabinets for Memphis. Important buildings include the 1970 Japan World Exposition (Expo '70), the 1981 Museum of Contemporary Art in Los Angeles and the 1992 Guggenheim Museum, SoHo, New York.

Issel, Alberto (1848–1926) Italian furniture designer who employed over 70 craftspeople in his Turin workshops. His pieces are marked by carved flowing, florid and floral features.

Isselburg, Peter (*c.*1580–*c.*1630) German engraver who worked in Nuremberg and Bamberg, where, in 1625, he published his handbook of grotesque patterns, bacchic subjects and ornaments, in 1625. It was aimed at painters, goldsmiths, embroiderers and other craftsmen. He published over 440 plates.

Issigonis, Alec (1906–1988) Turkish-born, car designer who became a naturalized British citizen. He trained as an engineer and first worked for Humber cars, before joining Morris Motors in 1936. His first success was the Morris Minor in 1948, before he briefly left to design luxury cars for Alvis. His triumph was the 1959 Mini, incorporating his signature minimalist features.

Itten, Johannes (1888–1967) German theorist and teacher who was a founding member of the BAUHAUS school and worked on his theories of design. Thought too cerebral by Walter GROPIUS, he was dismissed in 1923. In 1926 he founded the Ittel-Schule in Berlin to continue his work and, from 1932 to 1938, he was director of the Textlfachschule in Krefeld and director of Kunstgewerbeschule in Zurich.

Iwata, Itako (1922–) Japanese glass designer was president of Awata Glass, Tokyo. In 1984 he became a member of the International Council of Pilchuck Glass School, Washington and was a Trustee of the Corning Museum of Glass, New York State.

J

Jack, George Washington (1855–1932) British architect, born in New York, who became chief furniture designer from 1890 to 1900, when he took over the practice of Philip WEBB. His book *Wood Carving: Design and Workmanship* was published in 1903.

Jackson, Dakota (1949–) American furniture designer who started out as a consultant to magicians and rock music groups who wanted to use illusion in their acts. In 1970 he had his first furniture commission, from Yoko Ono for John Lennon. In 1991 produced his *Vikter* range, which included the *Stacking Chair*.

Jacob, Carl (*c.*1925–) Danish furniture designer who worked for Kandya in London, where he produced the popular 1950 Jason stacking chairs in bent beech for use in restaurants, offices and schools. It was widely used throughout the site of the 1951 Festival of Britain..

Jacobsen, Arne (1902–71) Danish architect and furniture designer who trained at the Copenhagen Academy. He started designing mass-produced furniture in 1950, including the *Egg* and *Swan* chairs (1959), constructed from fibreglass and with an aluminium base. He designed tableware in 1957 for Michelsen which was used in the film *2001: A Space Odyssey*. His 1967 *Cylinda* tableware in stainless steel was equally popular. His buildings include the St Catherine's College, Oxford, for which he also designed the lighting, textiles, cutlery and tableware.

Jacobsen, Jacob (1901–1995) Norwegian lighting designer who adapted the 1937 Luxo 2000 lamp from the British 1937 Anglepoise prototype. He bought the rights to produce it in Norway and by the 1940s had a near-monopoly on the lamp.

Jallot, Léon Albert (1874–1967) French craftsman who started to make furniture in 1880. From 1898 to 1901 he was manager of Samuel BING's shop L'Art Nouveau, in Paris. In 1903 he established his own decorating workshop, where he designed and made everything for the home. He was the first to react against the excesses of ART NOUVEAU, simplifying his designs until, as early as 1904, they were restricted to the natural grains of the wood. He believed in rich materials rather than over-rich decoration. In 1921 his son, Maurice JALLOT, joined him in the business. At this time they began to use newly-created synthetic materials and metal in their designs. they pioneered the use of indirect lighting in their interior designs. They produced fluted columns lit from within for the 1920 Salon of the Société des Artistes Décorateurs.

Jallot, Maurice (b.1900) French furniture designer with his father's workshop in Paris. After the semi-retirement of his father in the 1950s, he designed many stores and apartments, rugs, stained glass and furniture panels.

Jaulmes, Gustave-Louis (1873–1959) Swiss architect who turned to decorative painting in 1901, to furniture design in 1910 and tapestry design in 1915. Working in Paris, he carried out important commissions for the Musée Rodin and several important tapestry designs including one depicting American troops departing for France. After the First World War he decorated the Champs Elysées and designed the Cenotaph. He also painted murals for the Théâtre de Chaillot and the Paris Musée des Arts Decoratifs and the curtain for the Grand-Théâtre, Lyons.

Jamnitzer, Christoph (1563–1618) German goldsmith, based in Nuremberg, in the employ of Emperor Rudolph II. He published a book of 62 plates of grotesque and fanciful ornament, to be used as models for jewels or furniture decorations.

Jeanneret, Pierre (1896–1967) Swiss architect and designer and cousin of LE CORBUSIER, for whom he worked in Paris. They collaborated on important furniture designs. His best-known pieces include the 1947 *Scissors Chair* for KNOLL. It was made of birchwood, with a chromium-plated steel bolt, with rubber cushions, upholstered in linen-and-jute fabric.

Jeannest, Émile (1813–57) French sculptor who emigrated to Britain in 1845 to work for MINTON, then moving to Elkington's about 1850. He also designed furniture and taught at the Stoke-on-Trent School of Design. He designed the Minton majolica shown at the 1855 Paris Exposition.

Jefferson, Thomas (1743–1826) American politician, landowner and surveyor, he was presidend of the United States from 1801–1809. He designed and furnished his house at Monticello, Virginia and in 1789 devised a NEO-CLASSICAL silver coffee urn and goblets. In 1803 he designed a mosaic floor for Monticello, as well as a revolving door-cum-shelf unit and other furniture.

Jencks, Charles A. (1939–) American architect who designed limited-production furniture, including the 1984 *Sun* table, with the image of a *trompe l'oeil* sun. He was one of eleven designers who contributed to the Alessi *Tea and Coffee Piazza* project, his designs being influenced by classical columns.

Jensen, Arthur Georg (1866–1935) Danish metalworker who started out making ceramics for Mogens BALLIN in Copenhagen around 1884. He also worked for BING AND GRØNDAHL Porcelain, taking up jewellery and silver design in 1904. He aimed to make Modern design popular, taking his inspiration from nature. His silversmithy gained a reputation by employing the talents of the best designers of the time, including Johan Rhode and Sigvaard BERNADOTTE. Jensen's designers pioneered the use of stainless steel, originally a substitute for silver during the Second World War, for jewellery. Pre-war silver and post-war stainless steel pieces are still in production. In 1920, Jensen opened a showroom on Fifth Avenue, New York, its success being guaranteed, as newspaper magnate William Randolph Hearst had bought the entire stock of the Jensen exhibit at the 1915 San Francisco Exposition.

Jensen, Jakob (1926–) Danish industrial designer who was trained by Sigvaard BERNADOTTE, before setting up his own consultancy in 1961. He designed audio equipment for BANG & OLUFSEN, including the 1960 *Beolit 600* radio with ergonomic controls, the 1976 *Beogram 4000* record player and the *Beosystem 5500* four-unit music system with remote control.

Jensen, Jens Jacob Herring Krog (1895–1978) Danish ceramicist who moved to Cincinnati, America, in 1927. He worked for Rookwood Pottery, producing decorated pottery, often inspired by contemporary European painters.

Jensen, Jørgen (1895–1966) Danish designer, the son of Georg JENSEN. From 1923 to 1936 he designed silver flatware and jewellery at his own smithy in Stockholm. After his father's death in 1935, he returned to Copenhagen to head the Jensen company.

Jiricná, Eva (1938–) Czech architect and interior designer who works in Britain. Her major architectural projects included the Brighton Marina, before she set up as an interior designer. She designed fashionable shops for Joseph and Kenzo, salons for Vidal Sassoon hairdressers, Legends nightclub and Le Caprice restaurant. She designed a folding table and chair for Formica and collaborated with architect Richard Rogers on the interiors of the Lloyds building in the City of London. She also worked on the 'Way In' department of Harrods department store.

Joachim, Christian (1870–1943) Danish ceramicist who worked with Georg JENSEN from 1897 to 1900. From 1901 to 1933 he worked for Royal Copenhagen Porcelain, producing NEO-CLASSICAL shapes. For the last eleven years he was artistic director.

Joel, Betty (b.1896) British furniture and textile designer, who set up her eponymous company with her husband in 1919. She was noted for her luxurious furniture designs, using exotic fabrics, in a fussy style, aping that of Paris in the 1920s. Her carpet designs were hand-knotted in Tientsin, China, with clipped patterns. She retired at the height of her popularity in 1937.

John, William Goscombe (1860–1952) Welsh woodcarver to the 3rd Marquess of Bute. In 1884 he attended the Royal Academy Schools, establishing himself as Wales' leading sculptor. He was responsible for the 1989 Hirlas Horn of the Gorsedd of Bards and the 1911 regalia for the investiture of the Prince of Wales. He designed the seal of the National Museum of Wales and medals, including those for the 1899 National Eisteddfod and for the 1935 jubilee of George V.

Johnson, Philip (1906–1995) New York-based American architect who was influential in promoting design, through major exhibitions at the Museum of Modern Art, New York. Major buildings include many private houses through the 1930s and 1940s, the garden extension of the Museum of Modern Art in 1953, the Seagram Building, New York, in 1954 and the New York State Theater, Lincoln Center, in 1960.

Jones, Inigo (1573–1652) British theatre designer and architect. He travelled to Italy in the party of Lord Roos, acquiring knowledge of classical ideals. In 1905 he designed sets and costumes for Ben Jonson's *Masque of Blacknesse* at Whitehall for Anne of Denmark. Until 1840, stage design was his main activity. From 1609, when he designed the New Exchange, he developed as an architect, travelling to Italy again to acquire drawings by PALLADIO. In 1616 he began the design of the Queen's House in Greenwich for Anne of Denmark, whose hearse he designed in 1619. He designed interiors for Queen Henrietta Maria at Somerset House, in 1626. He was influenced by contemporary French designers, as well as Italian. The King's Bedroom at Queen's House was decorated with splendid palm trees, inspired by Spanish prints of King Solomon's Temple.

Jones, Owen (1809–74) Welsh architect, designer and theorist, who travelled widely across Europe and the Near East collecting designs. He published several books of views and architectural details, including his great *Grammar of Ornament*, in 1856, which became a bible for contemporary and later designers. He designed fabrics, carpets, playing-cards and book-covers. In the 1840s he was a leading tile and mosaic designer, for Herbert MINTON and the terracotta manufacturer, John Marriott Blashfield. In 1844 he showed designs for the floors of the New Palace of Westminser, but they were considered too Moorish. In 1850 he decorated the apse of All Saints, Ennismore Gardens, London and, in 1851, Christ Church, Streatham. In 1863 he decorated the Indian, Chinese and Japanese Courts at South Kensington and, in 1865, the Fishmongers' Hall. He was a close friend of the authoress, George Eliot and George Henry Lewes, whose house he decorated in 1863. He advised them on the book-cover for *Middlemarch*.

Joseff of Hollywood American costume jewellery company, at Burbank, California. Eugene Joseff moved to Hollywood and started making jewellery for the cinema, which he sold or rented for various productions. These included *Gone With the Wind* in 1939 and *The Thief of Bagdad* in 1940. Private clients have included stars of these films, such as Vivien Leigh.

Jourdain, Francis (1876–1958) Prolific French painter and designer, exhibiting alongside Paul Cézanne, Henri Matisse and Henri de TOULOUSE-LAUTREC in 1912. In 1912 he set up a workshop to design and make mass-production furniture, using cheap materials, in simple classic styles. By the end of the First World War he had set up a factory to supply his showroom and retail shop, Chez Francis Jourdain, Paris. Apart from furniture and furnishngs, he designed the smoking car for the Compagnie Paris-Orléans railway, the Bally shoe shop, Paris, including all the metal furniture and showcases, and a fresco for the Samaritime department store. For Jean Vigo, he designed the barge in the film, *L'Atalante*. In public areas he was innovative, incorporating clocks into walls, with only the numerals and hands showing.

Jouve, Paul (1880–1973) French illustrator whose major work, Rudyard Kipling's *The Jungle Book*, took over ten years to complete. It contained 90 woodcuts. He participated in the decoration of several liners, including the 1935 *Normandie*.

Jugendstil *see* **Art Nouveau**.

Jujol, Josep Maria (1879–1949) Spanish architect who designed metalwork for Antoni GAUDÍ's buildings, including iron railings for the 1906 Casa Milá. He also created mosaics for Park Güell and the Battlo apartment block. His work heralded the Surrealist and Expressionist movements. As an architect he used free forms, as exemplified by his Casa Dels Ous, the House of Eggs, so-called because of its curving lines.

Junkers, Hugo (1859–1935) German airplane designer and manufacturer, whose company was founded in 1895 for the production of water heaters. In 1907 he patented a twin piston engine, which was adapted in 1910 for aicraft. In 1919 he founded Junkers Flugzeugwerk, Dessau, where he designed and produced the first all-metal airplane. In 1929 he designed the first airplane passenger cabin.

K

Kåge, Algot Wilhelm (1889–1960) Swedish ceramicist, known at first as a poster designer. Joined the Swedish Ceramic Company in Gustavsberg in 1917, remaining there until 1960. He encouraged the use of modern designs and introduced stacking designs, simple forms and heat-resistant dinnerware. His 1917 *Liljebala* (Blue Lily) dinnerware was his first attempt to raise the standard of design available for the masses. Other series included the 1933 *Praktika, Marina* and *Pyro*. His moulded stoneware in the 1950s was named *Farsta* after the island on which the works is located. It was influenced by Mexican and Chinese forms.

Kan, Shiu-Kay (1949–) British lighting designer, from Hong Kong, working in London. He worked for Foster Associates and Fiorucci, both London, before founding SKK Lighting. His first design was the *Kite Light* and he went on to experiment with new techniques and mobile lighting, often motorized. His 1988 *Motorized Robotic Light* could move across the ceiling on horizontal cables by programmable, remote control. It was installed in the Design Museum, Butler's Wharf, London.

Kandinsky, Wassily (1866–1944) Russian painter who began to design porcelain after teaching courses at the BAUHAUS, Weimar. His 1922 cups and sauces for the State (formerly Imperial) factory in Petrograd (now St Petersburg) were reproduced in 1972 by Haviland and LIMOGES.

Karnagel, Wolf (1940–) German designer and teacher who worked as an associate designer with the Staatliche Porzellan-Manufaktur, Berlin. For ROSENTHAL he designed *Joy* in 1969 and *Pandio* in 1983. He has also designed porcelain for Lufthansa.

Kastholm, Jørgen (1931–) Danish architect and furniture designer whose signature piece is the 1962 *Scimitar Chair 63* with its tractor-like seat. He also designs cutlery, textiles and lighting.

Katavolos, William (1924–) American designer, in partnership with Ross LITTELL and Douglas Kelley. They produced their first furniture designs for LAVERNE Originals from 1949 as part of the *New Furniture Group*, with models in leather, chrome, glass and marble. The 1952 *T Chair* was modelled in wood and manufactured in chromium-plated steel. With George NELSON, he devised the 1956-7 *Omni Pole* shelving system and exhibition systems for Williamsburgh Restoration and the Smithsonian Museum. In 1965 he designed office partitions for the offices of Time-Life, New York and surgical and hospital products for Johnson and Johnson.

Kauffer, Edward McKnight (1890–1954) American graphic designer who worked in London. He settled in Britain in 1914 and in 1915 received his first important commission, for London Underground, who remained a principal client for over 25 years. Other clients included Eastman (Kodak), Eno's Fruit Salts, Orient Steamships, Shell Mex and British Petroleum. He designed theatre costumes and sets including those for Ninette de Valois's ballet *Checkmate*. From the 1920s he designed carpets for the Wilton Royal Carpet Factory, as did his wife, Marian DORN.

Kay, John Illingworth (1870–1950) Scottish designer who worked in London in the Silver Studio in the 1890s. In 1900 he left for the Essex Wallpaper Company, where he was designer for 22 years.

Kenwood British kitchenware manufacturer, founded in 1947 by Kenneth Wood in his garage. Kenneth Grange became consultant designer and the company was in the forefront of good design. Its first product was the 1947 *A100* Turn-Over toaster, followed a year later by the first all-British food mixer, the *Kenwood Chef*.

Kieffer, Michel (b.1916) French bookbinder, the son of René KIEFFER. He started in his father's bindery in 1935, soon developing his own style, named *décor cloisonné*, which involved setting semi-precious stones into leather bindings.

Kieffer, René (1875–1964) French bookbinder who started out as a gilder, setting up his own bindery, in 1903. Originally working in the classical tradition, he became noted for brightly coloured

ART NOUVEAU designs. By the 1930s he was incorporating metal plaques and portrait medallions into his creations.

King, Jesse Marion (1875–1949) British designer who studied and, later, taught at Glasgow School of Art. She was part of the Charles Rennie MACKINTOSH circle and a follower of the ARTS AND CRAFTS MOVEMENT. She designed wallpaper and fabric and the *Cymric* range of jewellery for LIBERTY. She designed many books, murals and mosaics.

Kinsman, Rodney (1943–) British industrial designer who established OMK Design in 1966 to work for furniture manufacturers. He designed the *Omstack* chair, the 1984 *Graffiti* shelving system and, in 1990, outdoor seating systems for British Rail.

Kjaerholm, Poul (1929–80) Danish designer of simple, occasionally austere, furniture, influenced by the BAUHAUS. Specializing in mass production, he is best-known for his chromium, wood and leather furniture, including the 1957 *Armchair II*. He designed the 1977 dining room of the Royal Porcelain concert hall and the 1978 restaurant Kanalen.

Klee, Paul (1879–1940) Swiss painter who taught at the BAUHAUS from 1920 to 1931. He was director of the stained-glass workshop and the weaving and painting courses.

Klein, Jacques (1899–1963) French decorator and designer of wallpaper and rugs for the Galeries Lafayette store, Paris.

Klimt, Gustav (1862–1918) Austrian painter who wove elaborate, symbolic designs into his portraits. He was a founder member of the Vienna Secession.

Klint, Ebsen (1915–69) Danish industrial designer who was with Philips from 1938–39, designed school furniture and is best-known for his 1947 folded-paper lighting fittings, inspired by origami. He was the son of Kaare KLINT.

Klint, Kaare (1888–1954) Danish architect who set up his practice in Copenhagen in 1920, branching out into furniture design in 1924. Made mainly by Rud Radmussen, it included his 1933 deck chair. He designed furniture and furnishings for Fåborg Museum in 1922–25 and for the Thorvaldsens Museum in Copenhagen in 1924–5. He collaborated with his son, Ebsen KLINT, on the design of plastic-coated, folded-paper lighting fittings.

Knight, Laura (1877–1970) British painter who designed the form and decoration of the 1933–34 *Circus* range of tableware produced by Wilkinsons of Burslem, supervised by Clarice CLIFF. She designed 1937 coronation ceramics by Wedgwood and glassware by Stuart Crystal.

Knoll A design company of international renown, founded by Florence and Hans Knoll. They commissioned work from a wide variety of designers and architects, including MIES VAN DER ROHE, Eero SAARINEN and Isamu NOGUCHI. They were particularly successful in creating harmony between the architecture of a building and its interior design. The company was sold in 1960.

Knox, Archibald (1864–1933) British silver designer from the Isle of Man, where he studied and taught at the Douglas School of Art. He moved to London and worked with Christopher DRESSER. From 1898 he designed for LIBERTY and was the inspiration behind their *Cymric* and *Tudric* ranges. His refined silver pieces, interlaced and enamelled, together with his Donegal carpets, were amongst the most elegant of the age. He also designed the 1917 gravestone of Arthur Lasenby Liberty.

Koch, Mogens (b.1898) Danish architect who also designed furniture. His 1933 *Safari* chair is still produced by Interna, Denmark. He designed for most major Danish manufacturers, including Rasmussen, and silver and textiles for the restoration of Danish churches.

Koehler, Florence (1861–1944) American artist whose crafts style jewellery, made in Chicago, was popular in fashionable and artistic circles at the turn of the century. She led the revival of interest in American crafts.

Kogoj, Oskar (1942–) Yugoslavian industrial designer, best-known for his 1968 *Red Object* plastic wagon. He uses organic forms and works primarily in plastic, for cutlery, kitchenware and toys. His *Gondolai* range of chairs are based on impressions of the seated body.

Komoi, Ray (1918–95) American graphic designer who started out in advertising, moving into furniture design in 1949 with his moulded plywood chair with a split seat and bent-metal legs. From 1945 he produced wallpaper and textiles using motifs inspired by painters such as Pablo PICASSO and KLEE for LAVERNE International.

Kørbing, Kay (1915–1995) Danish designer of one of the earliest fibreglass chairs, in 1955, with bent-metal legs.

Kotera, Jan (1871–1923) Czech architect who was influenced by Frank Lloyd WRIGHT. He took to glass design at the turn of the century, designing a punchbowl in 1903, which was a milestone in modern glass design. In 1898 he designed railway-carriage interiors and, thereafter, many interiors for restaurants, banks and private clients.

Kramer, Ferdinand (1898–1985) German architect who designed the 1925 *Kramer-Stove* and furniture for housing developments in Frankfurt. A small version of his 1927 black-lacquered bentwood side chair was used in Frankfurt elementary schools. In 1938 he moved to America and worked for Norman Bel GEDDES. Between 1948 and 1951 he designed the *Rainbelle* range of furniture.

Kristian, Roald (b.1893) Norwegian artist who executed the woodcuts for the first two books produced by OMEGA WORKSHOP. He was deported from Britain in 1917 as an enemy alien.

Krog, Arnold (1856–1931) Danish architect who, while a student, worked on the interior decoration and repairs of the Frederiksborg Palace from 1978 to 1881. He became artistic director at Royal Copenhagen Porcelain Factory from 1885 to 1916, developing a special style of underglaze decoration.

Kroll, Boris (1913–91) American textile designer who worked with his brother, Hammond Kroll, setting up his own firm in 1938. From primitive beginnings, dyeing in the bath, weaving by hand, he began using power looms and, in 1946, set up Boris Kroll, New York. He used cotton and spun rayon and, in 1956, was invited by the government of India to advise on updating handloom production. By 1991 the firm had 16 showrooms in America.

L

La Falaise, Alexis de (1948–) French farmer who founded a craftsmen's cooperative in Wales, moving to Fontainebleau in the

late 1970s. He designed furniture in oak, sycamore and mahogany, including the *Opera TV* cabinet and the *Obelis* bookcase.
In 1989 made furniture for the Chateau Bellevue Laforet vine-
yard.

La Farge, John Frederick Lewis Joseph (1835–1910) American
stained-glass artist, who was born and worked in New York. Initially trained as a lawyer, he went to Paris in 1856 where he met
the writers Gautier and Baudelaire and started to paint, copying
old masters in the Louvre. On his return journey he stopped in
England to see works by the PRE-RAPHAELITES. In 1875, he started
to design stained glass, influenced by Edward BURNE-JONES, Ford
Madox BROWN and Dante Gabriel ROSSETTI. His methods changed
the face of stained-glass design in America. In 1876 he produced
murals and architectural decorations for Trinity Church, Boston,
and for St Thomas Church in 1877, Church of the Incarnation in
1885 and the Church of the Ascension in 1886. In the 1880s he
decorated the Japanese Parlour of the Vanderbilt residence.

La Mache, Didier (1945–) French designer who produces and
sells his own lighting, furniture and accessories, which includes
the 1987 *Ciel Bauhaus!* table lamp.

La Pietra, Ugo (1938–) Italian architect who set up his own studio
1964 to design furniture, accessories and lighting. He has worked
for all the major Italian manufacturers. His metal work for Alessi
includes anthropomorphic coffee pots. He is also a prolific author
and editor.

Labino, Dominick (*c.*1935–) American ceramicist and glassware
designer, concerned with improving glass technology. He developed free-form techniques and pieces made from several layers,
together with large random forms made by opening up asymmetric bubbles and stretching the glass.

Lachenal, Edmond (1855–1948) French sculptor who opened a
ceramics studio at Malakoff, near Paris, in 1880. He made pottery
in the 'Persian' style. In 1890 he perfected a partially dulled glaze
and metallic lustre glazes. He made ceramic sculptures based on
works by Rodin and others and developed an interest in enamelled glass. His later vase forms were inspired by fashionable
plant motifs.

Lachenal, Raoul (1885–1956) French ceramicist, son of Edmond
LACHENAL. He succeeded to his father's studio and, from 1904,
exhibited incised and geometric-motif stoneware and coloured
glazes within cloisonné. In 1911 he moved to Boulogne-sur-Seine,
producing one-off pieces and series, often using ovoid shapes, with
simple decorations. He was fond of black-and-white contrasts.

Lacombe, Georges (1886–1916) French carver who became a
member of the NABIS artists' group in 1892. He took up wood
carving in 1893, producing furniture and panels in a style influenced by GAUGUIN. He did not sell his work, preferring to give it
to friends and neighbours.

Lacoste, Gerald (1909–1995) British architect who designed
decorative glass. His best piece was the 1934 silvered, grey-green
glass fireplace, with a glass tile hearth and surrounding mirrored
wall, made by Pilkington, for Norman Hartnell's salon, Bruton
Street, London. In 1938 he designed the London flat of Lord
Mountbatten.

Lacroix, Boris-Jean (1902–84) French designer who began working for the couturier Madeleine Vionnet in 1924, as a designer of
handbags and costume jewellery. He also decorated and designed
her private residence. He became a prolific designer of wallpaper,
lighting, bookbindings and furniture, the latter often of Cubist inspiration. He designed modern lamps involving engraved mirror
and frosted glass tubes, as well as an enormous range of domestic
lighting, including illuminated ceilings and picture frames.

Lade, Jan (1944–) Danish interior designer who founded Møre
Designteam in 1970, with Sven Asbjørsen. They designed the
1970 *Ecco* chairs and the 1985 combined chair/bed unit, on
which the sitter could recline, with feet higher than heart.

Lahalle, Pierre (1877–1956) French architect who began designing furniture in 1902, in collaboration with Maurice Lucet. Their
simplified 18th-century style reflected the change from ART
NOUVEAU to ART DÉCO. They used fine woods, often with ivory
and mother-of-pearl inlays. They achieved dramatic contrasts of
wood and lacquer, often gilded. Georges Levard joined the company in 1907, collaborating on furniture for Les Grands Magasins
du Louvre.

Lalique, René (1860–1945) French jeweller and glass designer who founded his manufactury in 1885. His early work uses flowing flower forms. He bought a small jewellery workshop in 1885 and supplied jewellery to CARTIER, Boucheron and other major jewellers. In the early 1890s he experimented with enamel, creating new soft colours. During this period he created most of the stage jewellery for the actress Sarah Bernhardt, and started to assemble a spectacular suite of jewellery to show at the 1900 Paris Exposition. Museums started to buy his work, and between 1895 and 1912, he assembled a suite of 145 pieces for Calouste Gulbenkian. His interest in glass expanded, first in the form of small crystal figurines and then with a moulded glass panel for the front door of his house. In 1906 François Coty commissioned him to design scent bottles made of pressed glass. He then designed one for Marcel Rochas's *Femme* and the double-dove stopper for Nina Ricci's *L'Air du Temps,* both in 1907. Ahead of his time in realizing the place glass would have in contemporary architecture, he installed 200 decorative windows in the Coty building of Fifth Avenue, New York. He began to concentrate on glass, at the expense of jewellery, using semi-industrial techniques to produce basic pieces, the decorative finish being done by hand. In the 1920s his output was prolific; bowls, vases, tableware, car mascots, lighting and one-off art pieces. His style used clear, coloured and opalescent glass, often inter-cut, and featured free-flowing motifs, based on plants and the female form. In 1932 he began designing a large range of glass pieces for the 1935 liner *Normandie.* At the 1925 Paris Exposition he had his own pavilion, featuring a huge, luminous fountain.

Lalique, Suzanne (1899–1995) French painter and decorator, the daughter of René LALIQUE. She was a porcelain designer for Sèvres and LIMOGES and also created fabrics and wallpaper.

Lam, Izabel (1948–) American fashion designer who took up industrial design in 1988. She was Geoffrey BEENE's design assistant before going on to design a range of flatware, picture frames, candlesticks and letter-knives, in a neo-BAROQUE style.

Landberg, Nils (1907–1996) Swedish engraver and glassware designer who trained in Gothenberg and at the school of Orrefors

Glass, where he went on to work from 1927. He designed much
tableware, architectural embellishments and art pieces. He produced delicate pieces, including tall glasses with slender, delicate
stems.

Lane, Danny (1955–) American painter and designer who moved
to London in 1975 to work with stained-glass artist Patrick
Reyntiens. In 1981 he set up his own studio in the East End of
London. He specialized in one-off architectural pieces, some produced for Ron ARAD's One-Off shop. In 1986 he produced a
stacking chair and table made from hammered armour-plated
glass.

Lane, Edward William (1801–76) British Arabic scholar who
abandoned plans to enter the church and became an engraver. He
left for Egypt in 1825, where he compiled an Arabic dictionary
and promoted Islamic design.

Lanel, Luc (1894–1966) French designer who created a silver
service in 1935 for the liner *Normandie*.

Langenmayr, Albert (1951–) German furniture designer, based in
Berlin, who is noted for the technical detail of his pieces. His
1990 *Tension* table used the principles of suspension-bridge engineering and his *Storch* chairs were each held together by a single
screw.

Lanvin, Jeanne (1867–1946) French fashion designer who encouraged designers in other fields, including Paul IRIBE, who designed the symbol of her fashion house. It showed her dressing
for a ball, with her daughter at her feet. Part of her apartment, designed by Armand-Albert RATEAU has been preserved in the Museum of the Decorative Arts, Paris.

Laporte-Blairsy, Leo (1865–1923) French sculptor of great
monumental pieces in the ART NOUVEAU style, who took up lighting design in the late 1890s. The introduction of incandescent
bulbs allowed much more flexible use of materials. He designed
lamps, statuettes, vases and *epergnes* in bronze and marble. He
later worked in silver and gold, with enamelling. Some of his
lighting was inspired by stories, such as one about a little girl and
a balloon, for Les Grands Magasins du Louvre.

Larche, Françoise-Raoul (1860–1912) French sculptor known for his monumental pieces. By the turn of the century he was casting mass-produced smaller pieces. He was best-known for his table lamps in the flowing form of Loïe Fuller and her swirling draperies. He designed the group *La Loire et ses affluents* for the place du Carrousel, Paris.

Larcher, Dorothy (1884–1952) British textile designer who worked with Phyllis BARRON at Painswick, Gloucestershire, where they produced dress and furnishing fabrics using original or newly-carved French blocks. They designed the fabrics for the Duke of Westminster's yacht and the Senior Common Room of Girton College, Cambridge. They used vegetable dyes, often on unbleached cottons and linens.

Larsen, Johannes (1912–) Danish civil engineer who took up industrial design in the 1960s, producing a range of pieces, including milking machines and the 1968 *Cylinder Cushion 272* floor seat.

László, Paul (1900–93) Hungarian architect who started a design studio in Vienna in 1923. In 1936 he moved to Los Angeles where he designed mass-produced furniture, as well as decorating houses for film stars including Cary Grant and Barbara Stanwyck, and for the Woolworth heiress, Barbara Hutton. He designed department stores such as Orbach's and Goodwater's, and the casinos of Howard Hughes's hotels in Las Vegas.

Latham, Richard S. (1920–) American designer who first worked for Raymond LOEWY in Chicago, producing designs for televisions, radios and ceramic dinnerware. He set up his own studio in 1955 and produced tableware for ROSENTHAL. In conjunction with Latham Tyler Jensen, his clients included Xerox and BANG & OLUFSEN.

Laverne, Erwine (1909–1995) and **Estelle** (1915–) American designers and entrepreneurs who worked in New York. They established Laverne Originals on the Tiffany estate at Oyster Bay, New York. They produced fabrics and wallcoverings, including the *Marbalia* marbled murals. Ray KOMOI designed for them from 1949 to 1955, In 1957 they designed the *Invisible* range of clear plastic furniture, using a technique they later licensed out to other companies.

Law, David (1937–) American designer who started as executive director of Unimark International in 1967. In 1972 he co-founded the Design Planning Group, going on to become head of packaging design for J. C. Penney, New York, in 1985. During the 1970s and 1980s he was a prolific designer of graphics, packaging, furniture, products and interiors. He collaborated with the Vignellis on the crystal ranges *Bordin* and *Aneic* for Sasaki Glass, and on the *Handkerchief* chair for KNOLL.

Leach, Bernard Howell (1887–1979) British potter who worked in St Ives, Cornwall. From 1909 he lived in Japan where, in 1911, he took up pottery with Ogata Kenzan VI, the master potter. He returned to Britain to found his own pottery with Shoji HAMADA and experimented in the re-creation of old-English techniques. He became the most influential potter in Britain, demonstrating, writing and lecturing. In 1936 he set up a pottery at Dartington Hall.

Le Blond, Jean-Baptiste Alexandre (1679–1719) French architect who worked in Russia on the Peterhof Palace in St Petersburg. He introduced the French ROCOCO style and a more intimate arrangement of public rooms.

Le Corbusier (1887–1965) Born Charles-Édouard Jeanneret in Switzerland, Le Corbusier trained as a metal engraver before being encouraged to study architecture. He worked in architect's office in Paris from 1909 to 1910 before travelling to Germany where he studied decorative arts, working, for a while, in the office of Peter BEHRENS. He became interested in mass-produced furniture in the 1920s and set out his ideas for architectural and decorative design in various journals and exhibited at the 1925 Paris Exhibition. In 1928 he collaborated with Pierre JEANNERET and Charlotte PERRIAND on the design of a range of furniture, all in tubular steel. From the late 1920s, Le Corbusier's reputation as an architect began to gain international recognition and in the following decades he worked on a variety of projects, including the Unesco building in Paris. His designs for both architecture and furniture have had a profound influence on succeeding generations of designers and he is regarded as one of the most creative figures of the 20th century.

Ledru, Auguste (1860–1902) French glassmaker who, together with Cheret and Larche, was one of the first designers to use the female form in Art Nouveau design.

Ledru, Léon (1855–1926) French glassmaker who, for 38 years, managed the Cristalleries du Val-Saint-Lambert, in Belgium. He promoted avant-garde design at the 1897 Brussels' Exposition, showing similar pieces at the 1900 Paris Exposition. His floral decorations were influenced by Gallé. He was innovative in technique, colour and design.

Leighton, John (1822–1912) British designer of the title page of *The Art-Journal Catalogue of the Great Exhibition,* 1851. He was a founder member of the Photographers' Society of Great Britain. His stained-glass designs were exhibited at the Royal Academy in 1854. He also designed book decorations and bank-notes.

Leischner, Margaret (1908–70) German-born textile designer who taught weaving at the Bauhaus in 1931, becoming head of the weaving department at the Modeschule in Berlin, until 1936. In 1937, she moved to Britain to become chief designer at R. Grey and Fothergill and Harvey, producing fabrics for car uphol-stery. From 1948 to 1963 she was head of the weaving depart-ment at the Royal College of Art, London. She designed Tintawn sisal carpeting in 1959 and advised Chemstrand on the use of their Acrilan fibre.

Leleu, Jules-Emile (1883–1961) French sculptor who, with his brother Marcel, took over their father's painting business in 1901. He began working as an interior designer, opening his own studio after the First World War. In the 1920s he produced large baroque Art Déco pieces, refining the style in the 1930s, with the use of exotic woods. His monumental style was well suited to official buildings such as ministries and embassies. He designed decor and furniture for over 20 liners, including the lecture room on the 1926 *Ile de France*, the 1931 *Atlantique*, the 1935 *Normandie* and the 1961 *France*. In 1937 he designed the dining room of the Elysée Palace, Paris.

Lemmen, Georges (1865–1916) Belgian painter who revived in-terest in the decorative arts. He designed rugs, tapestries, ceram-ics and mosaics. Toulouse-Lautrec bought a tapestry he had designed the emblem for and he designed the typeface for the 1908 edition of Nietzsche's *Also Sprach Zarathustra.*

Lenci, Fabio (1935–) Italian designer who set up a shop in 1966 to sell his contemporary furniture, which was made of recently-developed plastics using new manufacturing techniques. His *Chain* chair was formed from suspended upholstered rolls between plate-glass sides. He also designed the 1974 *Aquarius* bathshower unit for Teuco-Guzzini.

Lenoble, Émile (1875–1940) French ceramicist who originally worked in earthenware, before turning to stoneware, in 1904. He became influenced by Korean pottery and then by Sung Dynasty ceramics. He produced many pieces, including cylindrical vases, bottles and bowls, adding kaolin to stoneware, to achieve a finer finish. He used simple, geometric and floral motifs.

Lepape, Georges (1887–1971) French painter who moved in the same circle as Georges Braque, Francis Picabia and Marie Laurenáin. In 1909, he was discovered by Paul POIRET, whose couture creations he illustrated. In 1912 he started to do theatre design, the first being *La Nuits Persane* at the Thêàtre des Arts, Paris. In 1923 he designed Maurice Maeterlinck's *L'Oiseau Bleu.* He went on to design film sets until 1938, when he moved to New York, where he taught at the School of Fine and Applied Arts.

Le Pautre, Jean (1618–82) French engraver and designer who introduced a simpler, lighter design style for chimney-pieces.

Lescaze, William (1896–1969) Swiss architect who worked widely in Europe and America. In Britain, he designed buildings at Dartington Hall, Devon. In the 1930s, he started product design, the most notable being metal, cantilever chairs, the 1932 clock, desk-set, coat racks, lighting fixtures for the Philadelphia Savings Fund building and the 1936 microphone and 1945 mobile truck unit for CBS.

Lethaby, William Richard (1857–1931) British architect and theorist who promoted the ARTS AND CRAFTS MOVEMENT. He started out as Norman SHAW's assistant in 1881 and, in 1893, he was appointed joint principal, with George FRAMPTON, of the Central School of Art. In 1900, he became the first professor of design at the Royal College of Art, London.

Levanti, Giovanni (1956–) Italian designer of the 1987 *Nastassia* chair and 1987 *Alfonso* leather and metal bench for Memphis. He went on to become a tutor at the Domus Academy.

Léveillé, André (1880–1962) French artist and designer of jewellery and industrial textiles. In the 1920s, his paintings were adapted by jeweller Georges Fouquet for his pieces.

Lévy, Claude (1895–1942) French painter who worked for the Primavera decorating department of the Au Printemps store, Paris. She was an active decorator of shops and offices, as well as furniture and ceramics.

Lévy-Dhurmer, Lucien (1865–1953) French ceramicist, born in Algis. In the 1882 salon, he exhibited his copy in porcelain of Cabanel's La Naissance de Vénus. It is thought that he rediscovered the metallic lustre glaze technique used in Middle East ceramics from the 9th century. He often used gold highlights on generally sombre pieces. He was influenced by the Moorish style and painted extensive landscapes of North Africa. He painted murals and designed furniture for a private home on the Champs de Mars from 1910 to 1914.

Lewis, David (1939–) British designer who works mostly in Denmark. From 1960 until 1968, he collaborated with Jakob JENSEN on the design of radios and TV sets, becoming assistant designer at BANG & OLUFSEN. In 1965, he began work on the *Beolab 5000* range. He formed his own studio in 1968, designing the 1979 *Gori* boat propeller, the 1982 Odontoson range of dental instruments and the 1989 Multimec switch.

Lewis, Wyndham (1884–1957) British painter and writer who founded the Vorticist movement in abstract art. He was a member of OMEGA WORKSHOPS, but his style did not fit well with the flowery designs of fellow members and he left in 1914 to form the Rebel Art Centre.

Liaigre, Christian (1943–) French interior designer who furnished the Lloyds Building in the City of London, as well as French embassies in New Delhi, Warsaw, and Ottawa. In 1988, he designed travel goods for Louis VUITTON. He distributes and markets his own furniture, including rough-hewn tables inspired by the Romanian sculptor, Constantin Brancusi.

Liberty, Arthur Lasenby (1843–1917) British design entrepreneur who founded the eponymous store in Regent Street, London. From 1862 he worked in the Oriental Emporium of the Great Shawl and Cloak Emporium in Regent Street. The booming sales of Japanese goods led to the creation of his own store, which was expanded in 1883. He travelled to Japan in 1888, bringing back extensive collections of metalwork, which he had mounted in Britain. Liberty's designed and sold a wide range of furniture; Moorish and Arabic, Modern and Oriental. Their in-house designer, Leonard F. Wybyrd, was responsible for their rustic *Althelstan* range of furniture. Liberty imported a wide range of continental designs and, in turn, exported their own goods, with several concessions in stores such as the Serrurier-Bovy shop in Nancy. The shop was popular with the PRE-RAPHAELITES, from whom Liberty commissioned fabric and metalwork designs. He commissioned work also from Christopher DRESSER and Alexander KNOX, who designed the firm's 1899 silver *Cymric* and 1901 *Tudric* patterns. However, individual designers employed by the company were rarely named. Such was the influence of the company that, in Italy, ART NOUVEAU was known as Lo Stile Liberty.

Lichtenstein, Roy (1923–) American artist whose bold Pop art paintings, in primary colours, were easily adapted for use on ceramics, clothes and rugs, the latter for Vorwerk's *Dialog* range, which also used images by David HOCKNEY.

Liisberg, Carl Frederick (1860–1909) Danish ceramicist who was a sculptor and underglaze painter at Royal Copenhagen Porcelain, from 1885 to 1909. He innovated the use of slip in porcelain painting, adding relief to the image.

Liisberg, Hugo (1896–1958) Danish jewellery designer for the Georg JENSEN Silverworks, in the 1940s. Winner of the gold medal of the Danish Arts Academy in 1942.

Limbert, Charles P. (1854–1923) American furniture designer and manufacturer. In 1902, he started the Holland Dutch Arts and Crafts company, at Holland, Michigan. His designs were influenced by Charles Rennie MACKINTOSH, VOYSEY and BAILLIE SCOTT. His signature mark was pierced rectangles with rounded corners. His tables had flared bases and protruding sides. His

1905 *Square-cut Café Chair* and 1906 *Oval Center Table* were inspired by Mackintosh's chairs for the Willow Tea Rooms, in Glasgow, but executed in a more sympathetic style.

Limoges French factory at Limoges, which was established in 1736 for the production of domestic ceramics. The kaolin and petuntse (white powdered granite, originally used in China) were quarried nearby. In 1771, hard-paste porcelain was produced under the patronage of the Comte d'Artois, brother of Louis XVI. In 1784, the king took it over himself, and it became the Manufacture Royale, to produce plain white ware. After the 1789 Revolution, several factories were established in the area and, by 1840, there were more than 30 manufacturers. It is still the centre of domestic porcelain manufacture in France.

Lin, Maya (1960–) American architect who turned to monument design. Her design for the Vietnam Veterans' Memorial in Washington, a black granite sculpture, was widely opposed. She also designed the Civil Rights Memorial in Montgomery, Alabama.

Lindfors, Stefan (1962–) Finnish sculptor who designed the set for the evening news broadcast of the Finnish Broadcasting Company, in 1988. His 1988 *Scaragoo* articulated table lamp, lit up when touched. In 1989, he designed the interiors and furniture for the restaurant of the Museum of Industrial Arts, Helsinki.

Lindh, Richard (1929–) Finnish ceramicist who worked for Arabia, Helsinki, from 1955. He was head of the design department from 1973 to 1985. He received first prize in a competition at the Museum of Contemporary Crafts in New York and his work has been widely exhibited, including at the 1961 Finlandia exhibition, which toured Europe.

Lindinger-Loewy, Lone (1956–) Danish industrial designer who works with her husband, **Gideon Loewy** (1952–). Their studio designed the *Beolab Penta 2* tall speaker system for BANG & OLUFSEN and lighting for Poulsen. In 1983, they designed the *Beocom 1000* and *Beocom 2000* telephones for Bang & Olufsen. In 1987, they designed the *Stripes and Stars* dinnerware for BING AND GRØNDAHL.

Lippincott, J. Gordon (1909–) American industrial designer who set up his studio in 1935. He has styled appliances, including vacuum cleaners, office copying equipment, fountain pens and packaging, for clients including Waterman, Paramount Pictures, General Electric, RCA, Macy's, Johnson and Johnson and Northwest Airlines.

Littell, Ross (1924–) American designer who collaborated with William KATAVOLOS and Douglas Kelley on furniture, textile and dinnerware designs for LAVERNE Originals. Commissioned by Erwine and Estelle Laverne, they designed the 1949 *New Furniture Group* chairs and tables in leather, chrome, glass and marble. The team's three-legged chair, made in wooden prototype, was produced in chromium-plated steel.

Lloyd, Marshall Burns (1858–1927) American furniture manufacturer who started out as inventor of a sack-holder and scales, in South Dakota. He then invented a method of manufacturing bedsprings and mattresses. In 1906, he began producing reed baby-carriage bodies, patenting a system for producing wicker products. When supplies of rattan and cane were interrupted during the First World War, he used twisted craft paper. He produced over 100 furniture models and, by 1940, over 10 million pieces had been sold. His offices were covered in Lloyd Loom woven fibre. Lloyd Loom furniture was used on the liners *Ile-de-France* and *Champlaine*. Archetypal 1920s and 1930s designs are now collectors' items.

Loewy, Raymond (1893–1986) French designer who settled in New York, in 1919. He started as a window-dresser at Macy's, became a fashion illustrator for *Harper's Bazaar* and designed a logo for Nieman-Marcus. He designed advertisements for Kayser Hosiery and fashion brochures for Bonwit Teller. In 1929, he designed the housing for Gestetner's duplicating machine and then developed one of the largest industrial design practices. During the 1930s he was responsible for streamlining design, a new concept. Products his groups have been responsible for range from the 1934 Sears *Coldspot* refrigerator, to dinnerware for the Concorde airplane, the 1963 Studebaker Champion to the interior of President Kennedy's Boeing 707, Airforce One, and stamps, trademarks, radios and china. Popular ranges for ROSENTHAL include the 1967 *Aries*. He produced wallpaper patterns for Sanderson's 1960 *Centenary* collection. By the 1950s, he employed over 140 architects, engineers and designers.

Loffler, Berthold (1874–1960) Austrian designer, who was born in the Czechoslovakia. He taught in Vienna and, around 1904, founded Wiener Keramik, with Michael Powolny. Their style used the highly decorative idioms of late ART NOUVEAU, producing ceramics with folklore influences, at the WIENER WERKSTÄTTE. He also designed distinctive posters in the 1910s.

Lomazzi, Paolo (1936–) Italian designer who founded a design studio with Gionatan De Pas and Donato D'Urbino. Their best-known work included the innovative 1967 *Blow* clear plastic inflatable chair and the 1970 *Joe* seat in the shape of a baseball glove. In the 1970s they designed interchangeable units for modular seating and storage systems. These included the *Cube and Screw* range of knock-down plywood furniture.

Loos, Adolph (1870–1933) Moravian architect who worked in Vienna, after travel in America, where he saw the work of the Chicago School. He was an influential theorist, arguing against the excesses of JUGENDSTIL, such as the decorative works of Gustave KLIMT. He eventually abandoned all decoration and ornamentation on his buildings.

Lubetkin, Berthold (1901–1995) Russian architect who supervised the Soviet pavilion at the 1925 Paris Exhibition. In 1930, he settled in London, where he went into partnership with Anthony Chitty, Lindsey Drake, Michael Dibdin and others, to form Tecton. He is best-known for the penguin and gorilla houses at the London Zoo, in Regent's Park, the elephant house at Whipsnade Zoo and the giraffe and elephant houses at Dudley Zoo. In 1935, he won the competition for the design of working-class flats in reinforced concrete. His austere detailing was influential in the 1930s.

Lucci, Roberto (1942–) Italian designer of household and decorative goods. Designs include refrigerators for Candy, lamps and chairs for Artemide and furniture for KNOLL.

Lucino, Ennio (1934–) Italian packaging designer who has worked for Christian Dior, Estée Lauder (Aramis and Clinique cosmetic ranges), Du Pont, Pirelli and the Galeries Lafayette store.

Lundin, Ingeborg (1921–) Swedish glassware designer who worked at Orrefors Glasbruk, from 1947 to 1971. Her pieces include the 1955 *Apple* vase and the 1954 *Hour-glass* and *Bamby* vases, showing the dynamic and plastic qualities of her design style.

Lurçat, André (1894–1970) French architect noted for his furniture designs. In the 1920s, these were influenced by the geometric Cubist style, often made of tubular steel, echoing the work of Marcel Breuer. He was a fervent admirer of the Soviet Union and was the only foreign architect allowed to work there in the 1930s.

Lurçat, Jean (1892–1966) French painter who often decorated the buildings of his brother, André Lurçat. He designed tapestries, which were produced by his mother, including the 1917 Filles Vertes and Soirée dans Grenade. Influenced by 14th-century tapestries at Angers, he revived medieval techniques, producing a large number of hangings, including the 1957 Le Chant du Monde. He also designed wallpapers and ceramics.

Luthersson, Petur B. (1936–) Iceland's most important furniture designer, who also designed public spaces. The lighting for these included his 1969 aluminium hanging light. He also designed domestic lighting, including a range in spun aluminium.

Lutyens, Sir Edwin (1869–1944) British architect, most noted for his monumental buildings in New Delhi, India. He was a prolific designer of furniture, mostly in the Arts and Crafts style. His pieces often reflected historic styles, including four-poster beds, refectory tables and chairs inspired by Napoleon's meridiennes, which had one arm lower that the other, over which a leg could be draped. In 1905, he designed 21 chairs for the boardroom of *Country Life* magazine and furnishings for his 1934 Reuters building in London. He was the architect of the Cenotaph in Whitehall, London.

M

Macbeth, Ann (1875–1944) Scottish designer and embroiderer who was a teacher at the Glasgow School of Art for many years and wrote several influential textbooks. Her idiosyncratic designs were the result of losing an eye in childhood and, therefore, being deprived of stereoscopic sight.

Macchi-Cassia, Antonio (1937–) Italian industrial designer and consultant to Olivetti. He designed their *Divisumma model 18* adding machine, the *Copia 2000* copier and the *M20* personal computer. Other products include televisions for Condor and Radiomarelli, furniture components for Artemide and lighting for Arteluce.

Macdonald, Frances (1874–1921) British artist, the the sister of Margaret MACDONALD and the wife of J. Herbert MACNAIR Having studied at Glasgow School of Art she opened a studio with her sister in 1894 and worked on designs in embroidery, stained glass and metal as well as book illustration. From 1907 she returned to Glasgow School of Art to teach enamelling, silver- and goldsmithing.

Macdonald, Margaret (1865–1933) British artist, the sister of Frances MACDONALD and the wife of Charles Rennie MACKINTOSH, with whom she collaborated after their marriage in 1900. She studied at Glasgow School of Art and, with her sister, opened a studio in 1894. She specialized in painting and two-dimensional design and later in her career designed textiles.

Mack, Daniel (1947–) Canadian writer and broadcaster with the Canadian Broadcasting Corporation who began to make twig furniture, in 1979. He played a major part in the revival of 19th-century rustic furniture, made of natural materials fashioned into rectilinear designs, reminiscent of Charles Rennie MACKINTOSH and Frank Lloyd WRIGHT.

Mackintosh, Charles Rennie (1868–1928) Scottish architect whose major works include the Glasgow School of Art. In 1984, he, his wife, Margaret MACDONALD, J. Herbert MACNAIR and his wife, Frances MACDONALD, organized an exhibition of furniture, jewellery, metalwork and book illustration. They melded the styles of the ARTS AND CRAFTS, PRE-RAPHAELITE, Celtic and Japanese revival styles into the 'Glasgow School'. He designed two pieces of highly-regarded jewellery, a flight of birds necklace and a simple ring, both much reproduced. In the early 1920s, he designed textiles, silver flatware, including the *Black and White*

vase, bowl and ewer of 1904, the 1903 *Willow* bowl, the 1904
Cranston candlestick and the 1904 christening fork and spoon.
His distinctive black furniture was heavily influenced by the style
of Viennese JUGENSTIL, his popularity in Europe far outweighing
that in Britain. In spite of the outstanding quality of the Glasgow
Art School building, he had no major public commissions in Brit-
ain, although private commissions included Hill House in
Helensburgh, for the publisher W. W. Blackie.

Mackmurdo, Arthur Heygate (1851–1942) British architect who
spearheaded the Neo-GOTHIC Revival. He designed wallpapers,
furniture, carpets and metalwork for his buildings and was also an
important book and textile designer. His cover for his own book
Wren's City Churches, of 1883, featured stylized flames, which
are regarded as one of the earliest examples of ART NOUVEAU.

Macleish, Minnie (b.1876) Scottish textile designer who worked
with Charles Rennie MACKINTOSH and Constance Irving of Foxton
Textiles in London. She also designed for Morton Sundour Fabrics, in Carlisle, and many advertisements.

MacNair, J. Herbert (1870–1945) Scottish architect who was
married to Frances MACDONALD. Together with Charles Rennie
MACKINTOSH and his wife, Margaret MACDONALD, they formed the
group known as 'The Four'. Unsatisfied as an architect, he turned
to the decorative arts, practising in the ARTS AND CRAFTS and PRE-
RAPHAELITE styles. Such was the influence of his wife, that it is
difficult to make individual attributions for the design of jewellery, furniture or textiles.

Magistretti, Vico (1920–) Italian architect who designed the distinctive 1963 chair which bears his name. It has a brightly painted
wooden frame, with a rush seat; a mixture of tradition and Modern. Other notable chairs were the orange-dyed wooden 1960
Crimate, the 1971 *Pan chair* and the 1981 *Sinbad* chair, which
was based on a horse blanket draped over a piece of furniture. He
designed the 1966 *Chimera* and 1967 *Eclisse* lamps for Artemide,
for who he also designed the 1970 *Gaudi* and *Vicario* chairs. He
is a prolific designer of other furniture for a wide range of clients.
He was honourary visiting professor at the Royal College of Art,
London, and other institutions.

Magnussen, Erik (1884–1961) Danish metalworker, born in Copenhagen, but worked mostly in America. He opened his first workshop in Copenhagen, in 1909, producing pieces influenced by Georg JENSEN. In 1925, he was invited to America to produce Modern designs for Gorham Manufacturing, becoming art director in 1929. In the late 1930s, he designed for the International Silver Company at Meriden, Connecticut, producing everyday objects, including tea and coffee sets. His best-known work was the 1927 *Lights and Shadows of Manhattan* silver coffee set with a trapezoid tray. In 1939, he returned to Copenhagen, to work in a more conservative style.

Magnusson, Gunnar (1933–) Icelandic designer who specializes in furnishing public spaces. He has also designed furniture with exposed frames and simple shapes.

Maher, George Washington (1864–1926) American furniture designer, whose first pieces were monumental and ornate. By 1905, he moved to a simpler style, under the influence of C. F. A. VOYSEY. His chairs had architectural features, such as arches, as did his lamps.

Maiakkovskaia, Ludmilla (1884–1963) Russian textile designer who worked at the Muss silk mill in 1909 and was head of the painting workshop at the Prokhorovo Manufactury. Her designs were shown at the 1925 Paris Exhibition.

Maillot, Aristide (1861–1944) French painter who was greatly influenced by Paul GAUGUIN, Claude Monet and Puvis de Chavannes. He gave up painting in 1900 to concentrate on tapestry and sculpture. He established a tapestry studio at Banyuls-sur-Mer, dying his own wools. His sculptures are installed in the Jardin des Tuileries, Paris.

Mairet, Ethel (1872–1952) British weaver who married A. K. Coonaraswamy, the leading authority on Indian art. Travelling with him, she learned traditional weaving methods, which she introduced to the British market, through her workshop at Ditchling, Sussex, where Eric GILL also worked.

Makepeace, John (1939–) British furniture designer who set up a workshop in Farnsborough Barn, Banbury, in 1964, moving to Parnham House in Dorset, in 1976. He produces traditional and contemporary pieces, made by expert craftsman out of superior wood. He established the Parnham Trust and School for Craftsmen in Wood in 1977 and, in 1989, started training students in woodcraft. His best-known pupil is Viscount (David) Linley.

Malinowski, Arno (1899–1976) Danish sculptor who designed figurines for Royal Copenhagen from 1921 to 1935. He also painted pieces designed by others, including Christian Joachim. He designed jewellery for Georg JENSEN and the medal produced by Jensen for the 70th birthday of King Christian X that was worn by thousands of Danes during the Second World War as a symbol of resistance.

Mallet-Stevens, Robert (1886–1945) French architect who was influenced by Josef HOFFMANN's reaction against the excesses of ART NOUVEAU. His buildings were simple and functional and eschewed superfluous decoration. He applied the same principles to his furniture designs, using geometric shapes of painted metal and nickel-plated tubular steel. His side chair with a curved metal back and vertical flat stays, produced by Ecart International, is a classic of 20th-century design. He was invited by a French film producer to contribute towards the design of *L'Inhumaine* in 1923. He went on to design other films, including the 1926 *Le Vertige* and *Le Secret de Rosette Lambert*. He executed wall and ceiling lights for PAUL POIRET's salon and the entrance hall of the 1930 Union des Artistes Modernes exhibition.

Malmsten, Carl (1888–1972) Swedish furniture designer who used traditional Swedish designs for his chairs, wooden sofas and tables, creating austere rooms, which anticipated Modern Scandinavian design. He included elements of 18th-century and BIEDERMEYER paintings and experiments with rag and other paint finishes. In 1945, he founded the Nyckelvik School to promote folk art and handicrafts.

Maloof, Sam (1916–) American furniture designer who started out doing in-store design for Bullock's, Los Angeles. In 1948, he received his first furniture commission, a suite for industrial designer, Henry Dreyfuss. He built a workshop in Alta Loma, California, in 1953, and is still active there.

Mannerism A term that describes Italian architecture and design between 1520 and 1600. The word is derived from the Italian *maniera* to mean style and it describes detailed, highly-ornamented, often fanciful design that was later criticized for being self-indulgent and artificial. The term mannerism was coined in the 1920s when it was realised that a distinctive architectural and decorative style did exist in the period after Renaissance and before BAROQUE. Examples of mannerism do exist elsewhere in western Europe, particularly in Spain and France, but it was principally an Italian movement.

Manship, Paul Howard (1885–1966) American sculptor influenced by Hindu and Buddhist styles. In 1934, he started out on the design and construction of the Paul J. Rainey memorial gateway of the New York Zoological Park, which was to take five years. It is the epitome of the Streamline style. He designed other public monuments, the most famous being his gilded-bronze Prometheus of 1933, which is in the Rockefeller Center Plaza, New York.

Manzó, Pio (1939–69) Italian designer who studied at the Hochschule für Gestaltung, Ulm. He designed cars, taxis and tractors for Fiat, packaging for Olivetti, and the Parentisi lamp. He also wrote for the journals *Form, Style Auto* and *Interiors*.

Mappin and Webb British silversmiths founded in 1863. In the 1930s under its chief designer, A. Hatfield, they produced Modern silver by various designers, while they continued to produce the ARTS AND CRAFTS and ART NOUVEAU silver for which they were noted.

Mare, André (1887–1932) French painter who shared a studio with Fernand Léger from 1903 to 1904. In 1910, he began designing furniture in radical Cubist style. In 1912, he took to bookbinding in vellum and parchment dyed in the vivid palette associated with the productions of the Ballets Russes. In 1919, he decorated the cenotaph beneath the Arc de Triomphe for the 'Fàtes de la Victoire' and set up as an interior designer in Rue du Faubourg Saint-Honoré. He designed the costumes for Maurice Ravel's *L'Heure Espagnole* at the Paris Opera, in 1921. In partnership with Louis Süe, he designed ornate furniture, decorated with garlands and gilding. They designed glassware for Orfävrerie

Christofle and worked on the interiors of several liners and the Paris shop of Parfum d'Orsay, for whom they designed their scent-bottle. Similar clients included Helena Rubinstein and Jean Patou.

Margold, Emanuel Josef (1889–1962) Austrian architect who became assitant to Josef HOFFMANN at the WIENER WERKSTÄTTE. In 1911, he joined the artists' colony set up by the Grand Duke Louis IV of Hesse-Darmstadt, the last to do so. He produced much glass, furniture and porcelain. His silver umbrella handles showed fine beading, fluting and acanthus decorations. He also designed packaging for the Bahlens bakery.

Mari, Enzo (1932–) Italian designer who became interested in the design of childrens' toys in 1957, when his wooden puzzles were put into production by Danese. He experimented in plastics from 1959, his cylindrical umbrella stand and reversible *Vase 3078* were popular in the 1960s. Through the 1970s, he produced a wide range of furniture, fabrics for Driade and household goods for Le Creuset.

Mariscal, Javier (1950–) Spanish designer of a wide range of products, from posters to furniture, comic strips to textiles. His first piece of furniture was the brightly-coloured, asymmetrical 1980 *Duplex* bar stool, followed by the *Meubles Amorales*. He took part in Memphis's initial 1981 collection, designing the back-slanted *Hilton* tea cart in clear glass and metal tubing. He produced a ceramic range for Vináon and, in 1986, for Axis. His *Torero* and *Tio Pepe* chairs for the 1987 Pompidou Centre exhibition parodied Spanish culture. He designed the Cobi mascot for the 1992 Olympic Games in Barcelona and Expo '92 in Seville.

Martin, Camille (1861–98) French painter who designed bookbindings, involving transferring his paintings directly onto the leatherwork.

Marx, Enid Crystal Dorothy (1902–93) British textile and graphic designer who set up her own workshop in 1927. She designed patterned papers and book covers for Penguin and Chatto and Windus, wallpapers, fabrics, posters for London Transport, calendars for Shell and postage stamps. In 1937, she designed moquette fabrics for London Transport and was a member of the

Utility Furniture Advisory Panel, during, and after, the Second World War. She designed fabrics for EDINBURGH WEAVERS and for Morton Sundour, including her 1951 'Festival of Britain' fabric.

Masaki, Yuri (1950–) Japanese glass designer, president of the Masaki Glass and Art Studio. His works have been widely exhibited and in 1988 he won the grand prize at the 1988 Suntory Museum competition.

Massier, Clément (1844–1917) French ceramicist who learned pottery in his father's workshop, before setting up on his own in 1864. In 1883, he moved to Golfe Juan where he produced his first lustre ware in 1886, a style and form which was much copied by other potters. From 1885 to 1895, his workshop was overseen by the painter Lucien LÉVY-DHURMER. The company continues as a family business.

Mathieu, Paul (1950–) French designer who worked in collaboration with the American designer Michael Ray. Their furniture designs include a range of chairs and tables for Ecart International, recreating ART DÉCO and ART NOUVEAU in contemporary ways.

Mathsson, Bruno (1907–1995) Swedish architect who trained as a cabinet-maker. He designed furniture with organic, flowing lines, most often using natural wood, principally beech. His 1934 chair and compact 1946 extension table are still in production. He is best-known for the 1934 *Eva* chair, which was redesigned, with arms, in 1941. In the early 1960s, he collaborated with Piet Hein on the 'super-ellipse' furniture and pursued tubular steel construction, such as the upholstered *Jetson* and leather-covered *Karin* chairs.

Matsunaga, Naoki (1936–) Japanese designer who works in Milan, designing tables, seating, luggage and other domestic products for clients including, Olivetti, Candy, Fratelli and, in Brazil, Romi.

Matta (1911–) Chilean designer, born Roberto Sebastien Matto Echaurren. In the mid-1960s, he designed furniture, including the Malitte component seating system, which was promoted in America by KNOLL. It was made up of puzzle-like forms stacked into a cube when not in use.

Maugham, Syrie (1879–1955) British interior and furniture de-

signer who was the daughter of Dr Barnado, founder of the
Barnado Homes, and wife of the writer W. Somerset Maugham.
After a scandalous youth, she began her decorating business in
her own house, in 1926, which she painted entirely white as a
successful publicity stunt. Her clients were a roster of the rich,
famous and infamous of the 1920s and 1930s. Marion Dorn,
Oliver Messel and Christian Bérard designed rugs, furnishings
and murals for her clients, including Noel Coward, Tallulah
Bankhead, Mary Pickford and the Duke and Duchess of Windsor.
She was parodied as Mrs Beaver in Evelyn Waugh's *A Handful of
Dust*. Her 'white' period was followed by blue, red and Victorian
ones, ending with what Cecil Beaton called her 'lobster salad'
period. She was made bankrupt in the 1950s, but she left the
legacy of her white period, which affected a whole generation of
interior and film designers.

Mayodon, Jean (1893–1967) French painter who took up pottery
in 1912, producing pieces heavily influenced by Persian pottery.
It was made heat-restistant by the addition of powdered clay and
decorated with paint or low relief, highlighted with gold. During
the Second World War he became director at the Sèvres factory.

Mazza, Sergio (1931–) Italian interior architect who is best-
known for his work in plastics and his 1968 fibreglass *Toga* chair
and the 1969 *Bacco* low, fitted mobile bar. His *Torlonia* hanging
light was produced by Quattrifolio.

McArthur, Warren (1885–1961) American designer and manufacturer who patented the early use of aluminium in furniture design in 1930. His designs for over 600 models were not popular at
the time, but were recognized in the late 1980s, when many were
reproduced. In 1924, he designed the recreation vehicle
Wonderbus and, in 1930, he established his furniture manufacturing company in Los Angeles, where his clients included many
film stars. In the Second World War his designs were adapted for
use as seats in aeroplanes.

McClelland, Nancy Vincent (1877–1959) American designer who
worked in the advertising department of Wanamaker's department store in Philadelphia. In Paris, she studied fashion trends
and collected samples of wallpaper and textiles. On her return to

America she set up the first design studio in a store, Au Quatriéme at Wanamaker's. In 1922, she set up her own studio, showing French furniture in panelled rooms. She promoted historic wallpaper designs, through her reproductions and her book Historic Wallpapers of 1924. She advised on the restoration of national monuments, including the headquarters of General Robert E. Lee and Henry Wadsworth Longfellow's house, Portland, Maine.

McCobb, Paul (1917–69) American furniture designer who popularized modular furniture and moveable walls, which allowed flexibility of living and work spaces. He set up his first studio in 1945, producing higher-priced furniture ranges such as Directional, Predictor Linear and Perimeter. His interchangeable chests, cabinets and bookcases had bench bases which could be used as separate tables.

McConnico, Hilton (1943–) American fashion designer who worked for Ted Lapidus, Yves Saint-Laurent and Jacques Heim. He also designed furs for Nieman-Marcus. In 1974, he turned to film set decoration, winning a César Award for *La Lune dans le caniveau*. He also worked for the directors François Truffaut and Claude Chabrol. In 1985, he started to design glassware for DAUM, incorporating a cactus motif. In the late 1980s, he designed a silk foulard for the 1989 French Revolution bicentennial for Hermés, a museum of horse racing at Longchamps racecourse in the Bois de Boulogne, Paris, and a museum of costume history in Chateau Chinon. He designs his own-label range for Galeries Lafayette and has refurbished the Paris Métro station at Chaussée-d'Antin.

McGrath, Raymond (1903–77) Australian architect who worked in London. His interiors include those for the BBC Broadcasting House, Portland Place, the Embassy Club in Bond Street and for Atlanta aircraft. In 1932, he designed the lighting and the Synchronome wall clock for BBC studios, radio cabinets for Ekco and unit furniture for Easiwork. In 1934, he designed Six Ages of Architecture panels for the doors of the Royal Institute of British Architecture in London.

McGugan, Steve (1960–) Canadian industrial designer who works in Copenhagen. From 1982 to 1984, he worked for BANG & OLUFSEN, moving to the David Lewis Partnership in 1985. In 1988, he opened his own studio, designing electronic and medical products. He designed the widely publicized 1985 *Form 2* earphones for Bang & Olufsen and the 1989 NovoLet syringe for insulin injections for Novo Nordisk.

McLaughlin, Mary Louise (1847–1939) American pottery and porcelain decorator who was a pioneer of china-painting in America, influencing the generations which followed her. She founded the Cincinnati Pottery Club, disbanded in 1890. Her 40-inch Ali Baba pot was the largest made in America. For a time she worked in copy, returning to ceramics in 1895, producing carved ware known as Losanti. In 1904, she gave up pottery to write on history and politics. Her final works included metalwork, jewellery etching and painting.

Meier, Otto (1910–82) Swiss architect who opened an office with Ernst Mumenthaler, in 1925. They developed the modular furniture system 3M-Mîbel, which Meier constructed himself. Their award-winning *Das Neue Heim II* cabinets of 1928 were made of lightweight plywood.

Meier, Richard Alan (1934–) American architect who worked for various practices, including that of Marcel BREUER. His buildings reflected the ideas of LE CORBUSIER. His first furniture was produced in 1978, including chairs, stools and telephone stands for KNOLL. He designed a teaset for Alessi's 1983 *Tea and Coffee Piazza* project. For Skid Powell he designed the *Joseph, Peachtree* and *Anne* ceramic ranges and the glassware *Spiral, Lattice* and *Professor*. In 1991, he designed textiles for Design Tex.

Meier-Graefe, Julius (1867–1935) Romanian writer, art critic and entrepreneur, who worked in Germany and France. In 1893, he met William MORRIS, Edward BURNE-JONES and Aubrey BEARDSLEY, whose ideas he propounded on his travels across Europe. He wanted industry and art to work together, founding the journal *Dekoratiive Kunst* in 1897, to expound his views. He gave up the editorship in 1897 to open his shop, La Maison Moderne, in Paris, commissioning Henry VAN DE VELDE to design the exterior and interior. His aim was to bring together a cross-section of artists for commercial purposes. In 1904, he was forced to close the shop, selling the stock at half-price and losing his investment. In 1895, he was one of the first people to promote the stained-glass and enamels of Louis Comfort Tiffany.

Meinzer, Manfred (1943–) German industrial designer who worked for Ford in Cologne and Telefunken in Berlin. From 1965, he was chief designer at Revox, his first important design being the 1967 Revox stereo tape recorder.

Mellor, David (1930-) British metalworker, manufacturer and retailer. While still at Sheffield College of Art, his silver coffee set received a national prize and his 1951 version received wide publicity. The same year his *Pride* flatware was produced by Walker and Hall. In 1954, he set up his own workshop. In 1963, he designed the *Embassy* teapot for use in British embassies and, in 1965, the *Thrift* stainless steel range for use in government canteens. From 1969, he designed and produced cookware and utensils, establishing himself as a major retailer in London. Corporate clients include British Rail, the Post Office and the Department of the Environment. Silver commissions have been undertaken for The Worshipful Company of Goldsmiths, London, Southwell Minster and Darwin College, Cambridge.

Meneghetti, Renato (1947–) Italian designer who began his professional career in 1968. His clients include Felsina (watch bands), Caleppio (plastics) and Grundig Italiana (radio, television, record and hi-fi equipment).

Mengshoel, Hans Christian (1946–) Norwegian furniture designer, who collaborated with Peter Opsvik on the design of the 1979 ergonomic chairs in the Balans series.

Menzies, William Cameron (1896–1957) American film set designer who influenced interior and furniture designers. After studying at Yale University, he worked on special effects for Famous Players-Lasky in London, for two years from 1920. In 1923, he settled in Hollywood and became the most famous designer and art director of the 1920s and 1930s. He worked for Pickford/Fairbanks, Alexander Korda and David O. Selznick. For the 1924 *Thief of Baghdad* he used Art Déco and children's book illustrations. In 1929, he won his first Academy Award for art direction, for the 1928 *The Tempest* and the 1929 *The Dove.* He was overall art director on the 1936 *The Shape of Things to Come,* commissioning Vincent Korda as set designer and the Marchioness of Queensberry as costume designer, production designer of *Gone With the Wind* in 1939. From 1943, he went into directing and producing.

Merz, Johann Georg (1649–1762) German engraver of table designs and copies of other works. He published *Neue Inventiones auf Tobac Dosen,* a lively selection of designs for ROCOCO snuffboxes

Messel, Oliver (1904–78) British theatre, film and interior designer who took up mask-making at the Slade School of Art. These were seen by Serge Diaghilev, who commissioned him to design and produce some for the 1925 Ballets Russes production of *Zephyre et Flore.* In 1928, he designed sets and costumes for Noël Coward's *This Year of Grace* and, in 1935, for the film *The Scarlet Pimpernel.* In 1952, he designed the commemorative silk scarf and exterior decorations of the Dorchester Hotel to celebrate the impending coronation of Queen Elizabeth II and, in 1953, designed the *Oliver Messel* and *Penthouse* suites there. The decorations were inspired by his designs for *The Sleeping Beauty* for Sadler's Wells Ballet at the Royal Opera House, Covent Garden. In 1966, he retired to Barbados, where he started a new career as a house and garden designer. He designed houses for Princess Margaret on Barbados and Lord Glenconner on the tiny island of Mustique.

Meyer, Daniel (1576–1630) German son of a glass painter who published a book of architectural ornaments, including vases, cartouches and masks, in 1609. His *Architectura* of 1612 contained 88 plates of architectural orders and ornaments, such as brackets and strap-work. He is thought to be responsible for the book of jewellery and embroidery designs copied by Joseph Honervogt in 1618.

Michelangelo Buonarroti (1475–1564) Italian sculptor who was trained by the curator of Lorenzo de' Medici's sculpture garden. He worked there under the protection of Piero de' Medici until 1494. He then travelled to Rome, where he spent five years from

1496, progressing to Florence in 1501. He was summoned back to Rome by Pope Julius II, whose tomb took some 40 years to complete, from 1505. For it, he created superb Grotesque ornament, which were carved by Antonio del Pontasieve. In 1524, he designed the Biblioteca Laurenziana in Florence, including a carved ceiling. He also designed the carved reading desks there. From 1534 until his death, he worked in Rome. In 1537, he designed an inkwell for the Duke of Urbino and canopies for several churches, including Santa Maria degli Angeli. His ornamental style influenced MANNERIST designers. His design output was not large, as projects were invariably on a large scale, but they were all of superb quality. Excellent examples include the panels of grotesque ornament on Julius' tomb and the sinister melting masks in the Medici Chapel, on which he worked from 1520 to 1534. His marble candelabrum are in the same chapel.

Midavaine, Louis (1888–1978) French designer who learned the skill of lacquering whilst a prisoner in the First World War, after which he returned to France and opened a studio, under the patronage of the Duchesse de la Rochefoucauld. He designed many Modern lacquer animals and also decorated liners, such as the *Pasteur* and the 1935 *Normandie*. Amongst state interiors, he designed the dining room of the French President of the Senate.

Mies van der Rohe, Ludwig (1886–1969) German architect with an austere style, as exemplified in his German Pavilion at the 1929 Barcelona Exhibition. In 1927, he had designed the *MR* cantilever curved chair, in association with Lily REICH, and for Barcelona he created the eponymous chair, constructed out of tubular stainless steel and leather straps. It is still in production, together with most of his classic designs. He was the last director of the BAUHAUS, from 1930 to 1933. He visited New York in 1937, taking up an appointment in Chicago in 1938, where he became one of the most influential architects, designing little furniture. His own NEO-CLASSICAL house was sparsely furnished with his own classic pieces, Japanese tatami mats and paintings by his Bauhaus colleague, Wassily KANDINSKI.

Miklos, Gustave (1888–1967) Hungarian sculptor who served in the French army in the First World War. He discovered the art of

Greece and Byzantium, which influenced his work for Jacques Doucet's house in Paris. He produced decorative sculpture in the Cubist style and also designed stained glass and jewellery.

Minton British design company founded when Thomas Minto bought a pottery in Stoke-on-Trent in 1793 and soon began producing cheap, blue transfer-printed earthenware. His son took the company over, enlarging the range and employing more painters and decorators. In the mid-1800s Sir Henry Cole designed the shapes of tableware, with decorations by A. W. N. Pugin. In 1849, Leon Arnoux became artistic director and introduced majolica with bright colours and naturalistic shapes. From the 1840s, the firm produced large quantities of decorative tiles with designs by John Moyr Smith and Christopher Dresser. The tiles were used for floors and to decorate furniture. From the 1860s, the company's style became heavily influenced by both the Far and Near East. At the turn of the century they reflected Art Nouveau and Vienna Sezession styles following a period of classical design by immigrant French artists. The company is now part of the Royal Tableware Group.

Minton, John Francis (1917–57) Influential British painter and designer, with a high reputation as a teacher at all the London art colleges. He designed theatre posters and, in the early 1950s, wallpapers for John Line.

Miralles, Pedro (1955–) Spanish architect who worked in the office of fashion designer Jesus del Pozo. His designs include the 1985 *Acuatica* chair, the 1985 *Dry Martini* stool, the 1986 *Voyeur* folding screen and the *Egyptian* lamp. In 1988 he designed the *Andrews Sisters* suite of three interlocking tables. He designed the waste-bins at the 1992 Seville 'Expo '92', inspired by the 13th-century, 12-sided tower overlooking the Guadalquivir.

Modernism Rebelling against the florid excesses of Art Nouveau and paralleling the development of the geometrically decorative Art Déco movement, Modernism sought to strip away unnecessary ornament and decoration in architecture and associated design. Simple, stark lines were appreciated and industrial art, corn silos, ocean liners and motor cars were held up as examples of pure design. The prospectus of Modern designers was to strip away the clutter of the historic past and create design for the contemporary age. Rectilinear design replaced sensuous curves, concrete and steel replaced wood and precious metals. The function of the building and its furnishings was paramount. Though disregarding old institutions and academies, the movement founded one of its own at the BAUHAUS, where its principal proponents included Walter GROPIUS and Ludwig MIES VAN DER ROHE.

Moggeridge, Bill (1943–) British industrial designer who set up his first studio in London in 1969, to build models of scientific and consumer products for Pitney Bowes, Hoover and others. In 1977, he opened a studio, ID2, at Palo Alto, California, which was responsible for the design of the first portable computer, the 1982 *Compass,* for Grid.

Moholy-Nagy, László (1895–1946) Hungarian painter, photographer, film maker and stage designer who was invited to the BAUHAUS by Walter GROPIUS in 1923. In Dessau, he practised book-design and associated crafts. In Weimar, he succeeded Johannes ITTEN as director of the preliminary course, and Paul KLEE as director of metalwork. He left in 1928 for Berlin where he was active with the Piscator Theatre and produced his first modular, illuminated structure for the 1930 Exhibition. In the mid-1930s, he worked in London, contributing illustrations to *Lilliput* and *Picture Post,* making films and designing posters for International Textiles, London Transport and Imperial Airways. He created special effects for Alexander Korda's 1936 film *The Shape of Things to Come,* which were cut from the final version. He left London in 1937, to open the New Bauhaus in Chicago. When this closed in 1939, he set up his Institute of Design, which became a department of the Armour Institute of Technology, under Serge CHERMAYEFF.

Molesworth, Thomas (1890–1977) American furniture designer who perfected the 'Wild West' look originated by Colonel William F. (Buffalo Bill) Cody, at Cody, Wyoming, the town he founded to promote tourism. A typical Molesworth piece is his easy chair with Chimayo-weave cushions and moose-antler 'wings'. From the 1930s to the 1950s, his furniture was popular for hotel lobbies, dude ranches and private houses, including a den for President Dwight D. Eisenhower in Gettysburg, Pennsylvania. He used honey-coloured woods, fir and pine, with leather upholstery trimmed with brass tacks.

Molinis, Luigi (1940–) Italian designer who began his professional career in 1961. He worked for Zanussi, designing household electrical appliances, televisions and hi-fi equipment.

Mollino, Carlo (1905–73) Italian architect influenced by the organic forms of sculptors such as Henry Moore. He was also influenced by Charles Rennie MACKINTOSH, Charles EAMES and LE CORBUSIER. He designed a series of glass tables with one-piece bent plywood bases. Much of his output was for specific sites and not commercially available. Many of his pieces were lighthearted, approaching kitsch. He also designed sets, lighting, aeronautics and clothing.

Monk, John Lawrence (1936–) American industrial designer, based in Milan, producing electronic equipment for Lesa, vacuum cleaners for Oerre and medical equipment for Artsana.

Montagnac, Pierre-Paul (1883–1962) French painter and architect who designed furniture and interiors in the classical tradition, solidly made. From 1921, he collaborated with Maurice DUFRÁNE at La Maitrise and designed lighting, ceramics and tapestries, the latter for Gobelins. He designed suites on the 1930 liner *Atlantique* and the 1935 *Normandie*.

Moore, Edward Chandler (1827–91) American silversmith known for his fine craftsmanship. In 1852, he encouraged TIFFANY to adopt the British sterling standard. In 1868, Tiffany bought Moore's workshop, becoming director of the silver department. As there were no schools for smith in New York, he set up a training programme at the Tiffany workshops. After seeing Japanese pieces at the 1867 Paris Exhibition, he started to design Japanese-inspired pieces, from 1871. He also designed jewellery in the Japanese style for Tiffany.

Morandini, Marcello (1940–) Italian designer who started work in Milan in 1960, moving to Sydney, Australia, in 1963, and later to Singapore. He designed ceramics for ROSENTHAL, as well as the façade of their offices in Selb. He updated 1920s decorations and his *Corner* unit was made by ROSENTHAL in the 1980s.

Mørch, Ibi Trier (1910–1994) Danish architect who specialized in the design of glass and silver. She collaborated with Erik Herlow from 1951 to 1960 and designed the *Stub* range of stacking glassware with Grete Meyer in 1958, for the Kastrup glassworks.

Moretti, Carlo (1934–) and **Giovanni** (1936–) Italian grandsons of Vicenzo Moretti, who established a glass and bead factory near Venice, at the end of the last century. They expanded the company in 1958, to produce engraved glassware, coloured liqueur glasses and opaline goblets. In 1973, they began to make decorative pieces, mostly in Murano glass. Carlo designed hexagonal and octagonal glasses with gold borders.

Moreux, Jean-Charles (1889–1956) French architect and furniture designer who created massive, but elegant pieces, some of which were lacquered and inlaid with metal. His interiors included some for the Rothschilds and the 1928 music pavilion for the harpsichordist, Wanda Landowska. He designed a table, combining ebony, crocodile skin, crystal and ivory for the couturier Jacques DOUCET. He was one of the designers of Helena Rubenstein's 1938 apartment in Paris.

Morgan, David (1951–) British industrial designer who joined the design department of Thorn Lighting after graduating from the Royal College of Art, London. In 1981, he established his own studio to specialize in lighting design. His best-known piece is his award-winning 1986 *Burlington* lamp.

Morison, Stanley Arthur (1889–1967) British typographer who worked for the publisher Burns and Oates and Francis Meynell's Pelican Press, before founding the journal *Fleuron* in 1922, with Oliver Simon. In 1922 he was appointed typographical adviser to the Monotype Corporation, where he revived classical typefaces, including Garamond, Baskerville and Fournier, alongside new faces such as Gill Sans, by Eric GILL, and Albertus by Bertholde Wolpe. His own major achievement was Times New Roman, designed in 1932. He was also typographical consultant to Cambridge University Press from 1925 and designed distinctive bookjackets for Victor Gollancz.

Morris, May (1862–1938) British designer, embroiderer and lecturer, the second daughter of William MORRIS. Trained by her father, she designed textiles, wallpaper and embroidery for Morris & Co. She was a founder member of the Women's Guild of Arts in 1907. She created the jewellery her mother wore in portraits by Dante Gabriel ROSSETTI, and for herself in the triple-portrait *Rosa Triplex* in 1874. From 1886, she managed her father's business at Merton Abbey and taught at the Central School of Arts and Crafts, London.

Morris, Robert Lee (1948–) American jewellery designer who set up his business in New York in the 1970s. He designed sculptured pieces in Minimal style, which were sold at the Plaza Hotel. In 1977, he founded Artwear and collaborated with Donna Karan on her costume line in the 1980s. He also worked with Calvin Klein, Geoffrey BEENE and Karl Lagerfeld. He branched out into handbag, domestic product and dinnerware design. His *Rituals of Colour* cosmetics were produced by Elizabeth Arden and his leatherware by the Spanish company Loewe.

Morris, Talwin (1865–1911) British designer and metalworker who was a member of the Glasgow School with Charles Rennie MACKINTOSH and his circle. He specialized in beaten copper jewellery and was an innovator in his use of aluminium. He was art director of Blackie's, the Glasgow publishing house.

Morris, William (1834–96) British designer, craftsman, writer and political activist. He originally intended to make a career in the church, but while at Oxford he met Edward BURNE-JONES, and became interest in art and craft. He joined the office of G. E. Street, a leading GOTHIC Revival ecclesiastical architect, but decided that it was not his vocation. He moved to London with Burne-Jones and started to design large furniture pieces, with painted decorations, featuring medieval figures and inscriptions. Guided by Dante Gabriel ROSSETTI, he began to paint frescoes, together completing those in the Oxford Union. In 1859, he married Jane Burden, who became Rossetti's idealized PRE-RAPHAELITE woman. His partner, Philip WEBB designed his new house, the Red House at Upton in Kent. The experience gained in building and furnishing the house prompted Morris to set up a co-operative of designers and artists, which included Webb, Burne-Jones, Rossetti and Ford Madox BROWN. They were to exert a great influence on taste in Britain and abroad. At first they produced stained-glass, followed by tiles and pottery, painted by Morris's sisters Lucy and Kate, many based on designs by William DE MORGAN. In 1962, he started to design wallpapers, *Daisy, Fruit* and *Trellis* being in production in 1964. By the mid 1860s, the co-operative was were receiving major commissions, such as the 1867 refreshment room of the South Kensington Museum (now the Victoria and Albert Museum) and two rooms in St James's Palace, in London. By the mid-1870s, the company was in financial difficulties, so Morris bought out his partners and started Morris & Co., setting up looms in Merton Abbey, near his friend de Morgan. In 1883, he joined the Democratic Federation, Britain's first Socialist organization, for whom he lectured and wrote. He set up the Kelmscott Press in 1890, to produce beautiful, hand-made books. It published 53 titles, almost all designed by Morris himself, the craftsmanship involved demonstrating his belief in the alienation of industrialization.

Morrison, Jasper (1959–) British designer of wittily understated furniture and architectural ironmongery. He designed the 1988 *Door Handles I and II,* and in 1989 a range of aluminium handles. His wide range of clients include Vitra, SCP and Aram Designs. He specialized in limited-production designs, including the 1981 *Handlebar Table,* the 1983 *Flower-pot Table,* the 1987 *Hat Stand* for Aram, the 1984 *Wing-nut Chair* and the *Thinking Man's Chair* and *One-Legged Table* for Cappellini. Carpet designs include *A Rug of Many Blossoms,* 1985.

Mortier, Michel (1925–) French furniture designer who worked in the interiors department of the Au Bon Marché department store, Brussels. From 1963 to 1967 he worked on Expo '67 in Montreal and taught at the Institute of Applied Arts, before returning to Paris.

Morton, Alistair (1910–63) British textile designer and manufacturer, son of Sir James Morton, Chairman of Morton Sundour Fabrics. He joined the company in 1931, supervizing the company's first screen-printed fabrics. From 1932, he was artistic director and principal designer at EDINBURGH WEAVERS, where he commissioned designs from notable artists, including the

Constructivist Fabrics by Barbara HEPWORTH and Ben NICHOLSON. He designed dress fabrics for Horrockses and Edinburgh Fabrics, for whom he designed the 1946 *Unit Prints* series. He studied spinning and weaving with Ethel MAIRET at Ditchling, Sussex.

Moser, Koloman (Kolo) (1868–1918) Austrian painter and designer who was one of the founders of the Vienna Secession in 1897 and the WIENER WERKSTÄTTE in 1903. He was a founder of the Secesssion journal, *Ver Sacrum,* in 1897, with other members of the group including Gustav KLIMT. He was particularly influential as a graphic designer, employing Assyrian and Egyptian motifs. He designed book covers, posters, postage stamps, and bank-notes. He also designed stained glass, metalwork, ceramics, leatherwork and toys. Throughout his work the spreading influence of MACKINTOSH across Europe can be detected.

Motte, Joseph-Andre (1925–) French furniture designer who worked for the Au Bon Marché store in Paris. With Michel MORTIER and others, he set up the ARP design studio. He designed the chapel, transit hall and bar at Orly airport, the maritime train station at Le Havre. He participated in the renovation of the grand gallery of the Louvre Museum in Paris. His best-known furniture designs include the 1950 *Tripode* chair in steel, beechwood and rattan.

Mougin, Joseph (1876–1961) and **Pierre** (1879–1955) French ceramicists who set up a pottery with their sculptor friend Lemarquier. When he left, the brothers worked briefly at Sèvres, after which they set up a new kiln at Vaugird, where they produced some innovative pots. They exhibited their pieces widely and soon gained favourable notices, resulting in sales to museums, private collectors and the French government. In 1905, they moved to Nancy, where they became members of Émile GALLÉ's Ecole de Nancy. In collaboration with various artists, they produced pieces in the ART NOUVEAU style. After the First World War they made volume pottery at the Faïence de Lunéville. In the early 1930s, Joseph returned to Nancy to experiment with new forms and glazes, with his son, François, and daughter, Odile.

Mourgue, Olivier (1939–) French designer, the brother of Pascal MOURGUE, who opened an office in 1960 and became consultant to Prisunic, Mobilier National, Air France, Renault and many others. His furniture in stretched red Latex fabric, including the 1965 *Djinn Chaise Longue,* made by Airborne, featured in Stanley Kubrik's 1968 film *2001: A Space Odyssey.* In 1969, he designed seating for Prisunic and for Air France's Boeing 707. His simple, undulating style typifies French design of the 1960s.

Mourgue, Pascal (1943–) French interior designer who created furniture ranges for Mobilier International and KNOLL. Signature pieces include the 1985 *Lune l'Argent* chair and stool and the 1988 *Ikmisou* sofa for Fermob. He designed the 1986 glass and metal three-legged café table and 1987 *Atlantique* furniture collection for Artelino. He designs carpets for Toulemande Bochart and, in 1988, opened the Galérie Différences to show his fine art.

Mozer, Jordan (1959–) American interior and furniture designer, responsible for several restaurants in Chicago, including the Viveré. His 1990 suite of hospitality seating, including the *Cairo* bar stool, is widely used.

Mucha, Alfons (Alphonse) Maria (1860–1939) Moravian decorator and graphic artist who began his career in Vienna as a theatre designer, before moving to Munich in 1885 and Paris in 1887. He came to popular notice with his poster designs for the actress Sarah Bernhardt, in the 1890s. He designed the shop of George Fouquet, who produced the jewellery he created for Bernhardt. He also designed furnishings, giving three-dimensional form to ART NOUVEAU graphics. He made four trips to visit Louis C. TIFFANY in New York, sponsored by Charles Richard Crane, for whom he painted the Slav Epic series. He returned to Moravia (Czechoslovakia) in 1922, where his designs included postage stamps and banknotes.

Müller, Albin (1871–1941) German architect who taught at the School of Arts and Crafts in Magdeburg from 1900 to 1906. He then joined the Darmstadt artists' colony of the Grand Duke Louis IV of Hesse-Darmstadt. He became the leading architect there, designing exhibition products, including clocks and chairs. He produced silver- and pewter-ware, together with cutlery.

Müller, Karl (1888–1972) German silversmith who taught at Halle, producing more commercial pieces than the BAUHAUS.

When the Bauhaus moved to Dessau, several smiths moved to Halle to work under him, making domestic objects, cutlery and lighting.

Müller-Munk, Peter (1904–67) German metalworker who settled in New York in 1926, working for TIFFANY, before setting up his own workshop in 1927. He became associate professor at the Carnegie Institute, in Pittsburgh, establishing the first degree course in industrial design to be offered in America. His metal-work was angular and streamlined, exemplified by the sleek 1935 chromium-plated pitcher, based on the silhouette of the liner *Normandie*. It was mass-produced by Revere in Rome, New York State.

Munari, Bruno (1907–1995) Italian artist who began showing in Futurist exhibitions in Milan in the late 1920s. In 1933, he pro-duced his first suspended kinetic objects called 'Useless Ma-chines'. In the early 1950s he turned to industrial design, produc-ing his 1954 toy monkey. In 1957 he first experimented with plas-tics and produced the melamine cubic ashtray. He produced a se-ries of collapsible lamps and wooden puzzles for Danese, includ-ing the 1963 *Calza* light, made from metal hoops and stretched fabric. In 1971, he designed hanging shelves for Robots and the *Abitacola* bed-shelf living module for Zanotta.

Münchner Sezession In 1892 a group of over 100 artists broke away from the existing exhibition association named the Munich Society of Visual Artists. This grew enormously and became known as the Münchner Sezession to the press and public, so the title was officially adopted. It mounted the first show in 1893. Similar movements followed, in Vienna in 1897 and Berlin in 1898.

Munthe-Kaas, Herman (1890–1977) Norwegian architect who produced designs in MODERNIST style. His FUNCTIONALIST version of a wing-back chair was published in 1924 and he was one of the early exponents of tubular steel furniture in Norway, with his 1929 cantilever, bent-metal, nickel-plated range for Christiana Jernsenfabrik in Oslo.

Murdoch, Peter (1940–) British furniture designer who special-ized in children's designs. His 1964 *Spotty* child's chair was made of polyethene fibreboard printed with a large polka-dot motif. In 1967, he designed brightly-coloured cardboard furniture for Perspective Designs. He was a consultant to Hille and Price. With Lance Wyman, he designed the graphics for the 1968 Mexico City Olympic Games.

Murray, Keith Day Pearce (1892–1981) New Zealand architect who first worked part-time as a ceramics and glass designer at Stevens and Williams's Brierly Glassworks in England. From 1933, he worked at Wedgwood, producing pieces in a MODERNIST style. He was influenced by pieces seen at the 1925 Paris Exposition and at the 1931 Swedish Exhibition in London. In 1934, he designed a covered silver-and-ivory cup and a Modern silver-plated cocktail shaker for Mappin and Webb. His celebrated matt-glazed pottery for Wedgwood in the mid-1930s, are classic Modern pieces. In 1946, he returned to Wedgwood to design non-commercial sprigware, before returning to full-time architecture.

N

Nabis French artists' group formed in 1888 by Paul Sérusier, Jean-Edouard Vuillard, Maurice Denis, H. G. Ibels, Paul Ranson and Pierre Bonnard who had all studied together at the Académie Julian in Paris in the late 1880s. Joined by Paul GAUGUIN and the poet Henri Cazalis, they called the group 'Nabis', based on the Hebrew word for 'prophets', referring to the fact that their attitude to the painting of Gauguin bordered on religious enlightenment. The group emphasized colour and form, attempting to change the aesthetic in printmaking, posters, book illustration, furniture, textiles and stained glass. They opposed the naturalism of Impressionism and were attracted to linear distortion, influencing Symbolist painters and writers.

Nakashima, George (1905–1990) American woodworker who acquired the skills of Japanese carpentry when working in an architect's office in Japan, in 1937. He set up his first workshop in Seattle in 1941, being interrupted by a period of internment, when America entered the Second World War. After his release, he started a small business based at the farm owned by the architect Antonin Raymond, producing pieces which he thought of as fine art, rarely selling to retail clients. He worked with untrimmed slabs of wood, including black walnut and redwood, making virtues out of imperfections. Knot holes and rough edges featured in his work. He was influenced by SHAKER and Japanese craftsmanship. He made furniture for Nelson A. Rockefeller's home at Tarrytown, New York State and interiors for Columbia University, New York. For the Cathedral of St John the Divine in New York, he fashioned the 1968 heart-shaped *Altar for Peace* from a piece of English walnut weighing 1,500 lbs (700 kg). He worked up to the time of his death on part of a 111 piece suite of furniture for a private client in Princeton, New Jersey.

Nash, Paul (1889–1946) British painter who was an official war artist in both World Wars. He started out working at the OMEGA WORKSHOP in 1914. The Curwen Press produced his patterned papers in 1928 and in the same year London Transport used his moquette fabric for seating in railway carriages. He designed dress fabrics for Cresta Silks and his earliest textiles were all handprinted by Mrs Kennington at her Footprints workshop. He designed a dazzling bathroom for the dancer Tilly Losch, which featured silvered stippled glass in contrast to the black-glazed sanitary fittings. He designed decorations for ceramic tableware produced by Brains of Fenton and crystal for Stuart of Stourbridge. He was one of the eight founding members of the Society of Industrial Artists, and was its first practising designer president.

Navarre, Henri (1885–1970) French sculptor who executed a large number of monumental sculptures and carvings before 1924. At that time he began to make simple thick-walled glass vessels with internal decorations. In 1927, he designed a gilded reredos for the chapel of the liner *Ile-de-France*.

Naver, Kim (1940–) Danish weaver and designer who set up her workshop in 1966 for the design of ecclesiastical and industrial textiles and carpets. Her works include the five 1978 tapestries for the reception hall of the National Bank of Denmark, Copenhagen. From 1971, she designed jewellery for Georg JENSEN.

Neagle, Richard (1922–) American industrial designer who opened his own practise in 1954 in Westport, Connecticut. He was design director for Pye Electronics in Italy and design consultant to Montsanto in America. His range of objects include furniture, radio and TV sets, domestic electrical goods, plastic housewares and room dividing systems. His 1968 *Nike* chair was one of the first to be made in plastic by vacuum moulding.

Nelson, George (1907–1986) American industrial designer who promoted Modernism and introduced MIES VAN DER ROHE to America. He pioneered pedestrian malls in his 1942 *Grass on Main Street* concept. Though an architect, he preferred furniture, exhibition and urban design. Many of the individual pieces produced by his practise were collaborations. They include the *Bubble* lamp, the *Steel frame* storage system and the *Storagewall* concept. As design advisor to Herman Miller he produced clocks, tableware and furniture, including the 1956 *Coconut* chair and the 1933 *Sling* sofa and *Marshmallow* sofa. He designed several major exhibitions, including the 1959 America in Moscow exhibition, with Charles EAMES, and the 1964 New York World's Fair.

Neo-Classicism The ROCOCO style was being derided by the late 1730s as too frivolous and irrational. The reaction stemmed from students at the French Academy in Rome in the 1740s. They wanted a return to robust classicism, using boldly emphasized classical ornament, swags and frets, fluting and scrolls. PIRANESI was their example, but the ideas were not put into operation until the mid-1750s. A suite of furniture by Lorrain was the first important Neo-Classical statement. There was then a flurry of publications of plates suggesting suitable Greek and Roman models for inspiration. As Rococo did not have such strong expression in Britain, the establishment of Neo-Classicism was easier. The Palladian tradition of Inigo JONES and William Kent provided the basis for Neo-Classicism. The work of James 'Athenian' Stuart at Spencer House, London, was the first notable display of the new style, which was developed by John ADAM in the 1770s. In France the approach was more opulent as it became the official style of Napoleon I's empire. Palagi, who designed a monument to Napoleon in 1800, exemplifies the styles longevity in Italy. In the mid-

19th century it went into decline, but retained some strength in the commercial market. A more severe classical style took over, shown progressively in the work of LUTYENS, BEHRENS and Walter GROPIUS. This led to MODERNISM and the work of MIES VAN DER ROHE.

Nervi, Pier Luigi (1891–1979) Italian architect of monumental buildings who introduced the use of reinforced concrete. Though he did not design products, his neo-brutalist style influenced many other designers, and those employed to furnish his buildings.

Neutra, Richard Josef (1892–1970) Austrian architect influenced by Frank Lloyd WRIGHT, who made his buildings part of their surroundings. The division of interior and exterior space was blurred. He designed fitted units and often used chromium-plated steel. His 1929 *Cantilever Chair* was issued in reproduction in 1990. Pieces for specific houses include the high-backed bentwood chair for his 1947 Tremaine House and the 1940 *Camel Table* with wooden legs for the Sidney Kahn house.

Newill, Mary J. (1860–1947) British designer and embroiderer who was trained at the Birmingham School of Art and in Paris. She returned to teach at Birmingham and was a founder member of the Arts and Crafts Exhibition Society.

Newson, Mark (1962–) Australian industrial designer who worked in Milan and with Ron ARAD in London. He is best-known for his 1985 *Lockheed Lounge* steel chaise, which is in the lobby of the 1990 Paramount Hotel in New York. He designed the 1990 *Pod* clock, circular from the front and elliptical from the side. Its white, rotating dots were inspired by early CARTIER pieces.

Nicholls, David Shaw (1959-) British furniture designer who has worked mostly in Milan and New York. In 1980, he established Astflexi, to design and produce metal furniture and from 1984 worked for the SOTTSASS Associati, Milan, on projects including the Snaporazz Restaurant, Los Angeles, and the Academy Bridge, Venice. In 1987, he settled in New York where he designed his 1991 DSN sofa and chair and the *Arno* chair and *Aria* and *Ariane* tables. He designed a scent bottle and displays for Elizabeth

Arden, rugs for DSN and the *Mari, Bride n'Groom* and *Seven Palaces* dinnerware for Swid Powell.

Nicholson, Ben (1894–1982) British painter and sculptor who designed the 1937 *Constructivist Fabrics* range with Barbara HEPWORTH for EDINBURGH WEAVERS, under the artistic direction of Alistair MORTON. In 1948, he designed limited-edition screenprinted silk squares produced by Zika Ascher. He also painted the mural in the Regatta Restaurant at the 1951 Festival of Britain.

Nicholson, Roger (1922–) British painter who taught at St Martin's School of Art in London, becoming professor of textile design at the Royal College of Art, also in London, in 1958. He was a consultant designer to several manufacturers and in the late 1950s and early 1960s, and he designed wallpaper for Sanderson's *Palladio* Collection.

Nielsen, Erik (1857–1947) Danish ceramicist who was an apprentice woodcarver, joining the Royal Copenhagen Porcelain Manufactury around 1886. He collaborated with Arnold KROG on one-off ceramics, many influenced by naturalism and the Japanese style. From 1887 to 1947 he was a medal maker at Royal Copenhagen.

Niemeyer, Oscar (1907–1995) Brazilian architect of major buildings in Brazil and the United Nations building in New York. He designed a range of furniture in 1985, for Estel.

Nies-Friedlaender, Cordula Kianga (1958–) German industrial designer who worked for Schmidt Motor Sport in Nuremberg, before moving to London to work, firstly, for Moggeridge Design, and then for the architectural office Foster Associates. Her work included office furniture for Tecno, interior decoration and sales systems for Esprit.

Nizzoli, Marcello (1887–1969) Italian designer who started out as a painter, later becoming involved in the design of fabrics, exhibitions and graphics, including posters for Campari in 1926. With Eduardo Persico, he designed two 1934 Parker Pen shops in Milan and the Hall of Gold Medals at the 1934 Aeronautical Exhibition. In 1940, he became the most influential product designer at Olivetti, responsible for classic machines, including the 1948

Lexicon 80, 1950 *Lettera,* 1952 *Diaspron* typewriters. He also designed the 1956 *Divisumma* adding machine and, for Necchi, the 1956 *Mirella* sewing machine.

Noguchi, Isamu (1904–1988) American sculptor who made a major contribution to all aspects of industrial and stage design. From 1932, he lived mainly in New York. In 1937, he designed the helmet-like BAKELITE radio for Zenith and in 1940 a range of glassware for Steuben. His 1939 free-form glass-topped coffee table, made for the president of the Museum of Modern Art in New York, was commercially produced in 1944. His sculpture gardens, including that at the Bienecke Rare Book Library of Yale University, fused design, sculpture and architecture. His furniture for the Herman Miller Company includes the 1946 *IN70* sofa and matching ottoman, the 1949 *IN20* series rudder dining table, coffee table and stool. He has designed a range of lighting fixtures made of mulberry paper and spirally-woven bamboo called *Akari* (light) which are still in production. For mass production he designed the light-hearted 1954 rocking stooltable and the 1955 wire-and-Formica tables for KNOLL. He was also a noted stage designer, forming a special relationship with the modern dancer, Martha Graham.

Normandie French ocean liner, commissioned in 1935, which was decorated by some of the leading French designers of the day. The overall style was baroque ART DÉCO, with the exception of two suites which were in the French 18th-century style. René LALIQUE designed 48 wall panels, two large chandeliers and 12 ornate lighting fixtures for the 305 ft (93m) long dining room. Four huge panels showed Normandy village scenes. The walls were hammered glass with a ceiling in a honeycomb pattern of concealed lighting. In 1942, the *Normandie* burned in New York harbour and sank during the salvage operation. Some of the fittings were saved.

Novembergruppe An informal association of radical artists which was founded in Berlin in 1918. Influenced by the abortive November 1918 revolution, it was inspired by the painters, Cesar Klein and Max Pechstein. They rejected the past and promoted new expressive forms of communication. Members included architects such as Walter Gropius, Alfred Gellhorn and Ludwig Mies van der Rohe, painters including Lyonel Feininger, Wassily Kandinski and Paul Klee. The group was officially banned by the Nazis in 1933.

Noyes, Eliot Fette (1910–77) American architect who advocated Modern European design after reading Le Corbusier's treatise on architecture. After working in various architectural practises he joined the office of Norman Bel Geddes where he designed the 1946 IBM *Model A* electric typewriter. In 1956, he became corporate design director of IBM. He held similar positions at Westinghouse Corporation and Pan Am. In 1961, he designed the Selectric range of typewriters for IBM and shaped the image of many companies by appointing designers of like mind. They included Ivan Chermayeff at Mobil and Paul Rand at IBM. His 1964 Mobil filling station became the prototype for all their stations, throughout the world.

O

Obrist, Hermann (1862–1927) Swiss student of medicine and natural sciences who turned to art after seeing a vision of a radiant city in 1886. In 1888, he started studying ceramics, moving to Paris to study sculpture. In 1892, he moved to Florence to learn marble techniques. He established a studio for embroidery in Munich, In 1895, where, following the example of the Wiener Werkstätte, he founded the Münchner Werkstätte, with Peter Behrens and others, to sell everyday objects designed by Modern artists. He was one of the most important designers of Jugendstil.

Ohr, George Edgar (1857–1918) Eccentric American potter, dubbed 'the mad potter of Biloxi', where he set up his pottery in 1882. He produced boldly-coloured, bent and twisted earthenware pieces which foreshadowed the Modern works of others. He threw his pots on a handmade wheel, using clays from Mississippi river beds. His forms are totally his own, but show a slight similarity to the shapes of Christopher Dresser.

Olbrich, Josef Maria (1867–1908) Austrian architect who was a founder member of the Vienna Secession, designing the Secession House, after a preliminary drawing by Gustave KLIMT. In 1899, he joined the artists' colony founded by Grand Duke IV of Hesse-Darmstadt, where he was responsible for some ART NOUVEAU buildings. He designed silverware, including tea-table pieces and a candelabrum, many light fittings in pewter, brass and silver, electric ceiling models and gas wall fittings. His styles were functional, reflecting the angularity of Charles Rennie MACKINTOSH and members of the Viennese school.

Old, Maxime (1910–1994) French decorator and furniture designer who was an apprentice in Jacques-Émile RUHLMAN's workshop. He was one of the designers who furnished liners, including the 1926 *Ile-de-France*, *Liberté*, *Ville de Marseille* and *Flandre*. After the Second World War he designed furniture for the French Finance Ministry and the French Legation in Helsinki. His designs were refined and elegant. In the 1950s, he designed all the mahogany and woven-cane furnishings for the Hotel Marhaba, Casablanca. In the early 1960s, he experimented with the use of metal in his designs.

Olivetti, Camillo (1868–1943) Italian engineer and industrialist who founded the Olivetti office machinery company in 1908. He designed the company's first typewriter, manufacturing it on a moving assembly line, similar to that used by Henry Ford for car production in 1913. The 1911, M1 had similarities to an Underwood model.

Omega Workshops British cooperative for the production of furniture, furnishings, ceramics and textiles. It was set up in 1913 by the painter and art critic Roger FRY to make employment for his artist friends. His models were the WIENER WERKSTÄTTE and Paul POIRET's Studio Martine in Paris. The group designed the 1924 Cadena Cafe in London, including the waitresses' uniforms, murals, rugs and lighting. Many of the workshops designs presaged the Modern movement of some ten years later. Omega's designers included Vanessa BELL, Duncan GRANT and, for a time, Wyndham LEWIS. Other artists participated from time to time, including David Bomberg, Paul NASH and McKnight KAUFFER. The main motifs were nudes and flowers and Lewis's abstract patterns. Fry himself was the most successful designer of pottery and textiles, including the popular *Amenophis*. The workshop closed in 1921.

Opsvik, Peter (1939–) Norwegian furniture designer who collaborated with Christian MENGSHOEL on the development of ergonomic seating. In 1972, he produced his *Tripp-trapp* stool-chair and is best-known for the 1981 *Balans Variable* ergonomic stool.

Orders The Roman architectural writer, Marcus Vitruvius Pollio, whose works were discovered in the library of St Gall, detailed the orders of ancient architecture comprising columns with their bases, capitals and entablatures. The Doric order was expressive of power and appropriate for temples of Minerva, Mars and Hercules, Corinthian showed feminine grace and was therefore suitable for Venus, Proserpina and Flora, Ionic lying between these two, being suitable for Juno, Diana and Bacchus. The lesser-known Tuscan order was for castles, prisons and arsenals and the Composite allowed freedom of imagination. In 1662, Bernini expressed the profound significance of the orders for BAROQUE designers. 'The beauty of all things, including architecture, lies in proportion. It is a divine attribute taking as its origin the body of Adam, which was made by God's own hand and in his own image.' From 1758, when James 'Athenian' STUART designed a Greek temple at Hagley, the orders gained renewed significance in the NEO-CLASSICAL revival. Furniture designers, including CHIPPENDALE, prefaced their pattern books with an account of the significance of the orders.

O'Rorke, Brian (1901–74) New Zealand architect who studied at Cambridge University and practised in Britain. The 1932 music room he designed included a swirl-patter rug by Marian DORN. He opened an interior design studio and, in the 1930s, designed interiors for the liners Orion and Orcades and other ships of the Orient Line. In 1946, he designed the Vickers Viking and in 1947 the Orient Steam Navigation Building in Sydney.

Østergaard, Steen (1935–) Danish designer who set up his own studio in 1965, designing his first plastic piece, the 1970 *Chair 290* in polyamid. It was the first to be produced by a single-extrusion process, its fibre-glass shell upholstered on the inside, supported by a chromium-plated frame. He also produced a stacking range for Cado.

Ozenfant, Amédée (1886–1966) French painter and design theoretician who founded the journal *L'Elan* with Pablo PICASSO and Guillaume Apollinaire. He edited it from 1915 to 1917. He developed ideas on painting and the Purist manifesto with LE CORBUSIER, who developed these ideas in his 1925 Vers une Architecture. In 1924, with Fernand Léger, he founded a painting school and worked with Le Corbusier of the design of the Pavilion de l'Esprit Nouveau at the 1925 Paris Exposition. From 1935 to 1938 he lectured at the French Institute in London, moving to New York in 1939, to found a School of Fine Art and broadcast on artistic matters for Voice of America.

P

Pabst, Daniel (1826–1910) German furniture designer and cabinet-maker who settled in America in the mid-1800s. He opened his own workshop in Philadelphia in 1854, working in a Renaissance revival style, producing highly carved pieces for all the major stores. In the 1870s he turned the neo-GOTHIC style, being influenced by British designers such as Christopher DRESSER. He collaborated with Henry Pratt McKean on woodwork and furniture for Theodore Roosevelt's house on Long Island, New York. From 1860, he carved centennial spoons every year for the University of Pennsylvania. The workshop closed in 1896.

Pagano, Giuseppe (1896–1945) Italian architect and Fascist leader. He was technical director of the 1928 Turin Exhibition, moving to Milan in 1931. In 1933, he designed a streamlined train, shown at the Milan 1933 Triennale and, in 1939, he designed some simple laminated wood chairs. During the Second World War, he reacted against Fascism and joined the resistance movement. He was interned in Mauthausen concentration camp and died there.

Page, James (*fl.*1840) One of the earliest influential designers and design educators. He taught ornament and design at the School for Promoting Ractical Design in London, a forerunner of the Government School of Design which were set up across Britain.

Pahlmann, William (1900–1988) American interior designer who worked as a travelling salesman and actor before turning to interior design in 1933. In the 1930s he was noted for his colourful rooms at Lord and Taylor's store on Fifth Avenue, New York, where he worked from 1936–42. He opened his own studio in 1946 and designed numerous private homes in Texas and for Billy Rose and Abe Burrows, and, in 1959, the Four Seasons restaurant in the Seagram Building and the Forum of the Twelve Caesars restaurant, both in New York.

Palazetti, Sergio (1949–) Italian furniture designer and manufacturer who set up a showroom in New York in 1981, to sell both retail and wholesale. By 1991, he had eight showrooms across America, selling Modern classic and his own designs. He began furniture production with his *Maverick* collection.

Paley, Albert (1944–) American metalworker who trained as a blacksmith and became known for architectural metalwork, made with traditional wrought-iron techniques. He designed metal furniture, gates, staircases and railings, sometimes reflecting the ideals of ART NOUVEAU and simple Romanesque forms. He also designed jewellery in precious metals.

Pallucco, Paolo (1950–) Italian architect who established the Pallucco company to produce new furniture designs by himself an others and to reissue Modern classics. He designed the 1984 *Fra Dolcino* shelving and collaborated on the 1987 *Tankette* chair, which copied the threads of a trunk.

Palmqvist, Sven Ernst Robert (1906–84) Swedish glassware designer who trained and worked at Orrefors Glasbruk. He started designing in 1930 and returned to classical, graceful lines after the FUNCTIONALIST period. In 1954, he invented a technique for forming glass bowls by spinning molten glass in a centrifugal mould, thereby eliminating the nee for hand-finishing. He produced delicate crystal shapes in his bold-coloured *Ravenna* series, with simple inlaid patterns.

Palterer, David (1949–) Israeli designer and teacher who established a design and manufacturing firm with Borek Sipek in Amsterdam in 1983. Together they designed the interiors the San Casciano theatre, Florence airport and parks in Tel Aviv. They also designed furniture for a variety of clients, including Artleano and Zanotta.

Pankok, Bernhard (1872–1943) German designer who worked in Munich from 1892 to 1902, designing cumbersome furniture in a heavy ART NOUVEAU style. He was a founder member of the MÜNCHER WERKSTÄTTE, which aimed to sell everyday objects designed by MODERNIST artists.

Panton, Verner (1926–) Danish architect who collaborated with Arne JACOBSEN on experimental furniture, before setting up his own office in Switzerland, in 1955. He designed the laminated wood *Zig-Zag* chair and established his reputation with the 1957 *Cardboard House* and the 1960 *Plastic House*. Although he specialized in chair design, he also designed lighting, textiles, carpets and exhibitions. He designed the interiors of the offices of *Der Spiegel* in Hamburg and for Bayer ships. He pioneered the first one-piece cantilevered chair in a fibre-glass shell, although his best-known design is the 1960 *Stacking Chair*. Other well-known designs include the 1959 *Heart Chair*, upholstered in stretch-knit fabric. From 1969, he designed floor coverings and furnishing textiles, including the 1984 cotton chintz *Diamond* collection and the 1987 *Cubus* collection.

Paolozzi, Eduardo Luigi (1924–) Scottish sculptor who has also worked a lecturer in ceramics in many institutions, including the Royal College of Art, London. He has designed ceramics for ROSENTHAL and limited edition tableware for Wedgwood. In 1984 he designed the mosaic murals for London Underground's Tottenham Court Road Station.

Parent, Guillame (1961–) French furniture designer who started out as an apprentice cabinetmaker. In 1985 he became an independent cabinetmaker, designing furniture for Musée Carnavalet, Paris. In 1992 he designed pieces for the Réunion des Musées Nationaux, and signage for Chateaux Versailes and the Trianon.

Parish, Sister (1910–) Doyenne of American interior designers. In 1930 she married the banker Henry Parish II and while on honeymoon in Paris decided to become an decorator. Their Gracie

Square house has been designed by Eleanor BROWN of the McMillen company, and when the couple took a small house in New Jersey, she decided to decorate it herself. Her early commissions were for her well-connected friends and the Essex Hunt Club. Her decorative style, exemplified by her shop on Madison Avenue, drew on themes from the past, in particular the English country house style. She became well known in the 1960s through her work for the Kennedys. Her love of patchwork quilts, rag rugs and distressed paintwork created a great sense of nostalgia. In 1986, she advised the Duke and Duchess of York on the interiors of their house in Berkshire.

Parsons, Frank Alvah (d.1930) American teacher of interior design who has had a profound influence on generations of designers who have attended the Parsons School of Design in New York.

Pasini, Gianni (1941–) Italian designer who began his professional career in 1965 with clients such as Olivetti, Magneti Marelli and Crinospital. He designed electronic machinery, including a text-editing system and a mini-computer. In 1974, he formed the company Pasqui e Pasini with Sandro PASQUI.

Pasqui, Sandro (1937–) Italian industrial designer who started his career in 1963 working for Olivetti. His own studio worked for Magnetti Marelli and Crinospital. In 1974 he set up the partnership Pasqui e Pasini, with Gianni PASINI.

Peche, Dagobert (1887–1923) Austrian designer of ceramics and carpets for industry in a highly distinctive and unique style which was densely ornamented and decorated, but often used simple materials. He began designing for the WIENER WERKSTÄTTE in 1915 and exerted a great influence the group throughout the 1920s. His work also included designs for jewellery and wallpaper.

Peduzzi, Richard (1943–) French painter who turned to theatre design after meeting the director Patrice Chéreau in 1967. In 1968 he was commissioned by Mobelier National to design a furniture collection and he restored the library and museum of the Paris Opéra, designing the *Opéra* chair. He has designed more than twenty plays and operas for Patrice Chéreau and Daniel

Barenboim, for whom he designed Mozart's *Don Giovanni* at the 1994 Salzburg Festival.

Pentagram British industrial and graphic design consultancy which grew out of the firm Forbes, Fletcher and Gill.

Percier, Charles (1764–1838) French architect who became a designer after a stay in Rome studying classical artefacts. In 1793, he arranged the exhibits at the Museum of French Monuments, designing furniture, carpets, porcelain and bronze and silver work. He supervized every detail down to the braids and tassels. His style became the official style of Napoleonic France.

Pergolesi, Michelangelo (*fl.*1765–1800) Italian decorator, probably brought to England by Robert ADAM, though the only known work for him is the decoration on 62 pilaster in the Long Gallery of Syon House. His pattern books have been preserved, including his 1776 book of 66 plates, showing grotesque ornament and antiquities. The book was dedicated to his two patrons, Lord Scarsdale and the Duchess of Northumberland. A design for a table is housed at the Victoria and Albert Museum, in London, and his *Design in the Etruscan and Grotesque Style* was published posthumously in 1814.

Perriand, Charlotte (1903–1989) French designer who worked closely with LE CORBUSIER, being responsible for most of the furniture for the 'machines for living'. Her pieces included the 1928–29 *LC1* series of sling chairs, and the 1955 *Synthése des Arts*, Tokyo chair. She designed furnishings for chalets in the holiday resort of Méribel and, in 1950, kitchen prototypes for Le Corbusier's Unité d'Habitation in Marseilles. In 1957, she designed furnishings for the Air France offices in London and, in 1959, for the common room of the Brazilian House of the Cité Universitaire, south of Paris. She took part in the refurbishments of the United Nations in Geneva and in the 1980s oversaw the reproductions of Le Corbusier and JEANNERET furniture by Cassia.

Pesce, Gaetano (1939–) Italian architect who opened an office in Padua where, in 1959, he was a founding member of Gruppo N. In the 1960s he experimented with Pop Art designs and the use of plastics. His first, inexpensive chairs, which were produced by B & B Italia, included the doughnut-shaped *UP5* armchair. In the

1970s he designed the *Golgotha* and the *Sit Down* suite of arm-chairs. His 1987 *Feltra* chair is the nearest he has come to achiev-ing individual architecture-furniture. He also designed the unor-thodox *Tramonto a New York* seating (1980), on which a vinyl-upholstered 'sun' rose over foam-covered cushions, with a woven pattern suggesting the New York skyline.

Pevsner, Nikolaus Bernhard (1902–83) German art historian and critic who settled in Britain in 1933, lecturing at Oxford, Cam-bridge and London universities. He also worked as a buyer for Gordon RUSSELL until 1939. An influential writer on architecture and design, his best-known works include *Pioneers of the Mod-ern Movement* (1936), and the 46-volume series *The Buildings of England*, written over a period of 23 years.

Pfister, Charles (1939–90) American interior and furniture de-signer who worked on many interiors in San Francisco before be-coming active in mass production design. In the 1980s, he de-signed the 21 Club restaurant in New York, the Square One res-taurant in San Francisco, and the Shell headquarters in The Hague. He also transformed a 13th-century Italian monastery into a hotel. His office furnishings and accessories for KNOLL included the 1975 range of clear glass ashtrays and bowls, produced by Vistosi in Murano. His 40-piece Premier collection of Domestic furniture (1990), was inspired by 19th-century Russian and 18th-century Swedish designs.

Picasso, Pablo Ruiz (1881–1973) Spanish painter who was one of the first to design sculptures using *objets trouvés*. He was prolific as a lithographer, etcher, book illustrator and ceramicist. In 1947, he started to produce pottery at the kilns of Suzanne and Georges Ramié in the South of France. In 1956, he started to work in sil-ver.

Picasso, Paloma (1949–) French fashion and furnishings de-signer, the daughter of Pablo PICASSO. She began her design ca-reer by creating fashion accessories for TIFFANY, and her cosmetic range was launched in the late 1980s. Her range of glassware, ce-ramics and flatware is produced by VILLEROY ET BOCH, her fabrics (*La Maison* range) by Motif Designs and eyewear by Optyl.

Pick, Frank (1878–1941) British design theorist and administrator who was a founding member of the British Design and Industries Association. He oversaw the redesign of the London Underground in the 1920s and 1930s. He employed graphic designer Charles H. Holden, architect Edward Johnston, poster designer Edward McKnight KAUFFER to design the image of the unified underground system.

Piper, John (1903–92) British painter who was an official war artist in the Second World War. He designed for the stage, including Benjamin Britten's *Rape of Lucretia* (1946), *Albert Herring* (1947) and *Billy Budd* (1951). In 1959, he designed stained glass for Coventry Cathedral and, in 1965, for the Metropolitan Cathedral. In 1979, he designed the Benjamin Britten memorial window in Aldeburgh Parish Church, Suffolk. In 1965, he designed a tapestry for Chichester Cathedral, Sussex.

Piranesi, Giovanni (1720–78) Italian artist who was trained as an architect and engineer in Venice before moving to Rome. He became inspired by the architecture and ruins of the city and executed drawings and engravings of them along with reconstructions of how he imagined Ancient Rome would have looked. In 1740 Piranesi entered a studio which produced printed views of Rome and while there his work was published in *Varie Vedute di Roma* (1745) and *Archi Trionfali* (1748). Piranesi's work profoundly influenced the first generation of NEO-CLASSICAL designers, including Robert ADAM, with whom he enjoyed a close friendship. Piranesi later set up as a designer and print-seller, while also restoring and dealing in antiques. His prints were exported throughout Europe, compounding the influence he had on other designers and artists.

Piretti, Giancarlo (1940–) Italian designer who worked on office and domestic furniture at Anonima Castelli, where he produced his first piece in plastic, the 1969 *Plia* folding chair. Other innovative pieces were his prefabricated seating, suitable for mass production, including the 1969 *Plane* folding chair, the 1971 *Platone* folding desk chair and the *Pluvium* umbrella stand. With Emilio Ambasz he designed the 1980 *Logotec* and 1984 *Oseris* low-voltage spotlight ranges for Erco.

Pitman, Benn (1822–1910) British teacher and woodcarver and brother of Isaac Pitman, inventor of the phonetic short-hand system, which bears his name. After teaching his brother's system for ten years, he went to America to promote it. He settled in Cincinnati, where he took up wood carving and, in 1856, invented relief engraving. In 1877, he and fellow artists and pupils started the decoration of the great organ of the Cincinnati Music Hall. His designs, which were influenced by nature, can be viewed in his highly decorated house. His daughter, **Agnes Pitman** (1850–1946), was a ceramicist and wood carver.

Pittoni, Giovanni Battista (1520–83) Italian designer who published his suite of 16 plates of ACANTHUS friezes, putti and seahorses, anticipating BAROQUE ornament. In 1566, he published a further 50 plates of strapwork.

Piva, Paolo (1950–) Italian designer who began his professional life in 1970, designing kitchen units, seating and travel goods for clients, including Dada, B & B Italia, De Sede and Lumenform in Italy. For Open Products, he designed the *Easy System* seating and embassies in Kuwait and Qater.

Platner, Warren (1919–) American architect who worked in the office of Raymond LOEWY and Eero SAARINEN. He created vertical steel wire tables and chairs, produced by KNOLL. In 1967, he set up his own studio where he designed furniture for KNOLL and Lehigh, the Georg JENSEN Design Center and the Windows on the World restaurant in the World Trade Center, New York.

Plumet, Charles (1861–1928) French architect who practised in the ART NOUVEAU style before the First World War and promoted the Modern style after it. He designed furniture in the 1920s and built elegant townhouses in Paris. He was chief architect of the 1925 Paris Exposition, where he erected four massive towers to house restaurants.

Poilly, François de (1622–93) French engraver who studied in Rome from 1649 to 1656. In 1669, he became engraver to Louis XIV. He designed a suite of scrolled black ACANTHUS ornament for watches, boxes and flasks. He also published suites of designs for chimneypieces, doors and panelling.

Poilly, Nicolas de (1626–96) French designer of six plates of artisan designs for ironwork, handles, locks, bolts, keyholes, escutcheons, hinges and street signs. He was the brother of François DE POILLY.

Poillerat, Gilbert (1902–88) French metal engraver who worked for Edgar BRANDT from 1921 to 1927, creating wrought-iron furniture. In the 1920s, he designed much grille-work, consoles, screens, lighting and firedogs. In 1934, he designed the ornamental door with folk scenes for Maison-Alfort, inexpensive jewellery for Jacques Heim and a bronze door for the 1935 liner *Normandie*. Other commissions were for the Bibliothéque National and the Palais de Chaillot. In 1946, he set up his own workshop, concentrating on big public works, including the Palais de l'Elysée and, in 1957, the façade ironwork for the new synagogue in Strasbourg.

Poiret, Paul (1879–1944) French couturier and design entrepreneur who started out working for Jacques DOUCET, on his graphic and fashion designs. His costumes brought him great fame, particularly those for the actress Sarah Bernhardt. He became a pattern maker at Worth after a dispute with Doucet and Bernhardt, founding his own salon in 1904, were his main achievement was to free women from corsets, with his natural, free-flowing styles. He encouraged many painters, including André Derain and Maurice de Vlaminck. Paul IRIBE illustrated his 1908 portfolio of fashion, heavily influenced by the style of the Orient. After the Second World War his designs were out of touch with the times, but he continued to entertain generously, his guests including artists such as Raoul DUFY, Jean-Louis Forain and Kees van Dongen, and dancers such as Isadora Duncan and Carlotta Zambelli. In 1911, he founded the Martine Art School, primarily for young ladies to paint from nature. From these, textile designs were created, together with painted furniture. For the 1925 Paris Exposition he decorated three barges on the Seine, *Amours, Délices* and *Orgues*, with hangings by Raoul Dufy. In the same year his business went into decline and he was forced to sell his collection of paintings.

Polglase, Van Nest (b.1898) American film set designer whose ideas influenced interior design of the 1920s and 1930s. He worked at RKO where he was famous for his 'Big White Set' as seen in many Ginger Rogers and Fred Astaire films. Designing in white became possible as arc lamps (which produced pink and green glows) were replaced by incandescent lighting. His most striking design was the set for the 1935 *Top Hat*, for which he recreated Venice, two storeys high, on two sound stages. It had winding canals, three bridges, a piazza, dance floors, balconies and terraced cafés. Its angular, late ART DÉCO style was much copied by interior decorators.

Pollen, John Hungerford (1820–1902) British clergyman who took to painting in the 1840s. In 1844, he started painting the ceiling of St Peter-le-Bailey in Oxford and, in 1850, the ceiling of Merton College Chapel. From 1855, he served for two years as professor of fine arts at the Catholic University of Dublin, where he designed and decorated the remarkable Byzantine University Church. He met Dante Gabriel ROSSETTI with whom he became responsible for the Oxford Union's frescoes. He also decorated the 1857 Foreign Office building and the Oxford Museum. After a period as an editor at the South Kensington Museums (now the Victoria and Albert Museum) he took on commissions such as the decoration of the library of Blickling Hall, designed tapestries for Alton Towers and a carpet for Wilton Royal Carpets.

Pollini, Gino (1903–1993) Italian architect of the Olivetti building in Ivrea and designer of early experimental all-electric kitchens at the Milan International Exhibition, in 1932. He also designed the 1935 *Studion 42* typewriter for Olivetti.

Pollitzer, Sigmund (1913–) British painter and decorative glass designer who worked on the 1930 Cumberland Hotel and Marble Arch Corner House, both in London. From 1933 to 1938 he was chief designer at Pilkington Glass. He designed glass panels and decorations for the 1936 liner *Queen Mary*, the 1938 *Mauretania* and the Gaumont theatre in the Haymarket, London.

Pompe, Antoine (1873–1980) Belgian architect and designer, based in Brussels, who designed silver flatware and hollow-ware in the style of Henry VAN DE VELDE. He is the only Belgian silversmith of the turn-of-the century whose work has survived.

Pond, Edward (1929–) British designer of textiles and wallpapers for clients in Britain and abroad. In the 1960s, his designs employed Pop and Op Art motifs. In 1969, he founded the Paperchase shop.

Ponti, Gio (1891–1979) Italian architect who designed enamels, mosaics, printed fabrics, ceramics and car bodies from the 1930s. In 1951, he designed cutlery for Krupp of Essen and, in 1953, sanitary equipment for Ideal-Standard. His best-known furniture design was the 1952 *Superleggera 646* chair made by Cassina, a reworking of traditional Italian designs. Many of his ceramics were decorated by Piero FORNASETTI.

Porden, William (*c*.1755–1822) British architect who was the son of a labourer, but rose to be Surveyor to Lord Grosvenor (later the Duke of Westminster). He specialized in the GOTHIC style and designed Eaton Hall, Cheshire for Lord Grosvenor, including its Gothic furnishings. The hall was demolished by the present Duke.

Porsche, Ferdinand Alexander 'Butzi' (1935–) German designer, grandson of the founder of the Porsche car company. He became the company's chief designer, being responsible for two classic cars, including the celebrated *911*, which is still in production. In 1972, he started his own studio in Austria and began designing a range of accessories including watches, sunglasses and leather goods. He produced de luxe goods in the 1980s, for Artemide and InterProfil. His 1985 lighting range included the *Parete PL* wall light, the *Lettura PL* floor light and the *Soffitto* pendant lamp.

Porta, Guglielmo della (1485–1577) Italian sculptor who worked in Genoa in the Palazzo Doria. He went to Rome in 1537, where he was strongly influenced by Michelangelo BUONARROTI. He became a restorer of antique statues and designed metalwork, including twelve reliquaries ordered by Pope Pius V from the goldsmith Antonio Gentile. He went on to become Keeper of the Papal Seal.

Porthault, Madeleine (1905–79) French producer of household linens who was a designer and salesperson with couturiére Maggy Rouff. In the early 1920s, after a period in New York, she met and married Daniel Porthault, who owned a lingerie company. In 1924, they started producing household linens, establishing a factory in 1935 to weave linens for printing and embroidering. Their first clients were the wealthy Ford and Mellon families in America. In 1955, she designed the *Carnation* print for the Duchess of Windsor and, in 1956, the linens for Aristotle Onassis's yacht *Christina*, employing a goldfish motif. Other clients included the Rothschilds, the Shah of Iran and the Kennedys. She and her husband opened a boutique in New York in 1960 and a second boutique in Paris, in 1964. Her son, Marc, designed their 1986 *Tulip* print, the 1965 four-leaf clover motif and matching LIMOGES porcelain and the 1985 animals series. In 1991, they reissued satin sheets, with a Grecian maid motif, originally created for Woolworth heiress, Barbara Hutton.

Portzamparc, Christian de (1944–) French architect and furniture designer who was responsible for the Café Beaubourg in Paris.

Pott, Carl Hugo (1906–85) German metalworker who joined his father's company immediately after the First World War. In the 1920s, he became interested in the theories of the Deutsche Werkstätte and the BAUHAUS and completely changed the design of the firm's products. Hitherto, very ornate, he simplified the lines and abandoned decoration.

Povey, Albert John Stephen (1951–) British furniture and interior designer who opened his own studio in 1983. He designed the 1985 Diametric range of furniture, including the *Curved-Rail Bed*, the *Y Trestle Table* and the *Eclipse Sofa*, all in steel. In 1988, he opened the Diametric furniture shop in London's Covent Garden. He designed the *Stacking Steel Filing Tray* for the BBC and became known for clever re-interpretations of classic British styles such as Queen Anne and Charles Rennie MACKINTOSH.

Powell, David Harman (1933–) British designer who worked on the development of melamine tableware at British Plastics, before becoming chief designer at Ekco Plastics. He designed his 1968 *Nova* plastic stacking tableware, the Eckoware kitchen storage containers and the 1970 semi-disposable cutlery. He became the first tutor in moulded plastics at the Royal College of Art, London, in 1968.

Powell, Edmund Barnaby (1891–1939) British glassware de-

signer who joined the family firm in 1918. At Whitefriars Glassworks he became director and designer of decorative and domestic glassware, specializing in large-scale pieces.

Powell, John Hardham (1827–95) British jeweller and metalworker who entered the office of A. W. N. PUGIN in 1844. Pugin
educated him in true GOTHIC principles and from the mid-1840s
he worked on Pugin's designs for stained glass. He married
Pugin's eldest daughter, Anne, and, on his father-in-law's death,
became chief designer at the family firm, John Hardman & Co.
He also designed church plate and jewellery, some of which was
exhibited at the 1862 London Exhibition.

Prenzell, Robert (1866–1941) Austrian-born potter who visited
Australia for the 1888 Melbourne Exhibition and settled there. He
built up a business designing and manufacturing terracotta architectural ornaments. He went into partnership with a cabinet
maker and produced pieces in the 'Gumnut Nouveau' style, a sophisticated Australian version of ART NOUVEAU, inspired by native
Australian plant forms.

Pre-Raphaelites British artists' group led by Dante Gabriel
ROSSETTI and Edward BURNE-JONES, taking their inspiration from
fairy-tale imagery and the early Renaissance painters. Their
paintings of ideal women (as exemplified by William MORRIS's
wife, Jane) often included jewellery and furniture which inspired
other designers and furniture makers.

Pritchard, Jack (1899–1993) British designer and manufacturer
of plywood furniture. His designs were inspired by LE
CORBUSIER's 'L'Esprit nouveau' pavilion at the 1925 Paris Exhibition. He worked for Venesta Plywood after a period with
Michelin tyres in France. He, his wife Molly and Wells Coates
formed the Isokon partnership in 1931, to produce plywood furniture, including the 1936 bentwood dining table and chaise longue
by Marcel BREUER and the Penguin Donkey, a bookcase designed
to hold paperback books published by Penguin.

Prix, Wolf-Dieter (1942–) Austrian architect who designed most
of the furniture for the Coop Himmelblau, in Vienna. It included
the 1989 *Vodol* armchair and an 'exploded' version of LE
CORBUSIER's 1928 *Grand Confort* club chair, with its bent metal-

tube frame straightened. He also contributed to the design of a mobile kitchen.

Procopé, Ulla (1921–68) Finnish ceramicist who produced many designs for ARABIA where she was a model planner. They included the 1957 *Liekki* flame-proof stacking dinnerware range and the 1960 *Ruska* range.

Proetz, Miroslav (1896–1954) American designer who devised the entire furnishings for the John Lohman House in Connecticut. In 1937, he designed and decorated Lord and Lady Mountbatten's house in London. In 1943, the Lord and Taylor store in New York appointed him director of its interior design department.

Propst, Bob (1921–) American designer of architectural sculpture, ecclesiastical interiors and playground equipment. He designed the 1968 Action Office system for Herman Miller, the success of which made the company the second largest office furniture manufacturer in the world. Other pieces include the 1967 *Pediatric* bed and a 1970 timber harvester.

Prouvé, Jean (1901–1984) French metalworker, engineer and furniture designer, the son of Victor PROUVÉ, he was trained as a blacksmith in Paris. In 1918, he carried out his first commissions, for a grille and a lamp, and in 1923 he opened his own workshop in Nancy. By 1924 he was manufacturing chairs in the Modern style, using sheet steel. In the late 1920s he worked for LE CORBUSIER, moving into industrial building in metal and sheet-steel office desks and school furniture. After publishing his *Le Decor d'Aujourd'hui* he stopped designing and turned to architecture, inventing new engineering techniques.

Prouvé, Victor (1858–1943) French painter and sculptor who worked with Émile GALLÉ, designing glassware, ceramics and marquetry. In 1904, when Gallé died, he assumed the leadership of the Ecole de Nancy. He produced jewellery and decorative pieces and patterns for textiles, placques, caskets and bindings, inspired by the flora and fauna of the Alsace-Lorraine region. His best-known binding was of Gustave Flaubert's *Salammbo*.

Pugin, Augustus Charles (1769–1832) French-born architect who studied at the Royal Academy School in London and was employed by John NASH. He propounded the GOTHIC style and his various books were a vital source for designers and architects working in that style. From 1825 to 1827, he contributed furniture designs to Ackermann's Repository, which were reprinted in book form as *Gothic Furniture*.

Pugin, Augustus Welby Northmore (1812–52) The son of Augustus Charles PUGIN, he was trained by his father and began designing while still in his teens. He was responsible for the GOTHIC detailing of Barry's Houses of Parliament in London, designing masonry details, wallpapers, stained glass and tiles. He converted to Roman Catholicism in 1835 and designed many Catholic churches, often on very strict budgets. He was a member of the committee which selected objects from the 1851 Great Exhibition, to form the basis of the museum in South Kensington, which is now the Victoria and Albert Museum.

Putman, Andrée (1925–) French interior and furniture designer who worked in the 1960s as a stylist at Prisunic, where she created a range of inexpensive, well-designed furniture and housewares. She decorated the house of the French minister of culture in 1963 and founded a partnership with her husband, the Dutch businessman, Jacques Putnam, which developed into the furniture company, Ecart International. Their first commission was to design the YSL Rive Gauche shops in America, the office of Jack Lang, French minister of culture, and boutiques for Karl Lagerfeld, Thierry Mugler and Balenciaga. She is noted for her black-and-white interiors, such as the 1985 Morgan Hotel in New York.

Q

Quarti, Eugenio (1867–1931) Italian furniture designer who started work aged 14 in a factory near Paris. In 1888, he returned to Italy, where he worked for Carlo BUGATTI for a short time. He set up his own workshop and, after exhibiting in 1900 in Paris, gained a commission to furnish the Palazzo Castiglioni in Milan and in 1908 the Casino and Grand Hotel in Pellegrino. Working in the ART NOUVEAU, or Stile Floreale idiom, his pieces incorporated wood, silver, mother-of-pearl marquetry and cast bronze ornaments.

Queensberry, David Marquess of (1930–) British glassware and ceramics designer who worked in an industrial pottery in Stoke-on-Trent, before becoming professor of ceramics at the Royal College of Art, London. Notable pieces include the 1963 *Harlequin* range of cut glass for Webb Corbett. With Martin Hunt, a colleague at the Royal College, he founded the Queensberry-Hunt Design Group in 1964 and has collaborated on designs for ROSENTHAL.

Quinet, Jacques (1918–1994) French interior architect who was inspired by the Louis XVI style. He was a master cabinetmaker, designing the architectural interior and decoration of the 1953 liner *La Bourdonnais*.

R

Race, Ernest (1913–64) Briton who started out as a lighting designer, but turned to textile design after a visit to India, where his missionary aunt ran a weaving village near Madras. He opened a shop to sell these textiles woven to his own design. After the Second World War, he worked in an architects' office and then formed Ernest Race Ltd. to design furniture. His first success was the *B.A.3* chair, made from cast-aluminium. More than 250,000 were produced. For the 1951 Festival of Britain he designed the cheerful and popular *Antelope* and *Springbok* bent-metal chairs. Other successes included the 1952 *Woodpecker* chair and the 1957 Flamingo chair. He also designed furniture for the P&O and Royal Netherland shipping lines and the University of Liverpool Medical School.

Racinet, Albert Charles August (1825–93) French draughtsman and chromolithographer, who published his *L'Ornement Polychrome* in 1869, surpassing in quality Owen JONES' *Grammar of Ornament* which had inspired it. He also produced plates for AUDSLEY's *La Céramique Japonaise*.

Ranson, Pierre (1736–86) French painter and designer who was the nephew of the great Gobelins flower painter, Louis Tessier. In 1780, he became principal painter and designer at Aubusson. His application to become a painter at Gobelins was constantly refused. From 1778, he issued 471 plates of ornament, largely in rococo style, of flowers, trophies and vases. He also designed embroideries for waistcoats and bed linens, some in the Chinese manner.

Rasch, Heinz (1902–) and **Bodo** (1903–) German architects and designers who specialized in chair design. They founded a factory in Stuttgart in 1922 to pioneer the use of thin bent plywood. The brothers' 1924 *Radio* chair was designed for the hall of Süddeutscher Rudfunk and the 1927 *Sitzegeiststuhl* (Sitting ghost stool). Heinz was a pioneer of cantilevered chair design.

Rateau, Armand-Albert (1882–1938) French furniture designer and wood-carver who was director of the Avaloine interior decoration firm in 1905. After the First World War, he started his own practice working for private clients in the ART DÉCO style, including the Rothschilds in Antibes and the American art collectors, the Blumenthals. His style grew more NEO-CLASSICAL, though he had occasional lapses of taste, such as his fur-covered chairs and gold-lacquered walls for the duchesse d'Albe in Madrid.

Ratia, Armi (1912–79) Finnish textile designer who set up a weaving shop in Vyborg, producing rya rugs. In 1949, she began working for her husband, who was a manufacturer of oilcloth. She adapted the production of silk-screen printing on cotton sheeting.

Ravilious, Eric William (1903–42) British wood engraver and ceramics decorator who designed printers' ornaments for the Curwen, Golden Cockerel and Nonesuch presses, decorations for the BBC, London Transport pamphlets and advertisements for Austin Reed. He collaborated on the murals of the refreshment room of Morley College, London, and designed the British Pavilion at the 1937 Paris Exposition. In 1936, he designed a suite of furniture for the Dunbar Hay shop and designed bucolic images for transfer onto ceramic blanks, for Wedgwood. In 1935, he designed glassware for Stuart Crystal. He was an official war artist, and was lost on a flight from Iceland.

Redgrave, Richard (1804–88) British designer and administrator. After study at the Royal Academy Schools he taught drawing, becoming one of Henry COLE's assistants at the Somerset House, School of Design, He rose up the hierarchy to become Director of the Art Division of the Department of Education. Under the pseudonym of Felix Summerly he designed a glass jug, water bottles and glasses, decorated with water lilies, and paper hangings made by Simpsons. He was an advocate of the work of A. W. N. PUGIN and his formalized and conventional ornament. He was a member of the executive committee of the British Section of the 1855 Paris Exhibition.

Reiber, Émile Auguste (1826–93) Born in Alsace, which was variously German or French territory, he studied architecture, but was mainly a designer. He founded the influential pattern-book periodical *L'Art Pour Tous* in 1861 and defined renaissance revival designs. For the 1862 London Exhibition he prepared designs in the arabic style. From the 1860s, he designed metalwork for Christofle, becoming the artistic director of the firm in 1870. For the 1867 Paris Exhibition he showed imitations of Chinese cloisonné enamel and, throughout the 1870s, designed in the Japonese manner, being named the high priest of 'Japonisme'.

Reich, Lilly (1885–1947) German architect and furniture designer whose career is closely interwoven with Ludwig MIES VAN DER ROHE, who claimed title to many of her designs. Her first design was a rustic metal pitcher, completed before she joined the WIENER WERKSTÄTTE under Josef HOFFMANN. Her collaboration with Mies van der Rohe began at the 1927 Berlin 'Mode der Dame' exhibition, in which they designed the Silk section. She joined him at the BAUHAUS in 1932, becoming head of the weaving and interior design workshops. She designed the classic 1930 chaise, credit for which went to Mies van der Rohe, but it was undoubtedly all her work. It was recently put into production again by KNOLL. In 1933, she returned to Berlin, designing furniture for private residences. After a brief period with Mies van der Rohe in Chicago she returned to Germany, being forced to work for the Nazi state during the Second World War. From 1945, she concentrated on teaching, in Berlin.

Renwick, William Crosby (1814–92) American industrial designer who headed the product design department of Raymond LOEWY and became vice-president of the George NELSON practice, where he designed the seminal 1953 *Bubble Lamp*, which is still in production.

Ricketts, Charles de Sousy (1866–1931) Swiss illustrator who worked in Britain in the ART NOUVEAU style, influenced by William MORRIS. In addition to his book illustration, he designed for the theatre and produced small bronzes and jewellery.

Rie, Lucie (1902–1995) Austrian ceramicist who moved to Britain in 1938 setting up a pottery and button-making workshop. She designed her handmade buttons to match her customers' fabrics. In the 1940s, she designed sophisticated domestic wares, with Hans COPER.

Rinaldi, Gastone (1920–) Italian furniture designer who specializes in metal furniture. In 1955, he designed a dual-position chair in steel rods and raffia and, in 1958, the *Saturno* sofa. From 1977, he produced the *Aurora* stacking chair and the 1979 *Daphne* folding chair.

Robertson, Alexander W. (1840–1925) British ceramicist who worked in America. He settled there in 1853, opening the Chelsea Ceramic Art Works in Massachusetts. In 1884, he moved to California and worked in San Francisco at the Roblin Art Pottery, which was destroyed in the 1906 earthquake. They moved to Los Angeles until 1910 and then to Halcyon, California, a utopian Theosophist colony.

Robsjohn-Gibbings, Terence Harold (1905–76) British designer who gave up architectural studies to become an antique dealer in New York. In the 1930s, he became a successful interior designer in the NEO-CLASSICAL vein. From 1946 to 1956 he designed for the Grand Rapids furniture companies. In the early 1950s, he worked in the New England style, returning to the larger 'California' style, including his massive *Mesa* table.

Rococo From about 1735 the word 'rocaille', meaning rockwork, as in the decoration of grottoes, was used in France to describe the new fashion for shell and similar motifs in design. Strictly speaking rococo designs are based only on C or S scrolls. By the late 1700s it was used as a derogatory term for fussy design, but soon after became the accepted term for French design in the latter quarter of the 17th-century. Notable exponents of the style include the painter Boucher and the architect CUVILLIÉS. J. F. Blondel summed the style up as 'a ridiculous jumble of shells, dragons, reeds, palm trees and plants'.

Rogers, William Harry (1825–75) British woodcarver, the son of the celebrated carver, William Gibbs Rogers. He designed for him and others in the Renaissance manner, from the mid-1840s. He designed ornaments for the *Art Journal Illustrated Catalogue* of the 1851 Exhibition and a boxwood cradle for Queen Victoria shown in the exhibition. He also illustrated Shakespeare's *The Merchant of Venice*.

Rose, Joseph (1745–99) British head of a dynasty of decorative plasterers. He published Sketches for *Ornamental Frizes* (sic) in 1782, containing 331 designs by ADAM, WYATT and others.

Rosenthal German ceramics manufacturer founded by Philip Rosenthal who settled in America in the 1870s. He returned to Germany in 1880, to take over the family business, setting up an additional porcelain decorating factory near Selb. By 1954, the company was selling its wares through in-store outlets and was design-led. They established their Studio Haus throughout Europe and designed their first Studio Line range. Early pieces were designed by LOEWY and GROPIUS, a later generation including Bjørn Wiinblad, Tapio Wirkkala and Michael Boehm.

Rossetti, Dante Gabriel (1828–82) British painter and poet who shared a studio with Holman Hunt, with whom he and Millais founded the PRE-RAPHAELITE brotherhood, in 1848. Apart from his painting, which he gradually gave up after the death of his wife, in 1866, he was an influential designer. The style of the group influenced design of wallpapers, textiles and stained glass, in Britain and America. In the early years, he designed in all of these fields himself, being a founder member of the MORRIS, Marshall & Faulkney company. He also designed bookbindings, the most notable example being Christina Rossetti's *Goblin Market* of 1861.

Rossi, Angelo (1670–1742) Italian painter who worked as a decorative artist in Venice. His designs for chimneypieces, ceiling, doors and windows were published in London in 1753 as *A New Book of Ornaments*.

Rossi, Pucci de (1947–) Italian furniture designer who works in New York and Paris. He started as a sculptor, working in wood and then, metal. Many of his pieces are humorous, such as the 1982 *Tristan Table* and the 1985 *Bear Rug*. He also produced the 1991 *Lido* cocktail side table, *Lancelot* candelabra, *Parsifal* coffee table and *Maya* étagére.

Roupert, Louis (*fl.*1660s) German goldsmith and designer who published his suite of designs in 1668, comprising foliate scrolls, ACANTHUS and ornaments in black on white for engraving on silver. They feature putti and great branches of ornament and panoramic landscapes. A portrait of him accompanies the suite, showing another sheet of scrolling ornament and yet more scrolls emerging from a vase.

Rousseau, Clément (1872–1950) French sculptor who designed idiosyncratic pieces of furniture for wealthy clients at Neuilly, from 1912. He used rich materials, including inlays of exotic woods, shagreen, leather ivory and mother-of-pearl. He recreated the French styles of the 18th and 19th- centuries. In 1925 he collaborated with Jacques DOUCET.

Royal Copenhagen Porcelain Manufactury (Den Kongelige Porcelaensfabric) The first pottery in Copenhagen, which was established in 1755 under the patronage of King Frederick V. It produced soft- paste and Sèvres style porcelain. After the King's death the factory closed, reopening at the request of Queen Juliane Marie in 1807, when it was bombarded by the British fleet under Lord Nelson. The designs were undistinguished until the latter part of the 19th century. In the early 1900s, new forms and patterns were developed and workshops for stoneware and special glazes were set up. The 1790-1802 *Danica* pattern designed for Catherine the Great of Russia is still in production. In 1983, the company started to produce jewellery, merging with George JENSEN silversmiths in 1986. BING and GRØNDAHL joined the group, which is now owned by Carlsberg Tuborg.

Ruhlmann, Jacques Émile (1879–1933) French designer and

craftsman who began exhibiting furniture in the Salon d'Automne, in 1915. His exhibit at the 1925 Paris Exhibition combined classical luxury and Parisian modernism, exemplifying the ART DÉCO style. He decorated the tea-room of the 1926 liner *Ile-de-France*. He designed furniture, carpets and textiles for private clients including the Maharajah of Indore, using luxurious woods and metals. His best-known piece was the 1930 *Soleil* bed with rosewood veneer.

Ruskin, John (1819–1900) British writer and poet who won the Newdigate prize for poetry at Oxford. His aesthetic theories exerted a great influence upon such key designers as William MORRIS.

Russell, Gordon (1892–1980) British furniture maker and designer who worked in his father's antiques restoration business. He began to design furniture in 1910 in the ARTS AND CRAFTS style, but produced by machinery. He set up a shop in Wigmore Street, London, in 1929, with Nikolaus PEVSNER as manager and buyer. In 1931, he started to produce radio cabinets for Murphy. From 1939, he was influential in British furniture design, through his involvement with the Utility Scheme. He was an organizer of the 1951 Festival of Britain and was knighted in 1955.

S

Saarinen, Eero (1910–61) Finnish-born architect who was active in America. By the age of 19, he had designed furniture for his father's Kingswood School and, after studying at Yale, worked on further designs with Norman Bel GEDDES. From 1937, he collaborated with Charles EAMES, winning two prizes for their 1940 organic pieces. He later designed a bent plywood chair for KNOLL and the 1948 *Womb* chair of latex foam on a moulded plastic frame. He was a pioneer of sculptural furniture. His most notable building was the TWA Terminal at Kennedy Airport, New York.

Saarinen, Gottlieb Eliel (1873–1950) Finnish architect who was brought up in Russia, designing furniture early in his career, including pieces influenced by Charles Rennie MACKINTOSH and

Hugh BAILLIE SCOTT. He moved to America in 1923, and was appointed professor of architecture at the University of Michigan in 1923. Apart from his noted buildings, he designed rugs and textiles for the Cranbrook Academy of Art and a dining room to exhibit at the Metropolitan Museum in New York. He also designed silverware for the 1927 Paris Exhibition.

Sabattini, Lino (1925–) Italian metalsmith and designer whose early work is exemplified by the 1950 teapot for W. Wolff in Germany. Moving to Milan in 1955, he met Gio PONTI who included his works in the 1956 Milan Exhibition. He became director of design at Christofle Orfeverie in Paris, producing free-flowing forms such as the 1960 *Como* tea service. He also designed ceramics and glassware for ROSENTHAL and the 1976 *Sauciére*, manufactured by his own company, near Como. He also produced black titanium tableware, such as the 1986 *Insect Legs* service.

Saint-Aubin, Gabriel Jacques (1724–80) French painter who published engravings of vase designs in the BAROQUE manner, as well as snuff boxes, watches and other trinkets. His drawings of contemporary interiors and entertainments, found on the margins of sale catalogues, have been preserved and are a vivid illustration of the progress of designs of the time.

Sala, Bienvenue (1869–1939) Spanish glassmaker who settled in Paris in 1905, establishing a glass workshop in the Montparnasse quarter, He produced mainly vases, decorated with vegetable and animal motifs. He was the father of Jean SALA.

Sala, Jean (1895–1976) Spanish glassmaker and designer who worked in Paris with his father, Bienvenue SALA. He also designed vessels and chandeliers for the Cristalleries de Saint-Louis in clear crystal. He gave up glassmaking in 1953, to become an antiques dealer.

Sala, Pierre (1948–89) French furniture and stage designer who founded the Marie Stuart Theatre in Paris. In 1973, he set up his own firm, Furnitur, to produce his designs, which included the 1983 CLAIREFONTAINE desk, of which he sold 5,000. His lacquered chairs were also popular, including the *Piranha* and *Mare aux canards* models. He opened a shop at the Musée d'Orsay to sell his furniture, objects and clothing.

Sapper, Richard (1932–) German industrial designer who worked for Mercedes-Benz in 1956 and 1957, before moving to Milan to work for Gio PONTI in 1958. He is best-known for his high technology products such as the 1962 *Doney* and 1964 *Algol* television sets and the 1965 *Grillo* folding telephone for Siemens. For Artemide he designed the skeletal 1972 *Tizio* clock and the *Tantulo* clock. From 1981, he was product designer for IBM. His designs married the precision of Germany with the sensual qualities of Italy.

Schawinsky, Alexander (1904–79) Swiss designer who designed for the theatre from 1926, moving on to graphic design for Olivetti and Motta in Italy, in 1933. In 1936, Josef Albers invited him to teach in America at Black Mountain College, North Carolina. He collaborated with GROPIUS and BREUER on the design of the 1939 New York World's Fair and with Luigi Fugino on the 1936 Studio 42 portable typewriter for Olivetti.

Schlumberger, Jean (1907–) French jewellery designer who worked in Paris and New York. He collaborated with Elsa Schiaparelli, designing buttons and jewels for her *Circus* collection. From the late 1930s his best-known piece is an articulated cigarette lighter in the form of a fish. In 1940, he left Paris for New York, producing a stream of distinguished pieces in animal and vegetable forms, including angels and hippopotami, composed of semi-precious stones. In 1955, he became the first exclusive designer at TIFFANY, where he later became a vice-president.

Schmied, François-Louis (1873–1941) Swiss illustrator and designer who came to note through his illustrations for Rudyard Kipling's *Jungle Book*, some of which were printed in as many as 25 colours. To ensure good reproduction he set up his own printing press in Paris. He also produced lacquered panels with Jean Dunand, some of which he incorporated in his bookbindings. After the 1929 Stock Market crash he was declared bankrupt and all his possessions were auctioned. He retired to the Moroccan desert, to refurbish an old fort.

Schreiber, Gaby (1912–) Austrian designer who worked in London on interiors including National Westminster Bank branches,

Peter Robinson stores, Gulf Oil and Fine Fare Supermarkets. She was general consultant designer for the 1965 liners *Queen Elizabeth II* and *Cunarder*, and to Zarach, Allen and Hanbury and the BOAC airline (now British Airways). In the 1930s and 1940s, she designed a range of modern domestic plastic tableware, including her plastic meat tray. Later, she became consultant on plastics for Marks and Spencer and yachts for Sir Gerald d'Erlanger and Whitney Straight.

Schwanzer, Karl (1918–75) Austrian furniture designer whose chairs were intended for mass production. He designed the panorama of the Alps at the Austrian pavilion at Expo '67, in Montreal.

Scott, Giles Gilbert (1880–1960) Distinguished British architect whose buildings include the Liverpool Anglican Cathedral, Waterloo Bridge and Battersea Power Station. As a designer his signature piece was the 1936 *Model K6* red telephone box, known as the Jubilee Kiosk. When British Telecom announced plans to replace them in 1988, there was a public outcry and many were reprieved.

Scott, Isaac Elwood (1845–1920) American furniture designer and wood carver who worked in Chicago from 1873. He carved ornaments for Chicago Terra Cotta and, in 1875, became a partner in the architectural office of Frederick W. Copeland. He designed vases for the Chelsea Ceramic Art Works in Massachusetts in 1879. In the 1880s, he began designing textiles and embroideries. In 1888, he moved to Boston where he taught wood carving at the Eliot School.

Scott, William Bell (1811–1900) British painter who was a minor member of the Pre-Raphaelite circle. He produced numerous designs for urns, cups, picture frames, tables, stands and other furnishings. From 1844 to 1864, he taught at the School of Design in Newcastle. He published his illustrated thesis *The Ornamentalist* in 1845.

Seddon, John Pollard (1827–1906) British architect who worked with John Pritchard in Wales from 1852 to 1862 and with John Coates Carter from 1884 to 1904. He designed furniture for William Morris, including the *King René's Honeymoon* cabinet, decorated by Ford Madox Brown, Edward BURNE-JONES and Dante Gabriel ROSSETTI. Other pieces showed the influence of A. W. N. PUGIN. He designed many tiles and ecclesiastical garments.

Selmersheim, Pierre (1869–1941) French architect and decorator who decorated an apartment in 1902 that avoided 'superfluous ornamental forms and acrobatic accomplishments'. He designed many domestic articles, which were produced by Socard and GALLÉ.

Seymour, Richard (1953–) British industrial designer who formed the Seymour-Powell consultancy with Dick Powell, in 1983. They styled the Norton 1987 police/military *Commander* and *P55 Sport* motorcycles. They designed a successful line of Tefal domestic products, including the 1987 *Freeline* cordless electric jug-kettle.

Shaker An austere style of furniture design, produced by the Shaker sect on the east coast of America. They originated in England in 1747, as the United Society of Believer's in Christ's Second Appearance. To escape persecution, a group went to America, establishing their first community in 1787 in New Lebanon, New York State. The Shaker style developed from English country and farm house models and is known for its simplicity.

Shaw, [Richard] Norman (1831–1912) Scottish-born British architect whose early work was in the GOTHIC style. In 1862 Shaw set up his own office, then went into partnership with W. E. Nesfield in 1866 developing his designs through Old English and Queen Anne styles. Despite his own talents as a furniture designer, he employed others, including BURNE-JONES for the fittings of his churches in particular.

Sheringham, George (1884–1937) British interior and textile designer who started as a painter, designing fans and silk panels by 1911. He designed numerous sets and costumes for the Lyric Theatre, Hammersmith, London. He decorated Claridge's ballroom in 1931 and designed carpets for John Crossley and Sons.

Shire, Peter (1947–) American designer who was invited by Ettore SOTTSASS to design for Memphis. He came up with eccentric furniture in Pop Art colours and kinetic shapes. In 1989, he designed a 63-piece collection of furniture for manufacture in

Italy. He created exciting new shapes for Murano glass and his ceramic teapots verge upon sculpture.

Sinclair, Clive (1940–) British electronics engineer who produced the first pocket calculator, the 1972 *Executive* and the 1976 *Microvision* pocket television. In 1980, he launched the *ZX80* inexpensive personal computer, which outsold all others. His 1985 innovative *C5* electric car was a commercial flop.

Smith, John Moyr (1864–94) British decorative artist who began working in the 1860s in the design studio of Christopher DRESSER. In the 1870s, he executed some designs for Collison and Lock furniture makers and published his *Ornamental Interiors, Ancient and Modern*, in 1887. From 1875, he carried out designs for tiles for MINTON, some of which appear in his *Album of Decorative Figures*, published in 1882.

Solon, Léon Victor (1872–1957) French designer, son of the distinguished designer, Marc Solon, at Sèvres porcelain factory and later with MINTON at Stoke-on-Trent. He was Minton's designer from 1900 to 190g, when he emigrated to America. He decorated the Philadelphia Museum of Fine Arts.

Sottsass, Ettore (1917–) Austrian designer who started out as an architect in 1947, opening a studio in Milan. From 1957, he was consultant to Olivetti, designing computers, typewriters, adding machines and systems furniture. From 1966, his furniture design was affected by Pop Art. He produced ceramics influenced by Indian shapes and motifs. In 1980, he set up Sottsass Associati and created the Memphis furniture and furnishings group, which gave opportunities to many new designers. In 1986, he set up the advertising agency Italiana di Communicazione, which had more than 100 clients worldwide.

Spratling, William (1900–67) American architect and silversmith who worked in Mexico, after a teaching career in New Orleans. His hand-crafted wares took their inspiration from native and rustic shapes, carried out in unusual gems, the silverware often incorporating mother-of-pearl, feathers, baroque pearls tortoiseshell and coral. They were sold at exclusive stores, such as Nieman Marcus and TIFFANY, and ordered by film stars and presidents, including Orson Welles and Lyndon Johnson.

Starck, Philippe (1949–) French designer who produced his first piece of furniture, the 1968 folding *Francesca* Spanish chair, at the age of 18. In 1969, he became artistic director at Pierre Cardin, but did not make an impact until he designed the interiors of two nightclubs in Paris. In 1982, together with four other designers, he laid out a room for President Mitterand at the Elysée Palace. In 1984, he was commissioned to design the Café Costes, the chair he designed for it selling over 400,000 copies. In 1984 he designed a range of furniture for the mail-order firm Trois Suisses. His La Cigale discothèque was built in Paris in 1988, and he designed furniture for Driade and many other companies. Alessi produced his domestic goods and his 1988 crystal collection was made by DAUM. He always chooses unusual names for his pieces, such as the *Ubik* range, which were named after characters in Philip K. Dick's science fiction novel of that title. His impressive and innovative interiors include those of the Royalton and Paramount Hotels in New York, the 1991 *Royalton* chair being produced by Driade. He has designed a bottle for Vittel mineral water and his 1989 *Fluocaril* toothbrush and stand has been described as 'the ultimate designer toothbrush'.

Steuben American glasswork manufacturer based at Corning, New York State. It was founded in 1903, to produce glass blanks for T. G. Hawkes, a glass-cutting firm. Frederick CARDER came from England to be artistic director and he extended the range of goods, including vases, paperweights, candlesticks, goblets and light-shades. After the Second World War the company grew solidly, producing glass of the highest quality and crystal commemorative pieces. President Harry S. Truman presented a Steuben 1947 *Merry-go-Round Bowl* to the then Princess Elizabeth as a wedding present. In the 1950s, the company began commissioning British designers, including Graham SUTHERLAND and John Piper, together with the engraver, Laurence Whistler. The Corning Institute is one of the world's most important centres for the study or glass and glass-making.

Stevens, Brooks (1911–) American industrial designer of the first electric clothes drier and the first snow-mobile and out-board motor. He designed the 1950 Harley-Davidson motorcycle (with the twin engine, still in use today) and the 1959 *Lawn Boy* motor mower. Car bodies include those for the 1940 Packard and Alpha Romeo and Volkswagen. A major achievement was the first wide-mouthed peanut butter jar, which allowed access to the bottom. He worked with Formica to develop the wood-grain laminate and was responsible for the first use of avocado as a colour for bathroom fittings.

traub, Marianne (1909–) Swiss weaver who worked mostly in Britain. In the 1930s, she worked under Ethel MAIRET and revitalized the flagging Welsh weaving industry. In 1951, she designed for the Festival of Britain, became a consultant to HEAL Fabrics and taught at both the Central and Royal Schools of Art, in London. Her *Tamesa* range was used on the 1934 liner *Queen Mary* and the 1965-8 *Queen Elizabeth II*

Stumpf, Axel (1957–) German designer who works in Berlin in an avant-garde manner. His 1986 *Kumpel I* and *Kumpel II* tables were constructed from three pick-axes and plate glass.

Stumpf, Bill (1936–) American industrial designer who created the 1966 version of the *Ergon* chair for Herman Miller, where he was vice-president in charge of research from 1970 to 1973. In 1973, he set up his own company with Donald Chadwick, designing the 1979-84 *Equa* plastic chair and the 1984 *Ethospace* open-plan office system.

Süe, Louis (1875–1968) French architect and painter who designed German-influenced furniture in the first years of this century. He formed a design company with André MARE, called Compagnie des Artes Française, and employed leading artists as decorators. They included Marie Laurenáin, André Derain, Aristide Maillol and Raoul DUFY. The hallmark of the company's design was the spectacular, large-scale approach, with excessive decoration and gilding. They designed silver for Orfèverie Christofle and the interiors of several liners, including the lounge of the 1926 *Ile-de-France*. Apartments were created for the couturier Jean Patou and the actress Jane Renouard, and the salon of the d'Orsay perfume shop, for whom they also designed a bottle. In 1928, Jacques ADNET took over as design director and Süe returned to architecture, building for Helena Rubenstein and others.

Summers, Gerald (1899–1987) British furniture designer who rivalled the great continental designers in the 1930s. Comparable to the bent-wood and metal designs of AALTO and BREUER, his designs are milestones in the development of modern furniture design. His pieces were marked by a lack of ornament and the stressed the importance of function. His two classic pieces are the 1934 *Bent Plywood Lounge Chair* and the curved *High Back Chair*.

Sutherland, Graham Vivian (1903–80) British painter who, before 1935, worked as an etcher and engraver. He also produced decorations for tableware for Brain's Ceramics at Fenton and for Wilkison's Pottery, under the direction of Clarice CLIFF. His most popular design was the 1966 tapestry, *Christ in Glory*, for Coventry Cathedral.

Szekely, Martin (1956–) French furniture designer who began as a copper-plate engraver. In the mid-1970s, he designed furniture, including the *Ar* stool and a 25-piece range for the Sauvagnat company. His 1980 *Coin* range was made of wood and aluminium. He worked extensively in stark black carbon steel, such as the 1980 *Cornette* chair and *Pi* range. In Italy, he worked with Ettore SOSSTASS and designed the 1986 *Carbone* chair.

T

Tackett, La Gardo (1911–1994) American ceramicist and teacher at the California School of Design in Los Angeles. He and his students developed outdoor pottery planters, which led to the formation of Architectural Pottery in 1950. He was noted for his hourglass shapes for both indoor and outdoor pottery. In 1957, he designed a range of dinnerware for Schmid International and, from 1963, was manager of the object division of Herman Miller.

Taeuber-Arp, Sophie (1889–1943) Swiss artist and designer and wife of the artist and sculptor, Jean ARP. She made collages, embroideries, stage designs and puppets. At Meudon, near Paris, she founded the abstract art periodical *Plastique*, which lasted for only five issues.

Talbert, Bruce J. (1838–81) British architect of the Corn Exchange Hall in Dundee. In the early 1860s, he started to design furniture in the simple GOTHIC style and, shortly after, to work in silver and wrought iron. He settled in London in 1865, designing furniture for Holland and Sons. In 1867, he published his *Gothic Forms Applied to Furniture, Metalwork, and Decoration for Domestic Purposes*, which influenced cabinetmaking in Britain and America. His ecclesiastical metalwork was made by Cox, his wallpaper by Jeffrey. He also designed textiles and his ironwork was made by Coalbrookdale. His style developed from Gothic to Jacobean as he became one of the leading designers of the Aesthetic Movement.

Tapiovaara, Ilmari (1914–1995) Finnish interior and furniture designer who worked for Alvar AALTO in his London office in 1935 and 1936. He then worked for LE CORBUSIER in Paris. In the 1940s and 1950s he was one of the pioneers of knock-down furniture. For the 1952 Olivetti showroom in Helsinki, his stacking *Lukki* chair was designated 'the universal chair'. He designed cutlery, radio and stereo equipment, a colour-planning system for the paint manufacturer Winter and wall paintings and tapestries. Interiors included a concert Hall in St Petersburg, aeroplanes for Finnair and the 1973 Intercontinental Hotel, Helsinki.

Taylor, Michael (1927–86) American interior and furniture designer who frequently used logs and wicker for his furniture, to set of his beige-on-beige decors. He set up his practice in 1956, after working with Frances Mihailoff in San Francisco. He was influenced by the style of Syrie MAUGHAM and had many show-business clients.

Teague, Walter Dorwin (1883–1960) American industrial designer who opened a studio for advertising and book design in 1911. In the 1920s, he expanded his range and designed piano cases for Steinway. His first major client was Eastman Kodak for whom he designed the 1936 Baby Brownie camera. He designed coaches for the New Haven railroad, the 1937 Ford showroom in New York and Texaco service stations. His crystal designs were made by STEUBEN Glass. He designed the 1932 Philadelphia 'Design for the Machine' Exhibition. With Frank del Guidice he designed the Boeing 707 and 727 airline interiors. Much of his work was undertaken by teams, directed by him.

Templier, Raymond (1891–1968) French jewellery designer who joined the long-established family firm in 1912. He was known for his ART DÉCO designs made of gold, lacquer, silver and eggshells, in simple geometric shapes. His designs for cigarette cases, hip flasks and boxes were influenced by cars, planes and sports. He also designed jewellery for the Marcel l'Herbier films *L'Inhumaine* (1923) and *L'Argent* (1928). In 1929, Marcel Percheron joined the firm as a sketch artist, faithfully executing details of Templier's designs for 36 years.

Testa, Angelo (1921–) American fabric designer of the 1941 *Little Man* abstract floral fabric, which received wide publicity. It was hailed as a new direction in fabric design. He produced a range of similar abstract designs, some with matching wallpapers, for clients including KNOLL. He also worked on patterns for laminates, vinyls and fibreglass panels.

Thierrat, Augustin (1798–1870) French painter who was brought up in poverty following the 1793 Seige of Lyon, becoming professor of painting at the Lyon Ecole dea Beaux-Arts. In 1823, he was appointed professor of floral design and taught the next generation of designers. He designed textiles, before becoming curator of the Lyon Museum.

Thonet, Michael (1796–1871) German furniture maker and designer who employed renowned cabinet makers in his early days. In 1841, he was invited to Vienna by Count Metternich and sold furniture to members of the imperial court and the nobility. He was interested in the possibility of mass-production and, by 1856, had designed his own factory, from architecture to machinery, in the Moravian forests, near to a supply of beechwood for his bentwood furniture. He invented new ways of making simple, unornamented, pieces, which made him the most innovative of 19th-century furniture designers. He took out patents in several countries for his manufacturing process. The firm continued after his death and, in 1888, produced the folding theatre seat. Their *Chair No. 4* has sold 50 million copies worldwide and was much admired by LE CORBUSIER. The French branch of the company was opened in 1929, to produce chromium-plated steel furniture to designs by BREUER, Le Corbusier, JEANNERET and Charlotte PERRIAND. In 1932, Gilbert RHODE designed chairs in America for the company, which is still in existence.

Tiffany, Charles Louis (1812–1902) American design entrepreneur who opened a fancy goods and stationery store on Broadway, New York, with John B. Young. From 1841, he started to stock jewellery from Paris, glass from Bohemia and porcelain from Dresden. As the shop grew bigger, the stock grew grander and, in 1848, they started making their own pieces. They opened a Paris branch in 1850, where, it is reputed, they bought the diamonds of Marie Antoinette, the Esterhazy treasures and part of the French crown jewels. At the same time they started designing their own silverware and they were the first in America to adopt the English sterling silver standard. To satisfy the demand for Japanese design among their European clients, they hired Christopher DRESSER to bring back *objéts d'art* from Japan. A collection of 2000 pieces was sold in 1878. Louis Comfort TIFFANY joined his father in the business and became director of the jewellery workshops in 1902.

Tiffany, Louis Comfort (1848–1933) American designer and glass maker. He studied painting in New Jersey, before going to Paris in 1868. In the late 1870s, he developed an interest in the decorative arts and, in 1879, founded an interior design company. He had many successful commissions, on which he collaborated with fellow artists. He participated in the decoration of Mark Twain's house in 1880 and several rooms in the White House in 1882. He designed notable wallpapers, including his wild clematis and cobweb pattern. In 1885, his interest in glass, led to the founding of the Tiffany Glass Company in 1885. He visited the Paris 1889 Exhibition, where he met BING, who had supplied oriental goods to the family shop. Bing became Tiffany's exclusive European distributor. Tiffany glass specialised in stained, opalescent and lustre glass, the latter being patented in 1881. The Tiffany *Four Seasons* window was shown at the 1892 Paris Exhibition and, in 1895, Bing displayed Tiffany stained glass designed by Pierre Bonnard, Vuillard, TOULOUSE-LAUTREC and others. His Favrile glass, irridescent, elegant and colourful became the epitome of the ART NOUVEAU style.

Toft, Charles (*c.*1831–1909) British potter and metalworker who was educated at the School of Design, Stoke-on-Trent. In the 1860s, he designed metalwork for Elkingtons and taught at Birmingham School of Art. From 1872, he designed ceramics for MINTON, being particularly involved in the revival of the 16th-century French 'Henri II' ware. He later opened his own factory.

Toulouse-Lautrec, Henri (1864–1901) French painter and graphic artist who designed his first poster in 1891 for the Moulin Rouge cabaret. By 1900, he had done some 31 posters, influenced by Japanese prints. He was associated with the ART NOUVEAU movement in France and Belgium and designed stained glass windows for BING, made by Louis Comfort TIFFANY.

Traquair, Phoebe Anna (1852–1936) Irish-born enameller, jewellery and tapestry designer who worked in Scotland. She worked first on domestic embroidery, specializing in large panels in the medieval manner, influenced by medieval manuscripts sent to her by John RUSKIN. She produced enamels that were pale and sometimes executed on silver rather than copper, becoming deeper from 1905. She was the first woman to be appointed honourary member of the Royal Scottish Academy.

Tribel, Annie (1933–) French furniture designer who joined Atelier d'Urbanisme et d'Architecture in 1962, designing interiors for youth clubs, rest homes and theatres, including Le Theatre de la Ville, Paris. She has designed for public institutions including the French Embassy in New Delhi and private guest rooms of the Palais d'Elysée.

Tupper, Earl (1907–83) American chemist and inventor who saw the commercial possibilities of polyethylene, invented by ICI in 1939. He stumbled on a technique which enabled him to mould the material into a range of air-tight, lightweight and unbreakable kitchen containers. He founded Tupper Plastic in 1942 and devised the 'Tupperware Party' method of marketing, where housewives entertained friends and sold the products. He abandoned plans to expand his business in 1955 and sold the company to Rexall Drug.

Tschichold, Jan (1902–74) German typographer and design theorist who was influenced by a visit to the BAUHAUS in 1924. In 1926, he moved from Berlin to Munich where he designed many innovative posters for the Phoebus-Palast cinema. In 1928, he published *Die neue Typographie*, codifying the new typography as practised at the Bauhaus. At the invitation of McKnight KAUFFER, the publisher Lund Humphries sponsored the 1935 exhibition of his work in London. Commissions to design the *Penrose Annual* of 1938 and other books followed. He moved to England in 1947 for two years working for Penguin Books, designing over 500 titles. He returned to direct the publicity department of Hoffman-Laroche Pharmaceuticals.

U

Ungers, Oswald Mathias (1926–) German architect whose furniture and carpet designs are based on geometric forms and variations on the square. He contributed to Dialog's 1988 carpet collection.

Urban, Joseph (1872–1933) Austrian painter and architect who was a member of the WIENER WERKSTÄTTE. His work was craft-orientated as shown by his Austrian Pavilion for the 1904 St Louis Exposition. His illustrations show the influence of Aubrey BEARDSLEY, as did his stage designs when he worked briefly at the Boston Opera. In New York, he became resident designer of Florenz Ziegfeld's Follies for 12 editions. From 1917, he was artistic director at the Metropolitan Opera, New York, designing 55 productions. He designed the interiors of the 1931 Park Avenue Club and sets for a further 18 Broadway shows. He was the first designer to use Modern and ART DÉCO designs for films. In 1925, he returned to architecture, his buildings including the 1927 Ziegfeld Theatre and the Mar-a-Lago house for Marjorie Merriweather, now owned by Donald J. Trump, in Palm Beach, Florida.

Utzon, Jørn (1918–) Danish architect and town planner who worked in the style of AALTO and Frank Lloyd WRIGHT. His best-known building is the Sydney Opera House. He designed furniture in the late 1960s and early 1970s, including the 1967 range for Hansen, based on a system of component arcs locking at 45-degree angles.

V

Valentien, Anna Marie (1862–1950) and **Albert R.** (1847–1925) American ceramicists. Anne Marie Bookprinter worked in the decorating department of Rookwood Pottery, which was run by Albert Valentien. Restricted by the artistic policy there they left in 1905, leaving for San Diego where Albert was commissioned to paint California's wild flowers. They set up the Valentien Pottery where they could experiment with sculptural and organic forms. The pottery was active until 1914.

Van Alen, William (1883–1954) American architect whose signature building was the wildly creative Chrysler Building in New York, begun in 1928. There are decorative brickwork friezes of car wheels and radiator caps, and stainless steel gargoyles on the 31st floor, all the decoration being inspired by the Chrysler car. The building's lobby was one of the most striking examples of ART DÉCO in America, incorporating dramatic murals, cream and red marble walls and lift doors inlaid with African woods in abstract floral designs.

van de Velde, Henry Clemens (1863–1957) Belgian architect whose own house, designed as an organic whole from architecture to furniture, furnishings and fittings, was a classic of the ART NOUVEAU style. When BING saw it, he was so impressed that he invited him to design four rooms at his Paris shop. In Germany, he designed the interior of the Folkwang Museum at Hagen and silver for the court jewellers of the Grand-Duke of Saxe-Weimar. With the coming of the First World War he had to give up his teaching post at Weimar, moving to Switzerland, returning to Belgium in 1925. He founded the Instituts des Arts Décoratifs de La Cambrai and was professor of architecture, University of Ghent from 1926 to 1936.

van den Broeke, Floris (1945–) Dutch furniture designer who works in London, after study at the Academy of Art, Arnhem, and the Royal College of Art, London. He was one of the fashionable designers of the 1960s, exhibiting one-off pieces at the Whitechapel Gallery, in 1974, with a retrospective at the Design Museum, in 1991, both in London.

van Doesburg, Theo (1883–1931) Dutch architect who was one of the founding members of the DE STIJL group, which published the journal of the same name, in 1917, the manifesto of architects and artists who sought a radical review of art. He was known for his use of primary colours in his stained glass and floors. Interiors included the colour scheme for a little flower room at the de Noailles villa at Hyeres and the renovation of the Café L'Aubette in Strasbourg from 1926 to 1928. With his death, the de Stijl movement came to an end.

Vasari, Giorgio (1511–74) Italian glass painter from Arezzo who moved to Florence in 1524, studying under a goldsmith as well as painting. In 1530, he collaborated on the design of triumphal arches to commemorate the coronation of the Emperor Charles V. At the end of 1531, he moved to Rome to work closely with Michelangelo and Raphael. He began work on his monumental catalogue of architectural designs in 1550, reissuing a revised version in 1568. In 1554, he returned to Florence to work as painter, architect and artistic impresario for Duke Cosimo I de' Medici at the Palazzo Vecchio. His designs for Cosimo included a cameo, tapestries on the Life of Man, map cupboards and a table supported by two sphinxes. He also designed decorations at the marriage of Giovanna d'Austria to Francesco de' Medici, for whom he also designed vases. His many church fittings included the choir stalls of Arezzo Cathedral, a wooden tabernacle for the cathedral of Sante Croce in Florence and the carved organ case of the church of the Cavalier di Santo Stefano.

Vassos, John (1898–1985) Greek illustrator who was born in Bucharest and worked in Boston. He designed packaging, being a pioneer in the use of applied psychology to determine the effectiveness of labels, packages and containers. For Coca-Cola, he designed bottle dispensers that suggested coolness, the body of the bottle suggesting valuable contents. From the 1930s to the 1960s, he designed sound equipment for RCA and in 1939, he patented a streamlined child's tricycle and a harmonica. He also took commissions for interior design.

Vergottini, Bruno (1935–) Italian industrial designer who started his career in 1968 in fashion as well as industrial and interior design. He designs ceramics, textiles, furniture and umbrellas. For Innocenti he devised colour coordination for cars.

Villeroy et Boch German ceramics and glassware manufacturer, located at Mettlach. In the 18th century, François Boch and the Villeroy families founded separate factories. In 1936, these were amalgamated to produce tiles, sanitary fittings and tableware and glassware. From the early 1960s, the company broke away from its traditional shapes and began issuing striking contemporary designs. In 1973, they issued a melamine range and in 1991, Paloma Picasso's designs.

Vincent, René (1879–1936) French ceramicist and illustrator who drew illustrations for *La Vie Parisienne* and *L'Illustration*, the drawing slowly changing from Art Nouveau to Art Déco. He designed vases, table services, clocks and opened a workshop at Sèvres.

Viollet-le-Duc, Eugène Emanuel (1814–79) French architect and historian whose energies were mainly directed to the restoration of ancient buldings, with detailed research into styles and materials. His principal work was at Notre-Dame from 1845 to 1865 and the Chateau de Pierrefonds from 1868 to 1870. His first teaching appointment was as professor or ornamental composition in Paris at the age of 20.

Voysey, Charles Francis Annesley (1857–1941) British architect, he was the son of an Anglican clergyman, who was dismissed from the church for his unconventional beliefs. After the family moved to London, Voysey began work in the office of the architect John Pollard Seddon. He set up his own practise in 1882, designing many medium-sized houses, including H. G. Wells' Spade House, Sandgate, Kent. He also designed textiles and wallpapers for his houses and for other manufacturers.

Vuitton, Louis French luggage manufacturer which was founded by Louis Vuitton in 1860 to design trunks with flat tops which made them stackable in the holds of liners, or able to stand upright in staterooms. They were originally covered in elegant grey Trianon canvas. He was so successful that he became the Empress Eugénie's favourite 'packer'. To discourage counterfeiters, the 'LV' symbol was imprinted on paint impregnated canvas in 1896. Ironically it is one of the most counterfeited symbols today. The writing desk trunk, designed for Leopold Stokowski, is still available. In 1959, the company added accessories, scent bottles and manicure sets to its range. In the 1980s, the Epi non-mongrammed series in coloured leather was introduced.

W

Wagenfeld, Wilhelm (1900–1990) German architect and industrial designer who was an assistant instructor at the BAUHAUS at Weimar from 1925 to 1929. There he designed lighting fixtures, including one in nickel-plated brass with a disk base resting on three hemispherical padded feet, and a cylindrical column surmounted by a metal ring supporting the hemispherical shade. It was regarded as representing the basic Bauhaus philosophy. In 1929, he became director of the metalworking department, also designing in glass and carving wood cuts. While teaching in Berlin, he designed commercially, including the 1932 teapot and diffuser, the 1934 coffee percolator, both mass-produced. He designed pressed-glass utility units including cube-shaped dishes which stacked into a cube and a 1938 zig-zag-shaped ink bottle. His 1939 *Oberweimer* set of glasses, intended to introduce good design to the working-classes at affordable prices, outsold any other set of glasses made worldwide. After the Second World War, he designed porcelain for ROSENTHAL, appliances for BRAUN and inflight catering packs for Lufthansa.

Wall, James E. (d.1917) American furniture manufacturer who produced pieces made from imported bamboo and lacquered panels, ranging from fire screens to chairs, curtain poles to plant stands. In 1896, he became a stockbroker, returning to furniture making in 1901 as a partner in the wallpaper hangers Wall and Brackett. They imported wallpapers from Britain and France, and grasscloth and leather from Japan.

Walton, Alan (1891–1948) British painter, decorator and architect who set up his textile company, with his brother, in 1925. He commissioned some of the most interesting screen prints of the 1930s from Vanessa BELL and Duncan GRANT, who also designed carpets for him. In the late 1920s, he became head of the design department at the Fortnum and Mason store, decorating many private homes. His 1925 design for the Restaurant Français in Leicester Square, brought customers to see his decor as much as for the food. Overseen by Clough Williams-Ellis, he also designed the Restaurant BOULESTIN.

Ward, Neville (1922–) British interior designer who designed the exterior of the Design Centre in London. He designed a Thameside restaurant for the 1951 Festival of Britain, interiors for Sealink Ferries, the line *Oriana* and products ranging from pianos to plastic laminates.

Webb, Philip (1831–1915) British architect who met William MORRIS in 1856 and became influenced by the writings of John RUSKIN. In 1859, he started to design Morris's Red House, with an asymmetrical and free ground plan, an early example of domestic architecture in the GOTHIC Revival style. In 1861, he went into partnership with Morris, designing solid furniture in oak, stained glass and metalwork with medieval overtones.

Weber, Karl Emanuel Martin (1889–1963) German designer who was stranded in America at the outbreak of the First World War, whe he was in San Francisco to design the German section of the 1915 International Exposition. He worked for various studios in Los Angeles, opening his own studio in Hollywood in 1927. Key pieces include two silver cocktail shakers with ebony handles that he designed for Friedman Silver in New York. They were starkly simple in the Modern idiom. Though he lived in California all his life similar silver pieces and multifunctional furniture inspired by the New York skyline had as great an effect on the city's design conscience as if he had lived there.

Weil, Bruno Austrian architect who adopted the pseudonym B. W.

(the German pronunciation of his initials) as a furniture designer, producing the designs of architects such as LE CORBUSIER and Charlotte PERRIAND. He was the director of the French branch of THONET and produced domestic and office furniture, the latter influenced by EAMES.

Weil, Daniel (1953–) Argentinian architect who worked in London designing a range of designer clocks and radios for his own company, Parenthesis. His 1984 deconstructed radio had coloured separate parts in a clear plastic bag, to be wall-hung. Other radios were screen printed in bright colours, with exposed workings.

Welch, Robert Radford (1929–) British product designer and silversmith who set up his workshop in Chipping Camden to work in the ARTS AND CRAFTS tradition. From 1955, was consultant to Old Hall Tableware for which he designed a classic stainless steel toast rack and cutlery. His designs became influenced by Scandinavian design in the late 1950s and he produced a whole range of products including door furniture, alarm clocks, bathroom fittings and cast-iron utensils. His 1979 professional kitchen knife produced by Kitchen Devils is still very widely used.

Wharton, Edith Newbold (1862–1937) American writer and interior designer who collaborated with Ogden CODMAN on interiors and the influential book *The Decoration of Houses* in 1897 observing 'We have passed from the golden age of architecture to the gilded age of decoration'.

Whistler, Rex (1904–44) British theatre designer and *trompe l'oeil* muralist. His best known decorations are in the restaurant of the Tate, Gallery, London and Plas Newydd, the Anglesey home of the Marquis. He designed the monumental carved wood urns to commemorate Sir Samuel Courtauld, catalogues for Fortnum and Mason, earthenware for Wedgwood and carpets for the Wilton Royal Carpet Factory.

Wiener Werksätte In 1897, a group of artists led by Gustav KLIMT made a break from the academic style of painting, the motto of which was 'To the age its art, to art its freedom'. The group, known as the Vienna Secession, included MOSER, GRASSET and

BURNE-JONES and it exhibited work by Josef HOFFMAN and Charles Rennie MACKINTOSH. In 1903, Moser established the Wiener Werkstätte and appointed Hoffman artistic director. In 1905, other members of the Vienna Secession left and the Wiener Werkstätte became a centre for progressive design, characterized by rectilinear styling. After 1915 the style began to change, the designs becoming more curvilinear. In the 1920s the Wiener Werkstätte employed the talents of less prominent designers and in 1932 it was dissolved.

Wieslthier, Valerie (1895–1945) Austrian designer who was head of the ceramic workshop of the Wiener Werkstätte, creating in a highly idiosyncratic style with coarse modelling and drip effects. In 1929, she moved to America to work for Contempora, New York, and Sebring Pottery in Ohio. She also designed glassware, textiles and papier-mache models.

Wilmotte, Jean-Michel (1948–) French interior architect with an impressive list of commissions including a bedroom for President Mitterand in the *Palais de l'Elysée* and the office of the French Ambassador in Washington. He has designed a huge range of furniture and lighting, projection facilities for Canal+TV and interiors below the Pyramid at the Louvre, Paris.

Wirkkala, Tapio (1915–85) Finland's greatest glass designers designing for the Littala glassworks from 1947. He has designed many suites of drinking glasses, the 1965 pattern being an instant success. In 1955, he founded his own studio in Helsinki and has designed for Rosenthal, Orfevrerie Christofle and Venini. He has designed major Finnish exhibitions, including their sections of the 1954 Milan Triennale and the Brussels Expo '58.

Wolff Olins British design studio established in 1955 in London. The original partners were Wally Olins and Michael Wolff and they specialized in corporate identities and store design. After the partnership was dissolved, the firm continued and designed the British Telecom corporate identity.

Wormley, Edward (b.1907) American furniture designer who worked in Chicago and New York, He was in the design studio of the Marshall Field store for three years from 1928, moving to New York in 1931 to work as designer for Dunbar Furniture of

Indiana, refining its range for wider tastes. In 1945, he opened his own office and extended his range to carpets and textiles.

Wright, Frank Lloyd (1867–1959) America's greatest architect, designer and theorist, who revolutionized the approach design. His houses are too numerous to mention, but he also designed seminal furniture. His designs are characterized by their angularity and exagerrated vertically, influencing the ARTS AND CRAFTS MOVEMENT. Late into his 70s he was experimenting with mass-produced plywood furniture, which could just as easily have been produced by a local craftsman.

Wright, Russel (1904–76) American designer of domestic goods and the first designer to have his name credited in the manufacturers' advertising. He was raised as a Quaker and this was reflected in his pieces. He dabbled in theatre design before producing household items in spun aluminium. Macy's *Modern Living* range was a success in 1935. He also introduced the term 'blone' for bleached maple wood. Other designs include a 1932 Wurlitzer cabinet and a range of glassware and pottery. So prolific and so popular was he in the 1930s and 1940s that almost every household in America had a piece of his furniture.

Y

Yamaguchi, Kazama (1946–) Japanese industrial designer who started his career in Milan in 1970, becoming known for his lighting and vehicle body designs.

Yamo (1959–) Algerian designer who works in Paris, where he created a lighting project, showing kites in glass, for a palace in Osaka. Designed several interiors for fashionable people and numerous glass and metal collections. His 1989 *Wacapou* furniture collection for Roche-Bobois and 1990 table service for Christofle were widely distributed.

Yanagi, Sori (1915–) Japanese industrial designer who worked in the Japan office of Charlotte PERRIAND. He retained a traditional Japanese sensitivity to materials and forms. His best-known piece of wooden furniture being his 1955 *Butterfly* stool.

Young, Dennis (1917–) British furniture and industrial designer who opened his London office in 1946. A consultant to major manufacturers and lecturer on design at Camberwell School of Art, his best-known piece is the 1947 *Shell Chair,* one of the earliest ergonomic designs.

Z

Zanini, Marco (1954–) Italian architect who has designed several collections of furniture with Ettore Sottsass Associati and the Memphis company.

Zapf, Otto (1931–) Important German industrial designer of system furniture for Knoll, which bear his name, and workstations for Pacific Telesis.

Zimmerman, Marie (1878–1972) American metalworker who used Egyptian, Far Eastern and Greek art as inspiration for her jewellery. She studied ancient patination methods to achieve similar, authentic results. Her work was widely illustrated in magazines such as *Vogue, Art et Decoration* and *House and Garden* in the 1930s.

Zwicky, Stefan (1952–) Swiss interior and furniture designer who worked in Zurich and then for Olivetti in Milan, before setting up his own studio in 1983, His 1980 *Grand Confort, Sans Confort— Homage a Corbu* furniture was a parody of Le Corbusier's 1927 *Grand Confort* airmchair. It had solid concrete for the cushions and iron rods for the frame.